Practical Spiritualities in a Media Age

Also available from Bloomsbury:

Spirituality: A Guide for the Perplexed, Philip Sheldrake
Capitalizing Religion, Craig Martin
Consuming Religion, Vincent J. Miller
Media, Spiritualities and Social Change, edited by Stewart M. Hoover and Monica M. Emerich

Practical Spiritualities in a Media Age

Edited by
Curtis D. Coats and Monica M. Emerich

Bloomsbury Academic
An imprint of Bloomsbury Publishing Plc
B L O O M S B U R Y
LONDON • OXFORD • NEW YORK • NEW DELHI • SYDNEY

Bloomsbury Academic
An imprint of Bloomsbury Publishing Plc

50 Bedford Square
London
WC1B 3DP
UK

1385 Broadway
New York
NY 10018
USA

www.bloomsbury.com

BLOOMSBURY and the Diana logo are trademarks of Bloomsbury Publishing Plc

First published 2016
Paperback edition first published 2017

British Library Cataloguing-in-Publication Data
A catalogue record for this book is available from the British Library.

ISBN: HB: 978-1-4742-2316-4
PB: 978-1-4742-2315-7
ePDF: 978-1-4742-2318-8
ePub: 978-1-4742-2317-1

Library of Congress Cataloging-in-Publication Data
A catalog record for this book is available from the Library of Congress.

Typeset by Newgen Knowledge Works (P) Ltd., Chennai, India

Contents

Illustrations

Contributors

Liz Barr is a PhD student in the Rhetoric, Politics, and Culture program in the Department of Communication Arts at the University of Wisconsin, Madison. With a background in Gender and Women's Studies, she brings queer and feminist politics and scholarship in conversation with queer and feminist rhetorical studies. She is interested in medicalization and bodies, and works on alternative constructions of mental health and illness, focusing on ways that queer politics can inform resistance to the medicalization of madness. In addition to her work on madness, she explores HIV, AIDS, and public memory, focusing on nondominant narratives of AIDS activism. Her work has been featured in *Feminist Collections, Rhizomes*, and will appear in a forthcoming edited collection on feminist rhetorical science studies.

Marion Bowman is senior lecturer in the Religious Studies department at the Open University, UK, vice-president of the European Association for the Study of Religions, and a former president of both the British Association for the Study of Religions and of The Folklore Society. Working at the interstices of religious studies and folklore/ethnology, her research interests are very much rooted in vernacular religion—the experiences, worldviews, beliefs, practices, and material culture of individuals and groups in specific locations and contexts. Her research tends to be fieldwork-based, with people within, on the margins of, and outside institutional religion. In 2012 she co-edited *Vernacular Religion in Everyday Life: Expressions of Belief* (Sheffield, Oakville, CT: Equinox, 2012) with Ülo Valk. She has conducted long-term ethnological studies of Glastonbury and also of contemporary Celtic spirituality and is currently working on a three-year project on "Pilgrimage to England's Cathedrals, Past and Present."

Curtis D. Coats is a scholar whose work explores the intersections among media, religion, identity, gender, tourism, and sacred space. His work has been published in a range of disciplines, including the peer-reviewed journals: *Tourist Studies, Journal of Communication, Journal of Men, Masculinities and Spirituality,* and *Journal for the Study of Religion, Nature and Culture.* Since 2009, Coats is associate professor of Communication Studies at Millsaps College where he directs the Communication Studies major and co-directs the interdisciplinary

Film Studies minor. He is co-author with Stewart M. Hoover of the forthcoming book *Does God Make the Man? Media, Religion and the Crisis of Masculinity* (NYU Press, 2015).

Monica M. Emerich is president of Groundwork Research and Communications, a consultancy specializing in the global Lifestyles of Health and Sustainability (LOHAS) marketplace. As a journalist, Emerich has focused on the social, political, and economic aspects of sustainable living since 1991. She teaches communication strategies in the Sustainable Practices Program at the University of Colorado. In her book, *The Gospel of Sustainability: Media, Market and LOHAS* (University of Illinois Press, 2011) she explores the spiritualization of sustainability narratives and the construction of sustainability culture. She is co-editor with Stewart M. Hoover of *Media, Spiritualities and Social Change* (Continuum, 2011).

Jeremy Garber is a graduate of the Religious Studies program in Theology, Philosophy, and Cultural Theory at the University of Denver and the Iliff School of Theology. Jeremy received his MDiv from Associated Mennonite Biblical Seminary in Indiana, concentrating in theology and ethics. Dr Garber's dissertation was titled "'Another Way': The Pneumatology of Deleuzean Minoritarian Communal Interpretation in Scripture, the 16th Century Radical Reformation, and Alternative 21st century Anabaptist Community." His primary research is on the idea of the Holy Spirit and the interpretation of popular culture in religious communities, using media theory and Deleuzean philosophy. Dr Garber has published articles on the perception of Anabaptism in contemporary literature, the authority of Scripture in young adults, and theology in popular culture. He has also taught courses at the undergraduate and graduate levels in constructive theology, philosophy of religion, religion and popular culture, ethics, and comparative religion. He is currently the team leader of the Academic Advising Center at the Iliff School of Theology. He and his daughter, Fiona, are members of First Mennonite Church in Denver.

Jenna Gray-Hildenbrand is assistant professor of Religious Studies at Middle Tennessee State University and serves as co-director of the Religious Studies program. Her doctoral research focused on religion and law in the United States with a particular interest in the criminalization of religious practice. Gray-Hildenbrand's current research and teaching interests include indigenous religions, new religious movements, and alternative spiritualities, religion and media, gender and religion, race and religion, and theory and method in religious studies. Gray-Hildenbrand is presently working on two projects. The first investigates the history of the criminalization of serpent-handling in Appalachian Christian churches from the 1940s to the present. The second, in collaboration with Martha Smith Roberts, analyzes the various spiritualities emerging within the hula hooping subculture.

Florence Pasche Guignard was a postdoctoral researcher in the Department for the Study of Religion at the University of Toronto after completing her doctorate in the comparative study of religions from the University of Lausanne. Her work engages issues at the intersection of religion and gender, embodiment, ritual, media, and material culture. Method and theory in the study of religions, in particular comparative research designs, also count among her research interests. Pasche Guignard's publications have focused on religion and ornaments in devotional Hindu poetry, religion and toys, games and dolls, and religious rituals and representations on video-sharing websites. Her current research project, titled "Natural Parenting in the Digital Age: At the Confluence of Mothering, Religion, Environmentalism and Technology" is supported through a fellowship of the Swiss National Science Foundation. Her forthcoming publications focus on the intersection of religious discourses with motherhood, pregnancy, childbirth, and breastfeeding, with a particular focus on ritual and media.

Graham Harvey is Reader and Head of Department of Religious Studies at the Open University, UK. His research and publications primarily engage with Jews, Pagans, and indigenous peoples. He is particularly interested in "animism" and is author of *Animism: Respecting the Living World* (Columbia University Press, 2005) and editor of *The Handbook of Contemporary Animism* (Routledge, 2013). In 2013 he also published *Food, Sex and Strangers: Understanding religion as everyday life* (Routledge) in which he argued for a thoroughly relational, material, performative, and this-worldly definition of and approach to religion, rooted in fieldwork among Anishinaabeg, Jews, Maori, Pagans, Yoruba, and others. He is president of the British Association for the Study of Religions.

Stewart M. Hoover is a professor in the Department of Media Studies and Professor Adjoint in the Department of Religious Studies and is director of the Center for Media, Religion and Culture, all at the University of Colorado, Boulder. A specialist in media audience studies, Hoover is an internationally recognized expert on media and religion and has consulted, lectured, or conducted research in eleven foreign countries. His research ranges from legacy to digital media and across a wide range of cultural and social effects and uses of contemporary media. He is author or editor of twelve books and numerous articles and has taught graduate and undergraduate courses on contemporary media cultures, media history, theory, and research. He holds the Master's and PhD degrees from the Annenberg School for Communication at the University of Pennsylvania, and has received awards for his scholarship, service, and teaching.

Anne Maija Huffman is an assistant professor at Sofia University in Palo Alto, California. Her research interests include spirituality, psychology, transpersonal studies, culture, LGBT studies, and generational research. She teaches both online and in-person. She maintains a private practice in spiritual guidance. She is currently the chair of the MA in Spiritual Guidance program at Sofia University. Her publications include the co-written chapter: "Feminist and Cultural Contributions to Transpersonal Psychology," in *The Wiley-Blackwell Handbook of Transpersonal Psychology* and her dissertation *Eternal Youths: A Narrative Inquiry into the Buffering Effects of a Generational Cultural Complex against the Anxiety of Aging and death in the American Baby Boom Generation.* Her research has included work with the Institute of Noetic Sciences (IONS) where she collaborated on curriculum and course development for conscious aging. Additionally she has presented on the "Wisdom of the Aging: Fostering Spirituality and Meaning-Making for the Older LGBT Adult" for the Institute on Aging and UCSF Division of Geriatrics.

Lucas F. Johnston is assistant professor of Religion and Environmental Studies, and Faculty Affiliate of the Center for Energy, Environment, and Sustainability (CEES) at Wake Forest University. He is the director of the university's Religion and Public Engagement Concentration, and Ollen R. Nalley Faculty Fellow. Johnston has authored *Religion and Sustainability: Social Movements and the Politics of the Environment* (2013), co-edited *Science and Religion: One Planet, Many Possibilities* (2014), and edited *Higher Education for Sustainability: Cases, Challenges, and Opportunities Across the Curriculum* (2012).

Rachael Liberman teaches media studies courses in the Department of Media, Film & Journalism Studies at University of Denver. She earned her PhD in Communication from the University of Colorado, Boulder, where she served as the senior fellow of the Center for Media, Religion and Culture. Her research tracks the construction, proliferation, and circulation of discourses on gender and sexuality in contemporary media culture; and in particular, the mediation of female sexual subjectivity. Other research interests include: negotiations of agency within cultural production, feminist interventions in media studies, the pornography industry, and the politics of media and memory. Her work has been published *Porn Studies*, *Women's Psychology Quarterly*, and *Media/Cultural Studies: Critical Approaches*.

Jeffrey H. Mahan holds the Ralph E. and Norma E. Peck Chair in Religion and Public Communication at the Iliff School of Theology in Denver, Colorado. His research and teaching interests focus on religion as it is embedded in mass media and popular culture. He has served on film festival juries at the Berlin, Cannes, and Montreal International Film Festivals. Mahan is affiliate faculty at the Center for Media, Religion and Culture at the University of Colorado, Boulder. He was the founding co-chair of the Religion and Popular Culture Group at the American Academy of Religion. His authored or edited books include: *Media, Religion and Culture: An Introduction* (Routledge, 2014); *Religion and Popular Culture in America* (University of California, revised edition 2005); *Shared Wisdom* (Abingdon, 1993); and *American Television Genres* (Nelson Hall, 1983).

RuthAnn Ritter is a consultant and educator pursuing doctoral work in Organizational Change and Leadership at the University of Southern California. She holds Master's degrees in Theology from the Iliff School of Theology in Denver, Colorado and in Education from University of California, Santa Barbara. Her publications and presentations focus on how spiritual practices such as mindfulness and meditation are appropriated from Eastern contemplative traditions and used in secular settings such as the Western workplace. The workshops and trainings she delivers to businesses focus on practical ways to marry spiritual wisdom with organizational leadership and performance management.

Martha Smith Roberts is a PhD candidate in American Religions at the University of California, Santa Barbara. Her current research and teaching interests include American religious diversity and pluralism, race and ethnicity studies, diversity and social justice, embodiment studies, Asian American religions, new religious movements, and material culture. Her doctoral research project is a critical analysis of post-racial and post-ethnic theories of American religious pluralism, with particular attention to the human body on display at public exhibitions promoting tolerance in twentieth-century US history, including World's Fairs, Holocaust Memorial museums, and Body Worlds exhibitions. In addition, she is working on a research project with Dr Jenna Gray-Hildenbrand, which analyzes the various spiritualities emerging within the hula hooping subculture. She also serves on the Board of Directors for the Institute for Diversity and Civic Life in Austin, Texas.

Garry Tregidga is director of the Institute of Cornish Studies at the University of Exeter at Penryn in Cornwall. His research interests include the regional politics of Britain and Western Europe, the use of cultural memory and oral history in studying indigenous communities and the global connections between Cornwall and countries such as Australia, New Zealand, and the United States as a result of emigration in the nineteenth century. In 2000 he established the Cornish Audio Visual Archive and is a regional networker of the oral History Society. Garry is author of *The Liberal Party in South West Britain: Decline, Dormancy and Rebirth* (University of Exeter Press, 2000), editor of *Memory, Place and Identity: The Cultural Landscapes of Cornwall* (Francis Boutle Publications, London, 2012) and co-editor (with Marion Gibson and Shelley Trower) of *Mysticism, Myth and Celtic Identity* (Routledge, 2012). He has recently become the editor of *Cornish Studies* and is currently preparing a monograph on the Celtic Revival in Cornwall in the nineteenth and early twentieth centuries and an edited collection on Celtic politics in Britain since the 1880s.

Acknowledgments

Any work of scholarship builds on a community of scholars. We thank the individual contributors to this book, and we thank our editors at Bloomsbury, especially Lalle Pursglove and Anna MacDiarmid, for their help in navigating the publishing process (and in keeping us on schedule). Also, we thank the Center for Media, Religion, and Culture at University of Colorado, Boulder and the International Society for Media, Religion, and Culture, both of which have given us an intellectual home and a fertile field of inquiry the last fifteen years. Curtis would like to thank his home institution, Millsaps College, for its support for his scholarship. We especially thank Lynn Schofield Clark and Stewart M. Hoover, both of whom are friends and mentors. Finally, we thank Frank Lampe and Heather Coats—our confidants, encouragers, and partners who keep us grounded in our own material practices and who make our ordinary lives extraordinary.

1

Introduction: The Webs We Spin—Relational, Mediated, Spiritual

Curtis D. Coats
Millsaps College

Monica M. Emerich
University of Colorado

7:00 a.m., January 26, 2015

This day is like most other days, following a night like most other nights. In a small town in the central United States, a woman hits the "off" button on her alarm as she rises. Instead of coffee, she grabs her Hula Hoop, opens up a YouTube video on her smart phone and begins her ritual of hooping. Elsewhere, another woman swaddles her baby in a wrap before running out to complete her morning errands. A thousand miles away, a group of young men stock their van for their pilgrimage to an improvisational rock music festival. Across town, a group of executives get together for yoga before the day's work begins. Some in this group are physically proximate. Others telecommute to the yoga session.

3:00 p.m., January 26, 2015

A group of women and men meet online to discuss their mental illnesses, not as "madness" as society defines it, but as gifts to their identity and their community. Across the Atlantic, a young woman, while touring Glastonbury, Snapchats to her friends back home. A little later, she buys a crystal in a shop to commemorate her trip. Elsewhere, a group of local community members strategize how best to promote the spirituality embedded in their Cornish identity, a promotion that engages their Cornish Methodist and pagan heritages.

11:00 p.m., January 26, 2015

A young woman reads confessions on PostSecret. Emboldened and inspired, she posts her own confession—something she had never told her priest. Across town, a group of Cultural Creatives[1] *meets to discuss the spiritual power of their art and their desire for spiritual community. Some hesitate to commit to the group and begin to distance themselves. Others embrace this group and, thus, further entwine their identity with this emerging community. As the day, January 26, turns to a new day, a Baby Boomer couple reaches sexual climax, embracing the youthful vitality experienced in the "little death." Then they ponder their own mortality as the climax wanes.*

What these banal practices—parenting, sex, leisure, work—have in common is the extraordinary, spiritual meaning attached to them by practitioners. According to McKian, "[S]pirituality does not always sit outside the everyday, suspended in particular moments and spaces; it is also witnessed across the banality of everyday life."[2] At its core this book is about these people and their practices.

Of course, this book is also about concepts related to "spirituality" and "the media." Our hope is that engagement with these concepts will enliven the practitioners, enrich the concepts, and generate productive debate within studies of media, religion, and culture about spiritual, mediated practice.

Our aims in this book are threefold. First, we wish to resurrect the exploration of spiritual practices and beliefs, products, and places within media, religion, and culture studies. We hope this book encourages conversations about spirituality *versus* religion, spirituality *and* religion, or spirituality *as* religion—as productive as the conversations about media *and* religion, media *as* religion, or mediation *versus* mediatization of religion. Second, we explore how and why the ordinary is made extraordinary, yet practical to the life of the participant at the same time. Third, we argue that these "practical" spiritualities, in capitalist societies at least, occur in a Media Age. We will elucidate the contours and boundaries of the media in this age in an effort to situate contemporary spiritualities within media technologies, mediated relationships, and media spaces. We hope to accomplish these aims by engaging the culturalist, relational, and spatial "turns" in media studies; religious studies; and media, religion, and culture studies.

Practical spirituality . . .

The idea and the name for this book came to us organically, in all senses of that term's usage. We were discussing our own research on the organic foods industry and sustainability and the expression among those workers about viewing their occupations as a sacred journey. We were interested in the genealogy of these meanings—how we could link them back to narratives in print, digital, and broadcast media and vice versa, that is, how those media reflected and intersected with other practices, from shopping to parenting, from work to funerals. We were mulling over the way in which those elements nestled into place with expressions we had seen in research on spiritual tourism and with similarities in understandings about spirit—as that generated through service to one's self and one's society and then filtered through to the planet in the form of good energy. We began to talk more about the ways in which spirituality was physiological—fermented in the vessel of the flesh through everyday practices imbued with extraordinary meaning and transformed from raw material of life into a spiritual powerhouse of health for the world, truly a healing of the self to heal the world.

Defining spirituality

> How astonishing it is that language can almost mean,
> and frightening that it does not quite. Love, we say,
> God, we say, Rome and Michiko, we write, and the words
> Get it wrong . . .
>
> —Jack Gilbert, *The Forgotten Dialect of the Heart*[3]

Like Gilbert's "God," it is astonishing that the language for "spirituality" eludes us. Yet, defining spirituality continues to perplex scholars of religion, so we will not pretend to finally solve this definitional quandary. In fact, the chapters in this volume may serve to further complicate the question. However, important conceptual work has been done to create definitional boundaries. Our purpose is to use the rich scholarly discourse to define our use of the term "spiritualities" in an effort to locate the participants in the case studies presented here.

We begin with the broad markers "quest culture" and "eclectic seeker" culture laid out by Roof.[4] The eclectic seeker, for Roof, included:

> New Agers (although the term is fading), the New Spirituality, Neo-Pagans, Wiccans, goddess worshippers, Zen Buddhists, nature-lovers, feminists, holistic people, "followers" of various spiritual masters, "seekers," and many without a name for themselves or who shift from one name to another so frequently it depends on which day you ask.[5]

Further, this late modern capitalist (and often "urban") culture is informed by Giddens's[6] notion of the reflexivity of modernity and, following Giddens, what

Roof called a "reflexive spirituality," "a more deliberate, self-conscious awareness that we must take charge of our inner well-being—our sense of self—and buttress it with symbolic resources, discipline, and practice."[7]

Sarah Pike noted that the "inward turn" in New Age and Neopagan communities was marked by a commitment to "personal spiritual progress [that] is central to life and is the best way to effect changes in the world."[8] Spiritual progress, for these groups, is decentralized and anti-authoritarian. It is focused on an eclectic mix of healing techniques for the body, mind, and spirit. Casting a broader net beyond New Age or Neopagan, Heelas dubbed this collection of spiritualities "wellbeing spirituality," spiritualities that seek to infuse all realms of life, mind, and body *with* spirit.[9] Heelas wrote:

> The inner-realm enables spirituality to infuse life, transforming the quality of those aspects of one's being which have previously been divorced from the inner-life. Mind-body-*with*-spirit; emotions-feelings-somatic experiences-*with*-spirituality; the experiential aspects of relationships-*with*-spirituality.[10]

At the core of well-being spirituality is the self, or the inner-realm. Heelas wrote, "What matters is delving within oneself to experience the primary source of the sacred."[11] This principle of life *as sacred* differentiates well-being spirituality from what he calls "transcendent theism," "the spirituality of theistic humanism," and "immanent spirituality."[12] The first is most commonly identified with traditions built on scriptural authority and a wholly Other God. While there are parallels of practice between this and well-being spirituality, transcendent theism is validated by scriptural authority, not by "inner-directed self-expression."[13] Spirituality of theistic humanism, on the other hand, is most often found in expressions such as liberal Protestantism. There is much more overlap between this and well-being spirituality, but theistic humanism is still dependent on a notion of a transcendent Godhead. The same is true of what he calls "immanent spirituality," notable in the Quaker and Unitarian traditions. Here also the inner spark of the Divine is connected to a Divine "without." In sum, well-being spirituality rejects the Wholly (Holy) other and instead embraces holism of the self. Following Roof, this type of spirituality involves "yearnings for a reconstructed interior life aimed at forging an integrated self and transcending the limits of the given."[14] Such transcendence should not be thought of in terms of disembodiment; rather, in the cases here, such transcendence is about transcending the limits of the Ego, of modern dualisms, of the logic of capitalism, and of the State. Further, as Harvey argues persuasively in this volume, these notions of spirituality should not confuse the "inward turn" with individualism.

The chapters in this volume speak to the fundamental relational interactivity of spiritualities and, thus, their turn outward. Here we pick up on Sarah Pike's ideas of spiritual practitioners' aspirations of "effecting change in the world" and Heelas's idea about the "experiential aspects of relationships-*with*-spirituality" noted above.[15] Much scholarship about spirituality has focused on "the inward turn."[16] Taking Graham Harvey's lead, we argue that understanding spiritualities requires a turn toward relationships and everyday practices, an "outward" or "relational" turn.

Many of the case studies in this book focus on well-being spirituality, as described by Heelas. Others might also be classified as New Age or Neopagan, as described by Pike. These spiritualities work from the inside out, working on the self while simultaneously working outward to the local and global. While the cases in this text are not connected with "transcendent theism," there will be overlap between well-being, immanent, New Age, and Neopagan spiritualities. The differences among these are important,[17] but these differences are less important for our purposes because all of these spiritual iterations emphasize the cultivation of an inner-life spirituality that manifests itself in practical and relational ways.

There is a reason we chose the word, "practical," over a host of other qualifiers for spirituality, including "wellbeing" and "alternative." While many of the spiritualities expressed in these case studies fit in Heelas's "wellbeing spirituality," all of them may not. Thus, we cannot simply collapse "practical spiritualities" into "wellbeing spiritualities." The same is also true of Pike's definitions of Neopagan and New Age spiritualities. Some of these case studies might fit in either of these spiritualities as she defines them, but many do not. All of the case studies in this volume, however, will fit in the post-1970s spiritual currents described by Sutcliffe—sensibilities that have "passed out of the hands of a supernatural apocalypticism into a this-wordly humanism."[18] We propose that the types of expressions we see in this book are viewed as desirable by practitioners because they are both conducted as a personal expression of power and authority and because they make manifest a vision of attainable change in this world. These practices are not only physical acts but also take place in vision, mind, and heart, as much as prayer and faith might in the religious.

The practicality of spiritual work centrally figures the powers inherent in body and mind of the human but does not focus solely on the "acts" or practices that have been segregated so often in academic study of spirituality (e.g., the pilgrimage, the yoga session, the séance). In this book we argue for a more grounded, relational view of the situation to see how and where practical spirituality expresses not just in the single focused act of "the spiritual" but also as it echoes through, informs, and shapes the everyday life where most of us experience our life history—the ordinary. Following Harvey in this volume, "spirituality is something that people do in a world of birth, growth, death, decay, and recycling."[19] Key for us was to try to expand the *de rigeur* decontextualized academic interview of the "practitioner-in-moment-of-practice" to the practitioner-in-life-reflecting-on-practice. MacKian typified much spirituality research this way:

> If practitioners are interviewed at all, this takes place within circumscribed times and places cut off from their wider everyday worlds, and the picture emerges of something quite transactional, materially focused and temporally and spatially bounded. These "transactions" are then neatly presented as expressions of consumer capitalism and narcissistic self-interest, 'quick fixes' with minimal spiritual substance. There is little attention given to what other meanings might be ascribed by the participants themselves, or to the social and spatial worlds they might sit within.[20]

We agree that much of spirituality research has been undertaken on a practice focus, which often seems unmoored from the vernacular of the person's life. The scope of research has so narrowly focused on the practices themselves of New Age, of Mind-Cure, of paganism, and more that our chosen word, "practical," raised some concern in this direction.

We are not only interested in what people *do* to express their spirituality but also what they might wish to do, change, speak, or create. Pamela Klassen noted, "Practice is a concept that attempts to bring together thought and action— both how people think about the world they live in and what they do in it."[21] So we are interested in these aspirations and actions *in relation*—with other humans, with nonhumans, with products, with the natural world. In short, we are interested in *discursive practices* of practical spiritualities, acknowledging Foucault's work on discourse[22] and Stewart Hoover's work engaging the intersections of practice, meaning, and "plausible narratives of the self."[23] Thoughts, dreams, prayers, and faith are no less practical to us than rituals or political actions. All of these are embodied. All are practical. Thus, while we want to explore how spirituality becomes something goal-oriented for practitioners, temporally and spatially defined—"practical" in its ability to do something to change the everyday reality of the practitioner—we also want to explore spiritualities that speak to mystery, enchantment, and, even, transcendence. These states are not at odds for practitioners anymore than faith in the afterlife for Christians is at odds with tithing.

To this point MacKian wrote:

> In most academic accounts of contemporary spirituality-beyond-religion there is a distinct lack of attention given to the "mystery" or "otherworldliness" of such spiritualities, and how this may affect the everyday world as we know it. Indeed, you will be hard-pushed to find any serious or explicit engagement with spiritual mystery, enchantment and its relation to the quotidian and mundane.[24]

In sum, the case studies in this volume encompass embodied, relational practices that are mundane and mysterious, everyday and enchanted. Some case studies might be classified as New Age; others, well-being spirituality. There will be overlap among immanent spirituality, theistic humanism, and well-being spirituality. The focal point will be on relational practice, considered broadly, and the focal point will be on practices *in the Media Age*, a concept to which we now turn.

. . . In the Media Age

The title of this volume draws on our positions as media scholars and on our intellectual commitments to the study of media, religion, and culture, with acknowledgment to Hoover and Clark's *Practicing Religion in an Age of Media.*[25] The notion of a Media Age is well established in this area of scholarship. Couldry noted, "media influence now extends to 'all the spheres of society and social life' (Mazzoleni 2008)."[26] Hoover, following Roof and Giddens, posited a Media Age where religious authority shifts from institution to autonomous, reflexive selves.[27] A key source of this shift is the proliferation of symbols in the media sphere, which has created a symbolic field fertile for the growth of "nones" and "spiritual but not religious" people. Of course, it is not just media studies or studies of media, religion, and culture that embrace a notion of the Media Age. In sociology, Anthony Elliott and John Urry, for example, discussed the "the mobilities paradigm" where media work in tandem with transportation infrastructures to transform identities and global politics.[28] Mary Chayko discussed how media fundamentally alter late modern community formation, making it portable.[29] Finally, in a negative sense, Zygmunt Bauman pointed to the media, especially digital media, in the transformation of society to what he called "liquid modernity," where "virtual proximity renders human connections simultaneously more frequent and more shallow."[30]

Despite its ubiquity, we recognize that the use of a term such as "Media Age" is ambitious and provocative since practical spiritualities and religions have always been mediating.[31] Yet, scholars of media, religion, and culture have commented that *something* has changed since the late nineteenth century, especially in elite, industrialized regions, and has been escalating with tremendous force since the 1970s, and, in fact, in the first fifteen years of this century.[32] "Media" are seen at the root of that change.

But to ask a rather elementary question, "What are media?" Or, put differently, "To what media are scholars referring in their discussions of change in late modernity?"

To unpack the particularities of the "Media Age"—indeed, to build the case that we are in a "Media Age"—we'll draw, in part, on concepts, discussed by Peter Horsfield in *Keywords in Religion, Media, and Culture*.[33] Horsfield noted a shift from an instrumental view of media as *mere* vessels to a more culturalist view of media.[34] Rather than "mere instruments," media are thought of "as part of the dynamic of society itself."[35] This shift led to a broad consensus in the field of media, religion, and culture of thinking about "media as culture,"[36] which involved thinking about media in ways that Raymond Williams famously thought about culture—"a whole way of life."[37] The "media as culture" trope thought less about particular technologies of mass media and more broadly about "the total process of mediation of life."[38]

This double move in the culturalist turn, "media as culture" and "religion as media/mediating," had the positive effect of moving studies of media and religion away from technological instrumentalism where media are neutral channels or technologies that merely carry the messages encoded in them. However, this move had the negative effect of taking such a broad view that everything was media, mediated, or mediating. Thus, the claims about a "Media Age" became contradictory. If everything is media, then there can be no Media Age (unless all of human history is the Media Age).

While it would be easier to change the title of this book, we agree with Couldry, Clark, Hoover, and others that there is something particular to this age.[39] The key to understanding media of the Media Age is to hold the general "media/religion as culture" in balance with the specific properties of the media of the Media Age (henceforth referred to as simply, "the media"). In fact, Horsfield points to these particular properties: "media as text,"[40] "media as industries,"[41] and "media as technologies."[42]

"Media as text" can easily slip into the same traps of "media as culture." Any number of material objects can be read (as well as performed and practiced). To use examples from this volume, objects of material culture such as baby wraps (Chapter 2), Glastonbury candles (Chapter 4), or Hula Hoops (Chapter 5) have particular uses but also have readable, symbolic meanings. Part of the task of better understanding "the media" is to isolate properties of distinction among texts. This involves turning attention to issues of form, genre, and aesthetics.[43] In addition, as Horsfield notes, understanding media as text must be considered less an engagement with nouns, for example, Hula Hoops, books, or television, and more an engagement with processes—"text" as "interaction between the person producing the message within a particular media form, the media form itself, and what the person who receives the communication does with it."[44] This more robust focus on textual practice mirrors a general move in the study of media, religion, and culture toward practice, but, too often, practices become generalized, losing distinctions among mediating forms, for example, the differences between "hooping" and watching a "hooping" ceremony on YouTube. These are categorically different media and mediating practices, and the latter—watching and participating with the hooping ceremony on YouTube—contains the particularities of "the media" referred to when speaking about a Media Age.

The most distinguishing characteristics of "the media" are also often the most underdeveloped in studies of media, religion, and culture: media as industries and media as technologies. The reasons for this involve the intellectual commitments of the field—on the one hand, the move away from "medium theory"[45] and, on the other, the embrace of a culturalist view that often stands in opposition to political-economic approaches to media. Yet, Klassen noted "analyses of religion and media could benefit from more attention to the material conditions of capital, colonialism and state regulation that have made possible media production in religious arenas."[46]

Perhaps the most obvious point about "the media" are their connections to "complex, global mobility systems."[47] "The media" are connected to an increasingly concentrated global media industry. As Horsfield noted, "Without these industrial factors, no medium will become established as a sustainable form of communication within a society."[48] Recognizing media industries does not necessitate a shift away from practice. Rather, it necessitates a broadening of practice—work practices, policy practices, commodity practices.

In this volume, RuthAnn Ritter and Jeffrey H. Mahan (Chapter 3) provide insight into the ways in which spirituality and media infuse work life. This focus on meaning and practice during work can be extended into other industries (including media industries) to consider the ways in which "servant leadership" or other forms of "remixed" practices shift expectations in a changing workforce and influence production (media and otherwise).[49]

Also, while a shift to the study of media policy is unwarranted (though not unwelcome) in media and religion scholarship, this field should draw on important policy histories and discussions relevant to the policy practices integral to the construction of "the media." In some ways, these policies have been directly intertwined with religion, for example, the role of Christianity in Hollywood film censorship and The Motion Picture Production Code in the United States.[50] Further many media policy concerns have moral and ethical dimensions, for example, the perceived right to media access.[51] Finally, recent policy debates can have implications for spiritual and religious identity and practice, for example, the "right to be forgotten,"[52] and even the regulation of media ownership.[53]

Another central feature of "the media" (particularly in capitalist societies) is the relationship of media to commodification. When the issue of commodification has been discussed in studies of spirituality, the tendency has been to conflate commodification with inauthenticity.[54] However, this conceptual move cuts off the productive generation of identity, community, and ritual *through* commodities and brands. Thus, commodification should not diminish the authenticity of mediated encounters, but this inescapable reality of mediated life need not be diminished either. Living in a Media Age means experiencing much of everyday life through media industries, commodities, and brands.[55] This reality has implications for the construction of self and implications for practical spiritualities that seek to heal the world.

Of course, much of material culture in late capitalist societies is commodified. Baby wraps, Hula Hoops, music, crystals, and YouTube videos are all commodities. "The media," however, are commodities of a different kind because the consumer of media content is also a commodity *and*, often, an unpaid producer of media content.[56] Commodification of audiences has intensified through mobile, networked, digital media technologies. To the extent that one experiences spirituality *through* networked, digital media technologies, the user *becomes* data that is aggregated. Thus, the spiritual practices, communities, and interacting people are, in an important sense, the products that are sold to corporations in the digital media complex. Further, not only are audiences commodified, but also spiritual audiences, participants, and practices are (often unpaid) producers to the extent that their spirituality, participation, and practices provide user-generated content for media corporations. This double sense of commodification—becoming a commodity and a laborer in media commodity production—is a central characteristic of "the media," especially "the media" often accompanied with the qualifier, "new."

As Elliott and Urry note, "the emergence of complex, global mobility systems involve the creation of new forms of mobile life, new kinds of daily experience and new forms of social interaction."[57] Scholars of media, religion, and culture have highlighted this reality and pointed to its productive capacities for identity, community, and social action.[58] What has been underplayed to date is the connection of these productive capacities to media industries and institutions.

To the extent that institutions are addressed, the discussion focuses on the power of media to collapse (or at least to change) religious institutions and authority. The reflexive, or inward, turn in spirituality is discussed as a turn to the self for authority, a turn facilitated by media and a turn that challenges religious authority (see Chapter 10).[59] These assessments are accurate, but as Harvey notes in this volume, this inward turn and its given authority are too often over-privileged. Harvey addresses this position of the inward turn as it relates to religious belief and practice, but also this over-privileging of individual authority often ignores the ways in which authority shifts forcefully toward media industries as religious and spiritual practitioners become "system dependent"[60] on media connectivity for identity, community, and action. Several authors in this volume, in fact, note this sort of dependency.[61] Media connectivity (and mobility) are expectations of modernity, and these expectations feed the practices (and profits) of media institutions, which reveals the power of "the media" over spirituality in everyday life. This is not a dogmatic power per se (though a dogma of *neoliberalism* may, in fact, be embedded in this power[62]); rather, it is a "system" power (technological and industrial) that influences *how* spiritual people practice, *how* they interact with communities, and *how* they understand themselves and others.

The final distinguishing characteristic of "the media" is "media as technologies." Both Horsfield and Hoover have warned about the pitfalls of instrumentalism and technological determinism in medium theory, and these warnings have tended to shift conversations away from consideration of technologies.[63] Yet, sociologists such as Elliott, Urry, Chayko, and Molz[64] are persuasive in their discussions about the ways in which mobile technologies shape identity, structure taste and desire, modify space, and mold communities.

Rather than ignoring technologies, we need to revive certain elements of medium theory via media sociology. The best way to avoid the pitfalls of medium theory are found *within* the culturalist turn, that is, considering technologies as practice.[65] Certainly, technologies are not only "things"—for example, iPhones, televisions, computers, and cameras—but also they are processes. If we can reconceptualize "the text" as an interaction among producer, form, and audience, then we can conceptualize technologies in the same way. Jonathan Sterne connects technology to Bourdieu's *habitus* and to fields of capital and power, that is, connecting practices of technology to practices of industry. Sterne wrote:

> Technology is not simply a "thing" that "fills" a predetermined social purpose. Technologies are socially shaped along with their meanings, functions, and domains and use . . . Technologies are associated with habits and practices, sometimes crystallizing them and sometimes promoting them. They are structured by human practices so that they may in turn structure human practices. They embody in physical form particular dispositions and tendencies–particular ways of doing things.[66]

Using this definition of technology might seem to open the definition too wide, similar to "media as culture." By this definition, religion and spirituality could be considered a collection of technologies, as could religious or spiritual objects, for example, Christian crosses, pagan drums, or Hula Hoops. Indeed, they could be, and we would argue that these are, technologies. But it is not enough to leave the conversation there. Instead, the task of scholarship in this area must be to uncover the different set of social practices and techniques that accumulate into material technologies in fields of capital and power. Indeed, while media and religion are technologies, examination of the social practices of each would reveal much overlap and distinctiveness.[67]

Consideration of media technologies would explore their role in the creation of spaces (Chapters 3, 8, and 10) and communities (Chapters 2, 4, 5, 6, 7, and 9). Such an exploration would examine how media amplify, frame, and reverberate.[68] Consideration of media technologies would engage "legacy" media[69] ("one-to-many" types of media technologies, e.g., broadcast or print), as well as newer, digital media ("many-to-many" types of media technologies, e.g., social media such as Twitter or Smule). Today, "legacy" and "new" media must often be considered in tandem as media converge.[70] Certainly media technologies facilitate transmission and amplification across space, great and small, and encompass any number of producer/consumer configurations, each of which must be considered in constructions of spiritual meaning, identity, community, and practice.

Conclusion: "The relational turn" in religious studies and media studies

Practical spiritualities occur in a complex web of mediated interaction.[71] To fully understand this web, and to understand the complexities of the Media Age, scholarship on media, religion, and culture must explore the cultural, textual, institutional, and technological aspects of media and their relationship to practices of spirituality and religion. Focusing on "media as culture" has not done enough to differentiate meaning making practices around material objects. A more holistic approach is warranted and can be found in the relational turns in religious studies and media studies.

In the concluding chapter of this volume, Graham Harvey takes up the relational turn in religious studies in greater detail. In that chapter, he argues that while people do talk about subjectivities and individualities when discussing their spirituality, they also talk about their relationships and the ways in which spirituality is ordinary. Spirituality is not something set aside or cordoned off as "the sacred." Rather, spirituality infuses the ordinariness of everyday life. And this ordinariness, he argues, is practiced, interactive, and, fundamentally, relational. Thus, communication is at the core of this relational turn, providing a bridge to media and communication studies from a different entry point than the "inward turn." The relational turn has implications for self, community, and authority that can connect questions of human longing to relations of power as people seek to construct spiritual, interpretive communities.[72]

A key concept developed in this volume that bridges religious studies to human communication studies is "disidentification." Liz Barr (Chapter 9) deploys Jose Esteban Muñoz's concept to discuss a subaltern "world-making project" that allows members of the Icarus Project to redefine discourses around mental illness and spirituality. This positioning against perceived mainstream definitions of religion and mental illness is the defining *glue* to their community. Adding the concept "disidentification" to Hoover and Echchaibi's use of Bhabba's "third spaces"[73] points to community formation as "the work of distinction, made particularly acute as it resists and renegotiates."[74] Considering the differentiating social practices of distinction and disidentification provides fertile ground that can be carefully cultivated by scholars of communication and religion.

The bridge from religious studies to human communication spans to media studies because of the ubiquity of media and the system dependency on media for spiritual meaning, identity, and community in late modern life, at least in the lives of those discussed in this volume.[75] In these pages, "the media" are central to the legitimating and differentiating practices of spiritual community formation. It is important, however, to embrace the cautions about medium theory and technological instrumentalism. Media are not just things. They are not just platforms. Rather, media are also accumulations of processes, all of which are deeply human and deeply relational. This points to the need to think about "the media" itself as relational, not simply as a platform for relationships.

We can bring together these two disciplinary turns regarding relationships through integration with two other disciplines: cultural geography and media sociology, especially the turn toward the relational dynamics of space in the former and "the mobilities paradigm" in the latter. Of the former, Ek argued that space is not a neutral container, but processes.[76] He wrote, "There are no spaces, only spacing."[77] In late modernity, media heavily influence the dynamics of relational spacing. Ek wrote:

> Relational space (and place) as performed events are . . . practically mediated through media and communication technologies, as language-based systems of symbols and material practices. And media and communication technologies are also primarily situated practices, verbs. They are (increasingly crucial) parts of the heterogeneous assemblages of human material-machines that perform spaces (and places). The technological development of media and communication technology enables the folding and the unfolding, the actualisation of the virtual in ways that have not been possible before.[78]

This folding and unfolding is central to what Molz called, "blended geographies," geographies where the virtual and the physical combine and collide, where the self and community become portable and where time-space are compressed.[79] Elliott and Urry noted, "In a mobile society, our ways of Being-in-the-world tend towards the individualized, privatized collecting of experiences, places, events, trips, acquaintances, data and files."[80] Elliott and Urry rightly point to the power of mobile technologies of media and transportation on our sense of self and the world, as well as on our ability to connect with others. However, Harvey's discussion herein of the relational turn in religious studies challenges overemphasis on the privatized individual, and Ek's spatial-relational turn in media studies challenges Elliott and Urry's more static conception of space and time-space compression.[81] Finally both Hoover and Horsfield caution against the technological instrumentalism that Elliott and Urry's paradigm could lean toward. Nonetheless, the mobilities paradigm and its emphasis on media technologies add depth to our understanding of mediating practices.

Citing Henri Lefebvre, Ek noted that "space is permeated with social relations," many of which are blended in late modernity.[82] The continuing task of scholarship on media and religion is to examine blended social relations—spiritual, religious, secular, mediated, technological, consumptive, productive, institutional—as differential and differentiating relational practices in late modernity. Considering the spatial, relational dynamics of religion and media are, we suggest, the best way forward for a holistic understanding of media environments.[83] Doing so involves continued engagement with differences among spiritualities and religions, with the intersection of inward concerns and outward practices, with media *as* religion and media *and* religion,[84] and with media audiences, technologies, industries, texts, and practices.

The chapters in this volume will probe these relational dynamics. Some of the authors will engage media from the broad perspective that material culture *mediates—media as culture.* Others will seek to parse the differences between mediating material culture and the media of the Media Age. Taken as a whole, the chapters in this volume will help highlight important boundaries of the debates about media and elucidate new lines of inquiry in this debate, as well as offer new sites and texts for rich exploration. If the chapters do not actually make the spatial and relational turn in media studies addressed above, they point to this turn and imply its approach.

In addition, the chapters in this volume will engage the various facets of the relational and practical side of spirituality. To do so, authors will engage ideas about lived vernacular religion[85] as well as different conceptions of religious and spiritual practices. Authors will consider how the banal, the everyday, the mundane, and the mediated are imbued with spiritual meaning and how this spiritual meaning constructs identity, community, aspiration, and action. Authors will also consider mystery and enchantment as practical on their own terms and as generators for practical (and aspirational) action.

This book is organized to highlight different way points along life courses. Florence Pasche Guignard highlights spirituality and parenting, focusing particularly on the mediated practice of baby wearing and the ways in which this practice is spiritualized. RuthAnn Ritter and Jeffrey H. Mahan explore mediated spirituality at work, particularly a model of servant leadership made desirable in the Media Age and the ways in which a "wired" and "remixed" generation of workers brings new expectations and metaphors to work, blurring the lines between sacred/secular and public/private. Marion Bowman connects labor to consumption in the spiritual marketplace of Glastonbury, drawing the reader's attention to material religion and to the relational aspects of commodification.

Jenna Gray-Hildenbrand and Martha Smith Roberts continue the discussion of consumption and explore individual practice and community formation through media and Hula Hoops. Jeremy Garber considers the relationships among spiritual identity, community, and art, and points to challenges of spiritual community formation. Lucas F. Johnston, Garry Tregidga, and Liz Barr extend the question of identity and community to broader political action, engaging questions of eco-piety, Cornish political identity, and disidentification with mainstream definitions of "madness." Rachael Liberman and Stewart M. Hoover return to the more intimate and personal, as well as the anonymous and public, in considerations of confessional space via PostSecret. Anne Maija Huffman considers Baby Boomer identities, exploring the tensions between mortality and an entrenched media mythology of eternal youth. Finally, Graham Harvey discusses the relational turn in religious studies in greater detail, using food and sex as a "merism that refers to ordinary lifeways and relations."[86]

In conclusion, we offer these eleven essays from scholars from different disciplines as a way to begin to push for terms and boundaries, to expand the discussion about the role of media in matters of practical, mundane, relational, aspirational, and mysterious spiritualities. Spirituality has become widely perceived as the more personalized part of religion, taking the "external elements of religion" and transforming them into individual expressions.[87] Yet spiritualities are also powerful, legitimating forces that bind individuals, communities, and organizations together. It is vital that we continue to explore the ways and places in which spiritualities form and are plied in a Media Age.

2

Mediated Babywearing as Aesthetic Orthodoxy

Florence Pasche Guignard
University of Toronto

Embodiment, values, and media: Babywearing in the twenty-first century[1]

Since the turn of the twenty-first century, digital media have become central to the form, content, and dissemination of contemporary babywearing, a practice articulated around the optimal use of a device designed for the specific purpose of carrying a baby or a young child and involved in the practice and beliefs articulated as natural parenting. This chapter highlights how some aspects of babywearing intersect with media representations and deeply held beliefs relating to parenting, early childhood, family relationships, and society.

Both embodied and embedded in materiality, babywearing is more than just a component of a "parenting philosophy." It can also be considered a form of "practical spirituality" as defined in the introduction to this volume. Drawing from Pamela Klassen's discussion of the history and uses of the concept of "practice" in the study of media and religions, in this chapter, I turn my attention "away from doctrinal and official discourses of religions, states, and elites [. . .] toward the 'everyday' actions, movements, and sensations of 'ordinary' people."[2] I explore how contemporary Western parents use a variety of online media in order to learn, perfect, and transmit what is to them an "everyday" practice sometimes imbued, though, with "extraordinary" meanings.

Babywearing can be considered as spiritual in the sense that it is based on and expresses values that are not appropriated exclusively by established religious institutions and that transcend the utilitarianism of babywearing and its devices.

Babywearing is much more than just "practical" and thus is at the center of discussions and debates about what constitutes good parenting. Motherhood, a contested institution, is culturally informed by traditions, including religious ones, and is constantly responding to norms that are, in turn, enforced, challenged, or rejected. Babywearing, along with its specifically related devices, is a kinaesthetic and material expression of a set of values related to a particular maternal identity.

Researchers interested in the intersection of religion, media, and everyday life practice might ask not only "What is practical about spirituality?" but also "What is spiritual about a particular practice?" Like other embodied practices such as yoga or martial arts in which scholars detect forms of spirituality emerging outside of traditional religious discourses and institutions or on their margins, babywearing, too, is a "discipline" (in a Foucauldian sense): a bodily technique at the intersection of physical exercise and sartorial aesthetics that holds a promise of practicality, well-being, and wholesome parenthood.

While in many parts of the world carrying young children with the help of different devices remains a normal routine for parents and caregivers,[3] it is now considered, in specific Euro-American contexts, as one virtuous option within a wide array of parenting styles and practices. There, babywearing emerges as a choice, often a conscious or a militant one. Sometimes, objects not only express but also create meaning and meaningful lives. Babywearing wraps, slings, and carriers now are part of the paraphernalia of "good mothering" as defined according to the norms of specific parenting subcultures, principally those of "attachment parenting" but also, increasingly, those of "natural parenting." In this respect, babywearing is a crucial component of these two intersecting, but distinct styles of parenting. These, in turn, are frequently in line with lifestyles of health and sustainability (LOHAS),[4] and lifestyles of voluntary simplicity (LOVOS). LOVOS, already identified as one "ideological component" of "natural mothering," is described as dictating a "lifestyle that derives meaning from relative austerity and minimized consumption,"[5] which does not mean a complete absence of consumption. LOHAS, on the other hand, tends to create meaning through consumption, and in particular through "ethical" or "conscious" consumption of certain manufactured goods, products, and services. "Natural" and "attachment parenting" are easily compatible with LOHAS and LOVOS because of the centrality of this ethical reflection over consumption and sustainability carried on in diverse social circles and through a variety of media. Both alternative parenting subcultures are well represented in online "mamaspheres" that constitute spaces of self-representation and expression for mothers[6] and, more rarely, fathers. This chapter investigates examples from francophone contexts that I surveyed for a larger research project. In those contexts, babywearing remains an uncommon and controversial practice to which spiritual meanings are attached and that reflects current debates about "family values" and parenting norms.

Media, mediation, and mediatization seem to be contested terms even within the field of media studies.[7] Scholars of religions attempting to fill the gap in the study of spirituality, material culture, and digital media, too, are left to work with unstable definitions. In this chapter, I understand media first in a concrete sense as the variety of *mediums*, of material supports, used to communicate information and symbolic meaning. As I will argue, a babywearing wrap itself can become the medium used to express particular identities and sets of beliefs and values. I also use the term in the more general sense of "traditional media" (e.g., print, press, TV, radio) and digital media (e.g., social networks, blogs, forums). Mediation then refers to the process of using such media, whereas I understand mediatization as also including the effects that this use of media may have on a practice, or as Friedrich Krotz formulates it "media change, but also its consequences."[8] Media now play a key role in advertising and advocating for babywearing and in the transmission of the necessary technical skills and of discursive strategies to account for the practice in terms of a "right thing to do" as a parent or, even, as a species. Because the practice itself is now influenced by its multiple mediations, babywearing is both mediated and mediatized: taking a selfie with one's baby in the wrap and sharing it online, or looking at such pictures and their associated comments in order to learn more about babywearing is now an integral part of the babywearing experience for mothers.

These mostly female[9] users form intentional communities of shared affinities, values, worldviews—and they position babywearing as a central topic of discussion on their specific online platforms. Mediation, thus, is a powerful force both in shaping this distinctive identity and in allowing the emergence of what Birgit Meyer calls "aesthetic formations."[10] Pictures, moving images, and other forms of verbal and visual discourses relating to a primarily kinaesthetic practice are relayed through a variety of online platforms and, in particular, through social media. Users participate in larger social processes shaping a narrative about babywearing as the *right* thing to do, not only in a technical sense but also in a moral one as well. This practice is assumed to have positive effects on the wearer and on the child, both in the short- and long run. Because of this implied morality and of the expectation that benefits cannot be achieved through practice, babywearing can be considered a practical spirituality.

Embodiment and mediation are at the center of this chapter, which explores the relationship between a predominantly maternal experience of embodiment and particular modes of mediation and representations of babies and mothers as well as their connection. These constitute selective aspects of this mediatized culture of babywearing in the dominant framework of neoliberal and material(ist) culture of "conspicuous consumption"[11] (Veblen 2007) in which (good) motherhood can be performed through the purchase and the use of specific goods,[12] now complemented by their display through online and social media.

Babywearing at the intersection of attachment parenting and natural parenting

"Natural parenting" is better known in North America as "natural family living," "natural mothering,"[13] "green mothering," "sustainable motherhood," or, for some of its components, "paleo parenting." It is constructed as "a gender-specific and individualistic environmentalism in a neoliberal society"[14] enacted in the domain of parenting and frequently extended to housekeeping or even homesteading. As mentioned above, babywearing is a crucial component of two compatible but nevertheless distinct styles of parenting: natural parenting and attachment parenting. In spite of their similarities, they do not exactly overlap (even if mainstream media tend to conflate both). In the same way that not all "natural parents" are into babywearing (even though most interviewed were), babywearing parents do not necessarily subscribe to environmentalist ideas and values, although many of them do. One can coherently claim to be an attachment parent—breastfeed, cosleep, and carry one's baby as much as possible—and yet still use disposable diapers, purchase toys regardless of their possible unsustainability, eat processed food from conventional agriculture, and forego recycling and composting. While sharing many tenets of attachment parenting, natural parenting adds to it an environmentalist agenda with an emphasis on health and sustainability.[15]

Natural parents not only hope to raise healthy and well-adjusted children, they also do their best to mitigate their impact on the environment. For instance, whenever possible, they use washable diapers and prefer alternative medicines and special (often organic, vegetarian, or locavore) diets. They engage in Lifestyles of Health and Sustainability (LOHAS) and make intentional choices for their everyday consumption that they justify through ethical discourses articulated around social justice and environmentalist imperatives. As shown by Monica Emerich (2011), LOHAS media construct sustainability as ethical practice, as the *right* thing to do. This idea of doing something right through ethical consumption, for instance, is taken as a moral stance by people who adhere to and engage in it. Acquiring, properly using, and displaying certain objects becomes an expression of how we should live with and treat one another as well as of respect not only for our immediate environment but also for the planet as a whole. From this perspective, an ideally constructed idea of "Nature" or, in the discourse of my francophone informants, of "the natural" (*le naturel*) becomes central, valued, and almost sacralized, although not as directly and intensively as in instances of what Bron Taylor calls "dark green religion."[16] Babywearing—as a key practice of natural parenting, and, in turn inserted into wider LOHAS and LOVOS frameworks—participates in a wider, spiritualized conversation and sentiment about how humans should relate to each other and to Nature.

Moreover, babywearing aligns with the idea that the mother's and the child's bodies must remain in proximity, especially during the first weeks after birth, and that "natural" processes should not be disturbed by anything artificial, in particular by medical technology. However, natural parents do not systematically reject technology per se, especially when it helps enhance "natural" processes such as bonding.[17] Neither do these parents shun high-tech communication technologies used to promote such generally low-tech lifestyles, online media in particular.

Whether this is frowned upon or prescribed in the context within which they parent, babywearers de facto embrace bodily proximity with their own children. This idea of bodily closeness and maternal intimacy is often brought up when parents are asked to account for their babywearing. They frequently characterize babywearing with a wrap as "natural" or as "physiological" (*un portage physiologique*), adjectives also used to describe a birth with no or very little medical intervention. The maintenance of maternal intimacy with the child and the attention paid to the closeness of two bodies can be read not only as "care" but also as "love," with the possible implication of a mothering of superior quality and morality. "Wrap you in love" is the title of a webpage in English promoting babywearing with wraps.[18] In French, babywearing instructors recommend that the head of the baby should not be "close at hand," but rather also "*à portée de bisou*" or "*à hauteur de calin*" ("close at kiss" or "at hug's height"). As Marcel Mauss noted in his 1934 essay *Les techniques du corps* where he addresses "the history of carrying," it takes the distinct bodies of "two interrelated beings, mother and child" to babywear—and the practice has different implications for both. Mauss points out the "psychic states [that] arise [from being carried as a child] that have disappeared from infancy with us,"[19] and that being carried "next to [one's] mother's skin for two or three years"[20] might give individuals a different attitude toward their mothers and, probably, a different sensory perception of the body and of the world as well. The debate as to whether such sensory practice or its absence also has spiritual implications is left open.

Francophone online communities of babywearing mothers: The JPMBB case

The following sections focus on a heterogeneous but long-standing online community of users who discuss their experience of babywearing with a specific brand of wraps and slings in a francophone context. This case study offers a remarkable contrast that shatters some of the claims to universality and several of the tenets and values that are often brought forward mostly by North American advocates of babywearing. My informants and the participants whose conversations I followed on a variety of blogs, forums, and social media live for the most part in France, but also in Switzerland, Belgium, and francophone Canada. As opposed to some of the mothers whom I interviewed for this research, I do not consider myself as a technical expert in babywearing. Nevertheless, through my personal practice, I have acquired proficiency in using different babywearing devices, including the specific type of wrap discussed in this chapter. I've learned from certified babywearing instructors and from mothers who were willing to share with me technical advice, their own motivations for babywearing, and what they believed about the effects of babywearing both on them and on their child/ren.[21]

Babywearing with "*Je porte mon bébé*"[22] (I carry my baby) or JPMBB wraps and slings is the main topic of the daily conversations of parents (mostly mothers) who contribute to the open Facebook group examined here.[23] While many online groups and pages are dedicated to babywearing, the peculiarity of this Facebook group is that it brings together users holding general consensus that JPMBB wraps and slings are the best or, at least, their favorites. The group does not feature the prominent debates about the "better" type of wrap, sling, or carrier that frequently take place within larger communities of babywearers. Most posted pictures are of mothers using JPMBB products. Other images include "bad babywearing" positions (such as "facing the world"), alternate uses for the wrap (for instance, as a hammock for a sleepy child), and customized wraps.

Users ask questions and provide answers, post comments on their experience of babywearing with JPMBB wraps, and share advice and information. They also use the Facebook group as a place to advertise babywearing workshops and to swap, buy, and sell new and used wraps. Other topics of discussions related to attachment parenting or natural parenting more generally are also discussed.

The wrap as media: Collecting colors and customizations

A wrap can be used as a medium to voice a critique or rejection of specific norms and beliefs and to proclaim the adoption of alternative ethics of parenting. But, it is through processes of mediatization that this social value is now articulated and made manifest. The wrap itself can be customized through dyeing, embroidery, or silkscreen printing. It reveals culturally determined and often implicit convictions about what constitutes appropriate care of children. By using a particular type or brand of wrap, the wearer expresses belonging in a wider social framework or in a specific subculture that resists that framework.

The issues of conspicuous consumption of babywearing wraps and of sartorial aesthetics in relation to mediation deserve a discussion that exceeds the scope of this chapter. As a way in which to contextualize this case study, however, some of the significant aesthetic and technical characteristics that distinguish the JPMBB wrap from other brands include the availability of a wide range of colors (with new additions every season) and a pocket at the center of the original wrap bearing the JPMBB logo.

As one of the Facebook group users pointed out in a discussion about the controversial practice of collecting wraps, there would not be all this "frenzy around the wraps if they were all of the same color" and if users would not share pictures of their "stash" on Facebook. "There is no such thing as too many wraps," responds another poster. Even as a fashion statement, wearing an empty wrap would not make any sense. One cannot babywear without a baby: babywearing is the privileged practice of people who, on a regular or temporary basis, care for young children. Because only one wrap can be worn (and displayed) at a time, social media have become the alternative public space where users can share pictures of their collection, which may include up to fifteen JPMBB wraps and slings in different colors (not counting other types of carriers which appear in some of the pictures including customized babywearing wraps that include not only images such as trees, hands, animated cartoons characters, and abstract designs but also mottos such as "Keep calm and carry on," "Close to my heart," or "I carry the treasure of my life"[24]). Some wraps are customized with the child's name. For instance, "*Lalie à portée de bisous . . .* " (Lalie close at kiss) was the motto printed on one of the pictures publicly shared on the JPMBB users Facebook group. A mother had customized her wrap with the name of her child and she considered as desirable that this baby should be close enough to receive maternal marks of affection (kisses) while in the wrap (and, probably, the rest of the time as well). As will be further explained below, such proximity is deemed suspicious within mainstream French culture (and more largely other European francophone contexts, too). Babywearing is considered by some as detrimental not only to the upbringing of the child, but also to the mother and to society at large.

Freedom and connection: Babywearing as "gift" and "experience"

To better identify the beliefs and values that underlie babywearing and to understand how the JPMBB online community contributes to the construction of a "practical spirituality," it is necessary to situate babywearing more precisely against the backdrop of attachment parenting and natural parenting. In turn, these two parenting subcultures must be considered in their contemporary francophone context.

The founders of JPMBB (the firm is legally and administratively established in France but operates internationally) present themselves as parents who have experienced the "adult-child connection" much valued in attachment parenting theory along with other benefits claimed by advocates of babywearing.[25] On the JPMBB webpage, they write:

> Our "philosophy" is to pass on babywearing not only as a convenient tool, but mainly as a great way for parents to listen to their child and to themselves, to gain self-confidence and regain free will and autonomy, which isn't [*sic*] easy to keep during pregnancy.
>
> To us, babywearing is as important as any other aspect of parenting, because it usually happens at the very beginning of parenthood and of the adult-child connection. It is decisive and helps build the foundation of the future communication between the adult and the child, who in turn will become an adult.
>
> We discovered babywearing when we were given a wrap as a gift after our first child was born.

> Babywearing started as a gift and remained a gift to us: a gift both to the adult and the child, that's how we experience it and how we want to share it.
>
> Babywearing is a lot about sharing "knowledge": know how to trust yourself, know your Baby, know his needs and reality.
>
> When doing the instruction booklet and tutorial videos, we were careful to keep on passing this on, with responsible sales and marketing practices, for those who cannot come to a workshop.[26]

JPMBB mediatizes itself as a dynamic brand created *by* parents *for* parents and their babies. The company clearly outlines their ethics ("responsible sales and marketing practices"), obliquely addressing potential consumers engaged in "ethical consumption," and pays attention to issues of social justice in line with lifestyles of health and sustainability.

The connection between adult and child, the reinforcement of this alleged special bond, the convenience afforded by the babywearing wrap, and a restored freedom for the wearer tend to receive a great emphasis in the francophone contexts studied. Child-centeredness was less prominent. Unlike in North American discourses advocating babywearing, immediate response to the baby's needs was rarely mentioned first. Rather, my informants gave "convenience," "practicality," or even "freedom to resume regular outings and activities" as their main reasons for using a wrap. This is the case for "Vanessa," a babywearing instructor and work-at-home mother in Switzerland. When she gave birth in 2009, she used the wrap for many activities including visiting museums and dining out with her husband. They lived in a big city at the time and Vanessa emphasized how much more convenient the wrap was than a stroller when using the subway system. Shifting the focus away from the child and placing it on practicality and on the freedom babywearing affords users to fulfill aspirations outside of motherhood is part of a discursive strategy used by many of the francophone mothers interviewed, especially those from France. This emphasis is also perceptible in the images shared with the Facebook group, and online generally. By posting pictures of themselves with their babies in the wraps not only in their homes but also in the cultural, historical, and natural sites they visit, mothers strive to present babywearing as a socially acceptable and public practice.

Some mothers post such pictures and captions as an explicit response to allegations that babywearing and attachment parenting practices (in particular breastfeeding) confine women to domesticity. Such criticism against babywearing is part of a more general condemnation of the "naturalist ideology"[27] that supposedly pushes women back into their homes for the sake of environmentalism and conflates "women" with "mothers." However, as opposed to the use of washable diapers,[28] babywearing does not require "more work" from parents. On the contrary, the babywearing advocates and practitioners interviewed such as Vanessa repeatedly stated that their JPMBB wraps allowed them more freedom to venture out and ensure continuity in their social life. In contrast with the prominence of the child-centered benefits of attachment parenting in its North American and Anglophone expressions, discourses of francophones tend to be more matricentric and rarely prioritize the child's needs over those of the parent.

French parenting versus babywearing: Exotic, marginal, and dangerous

Natural parenting locates a lost parenting wisdom either in the distant past or in far-away cultures, unblemished by harmful technological innovations. Like many discourses about health and spiritual well-being, natural parenting tends to revere these idealized past or distant "Exotic Others" as repositories of valuable relational, spiritual, and practical wisdom to be reclaimed and embraced. By contrast, prevailing French views on parenting are generally informed by an efficiently mediated ideology of "scientific motherhood,"[29] usually expert-guided, and driven by progress and technological innovation rather than by intuition. In spite of its increasing popularity, babywearing is still predominantly portrayed in a negative light in most European francophone contexts.

Babywearing mothers often are prompted to account for their practice both by relatives and strangers. A user on the JPMBB users Facebook group posted the following message (translated):

> Today, I persuaded a 50-ish years old lady who almost called me a bad mother when she saw my son in the wrap! She starts by telling me off, saying that my baby had no coat and must have been cold in my "rag" (*chiffon*) ([though] it is 20° C degrees . . .). . . that here we were not in Africa . . . Then I explained to her the benefits of babywearing! She asked me many questions, in particular "why not a baby carrier (*un porte-bébé*) rather than your "rag"? I explained [everything] to her, and then she completely changed her mind. This is pleasant, but when I heard her [initial] discourse, I realized her prejudice and this is desolating.[30]

Allusions to a generic Africa, recurring in many (usually negative) remarks about babywearing,[31] position the practice as exotic and foreign[32] and links it to imaginary contexts where mothers cannot access the technical comforts of modern motherhood. In the opinion of the older woman who confronted the JPMBB user, such a practice should not take place in France or is tolerable only for mothers who actually are of African origin and thus cannot fit into the (unachievable) stereotype of the "ideal French mother" anyway. Many mothers who share their experiences on the JPMBB Facebook group have experienced the prevailing negative prejudice against babywearing. They report that they are the only ones in their neighborhood or town to use a wrap or a sling. They recount uneasy feelings about situations of social surveillance similar to that above where people not only stared at them and their baby in the wrap, but also made comments (or even tried to touch the baby). Some comments are positive, humorous, or stem from genuine ignorance about babywearing or concern for the baby ("Can he breathe?"; "Won't she fall down?"; "Is he not too cold, warm, tight, loose?"; "When will she finally learn how to walk?") or for the mother ("Don't you have back pain?"; "Can't you afford to buy a stroller?"). Other remarks, though, are perceived as highly offensive and some tend to be implicitly racist.

According to Sharon Hays, who coined the term "ideology of intensive mothering," the current hegemonic model of motherhood in North America says child-rearing is (or should be) labor-intensive, child-centered, and expert-guided. Mothers must devote time, resources, and energy to child-rearing. The success of attachment parenting theories has certainly contributed to the rise of this ideology, but its hold on francophone mothers living in Europe seems more limited. Detractors fear the progress of what they coin a new "maternalism" and its alliance with environmentalist agendas and the so-called naturalist ideology.[33] Even though they are not restricted to the geographical boundaries of France, some principles can be considered more typical of a French child-rearing style than of most contemporary parenting trends in North America: the desire to render the child autonomous as early as possible, early socialization and schooling, and a rather strict training to comply with parents' and caregivers' instructions. All of this is embedded in the generally guilt-free use of state-sponsored collective structures. Moreover, prevailing in this context is the idea that a woman should find satisfaction and self-realization not only through motherhood and domestic and family life but also through her relationships with adults of both sexes and through personal activities.

The belief that child-rearing requires training and regular schedules defined more by society's and adults' convenience than by the child's physiological needs (though both can coincide) is still widely accepted in this context. It is seen not only as necessary but also as highly desirable that a child be autonomous as early as possible and be fit to be cared for by caregivers other than the mother. This affects the prevailing perception of babywearing as a marginal, exotic, dangerous, and socially unfit practice (sometimes all together). If the baby is carried in the arms or in a wrap too much, too often, or at her own will, she will grow into *un enfant gâté* (a spoiled child). From this perspective, babywearing, or at least its intensive practice chiefly determined by the baby's needs rather than by those of the caregiver, is better avoided lest the mother wants to turn her child into a "tyrant" and herself into a "slave." Media relay and amplify such fears and suspicions, in particular when mainstream medical professionals are featured as experts and discourage the practice, mostly on social rather than on medical grounds: the fear is that the child will become *capricieux* ("fussy and picky"). Because babywearing is suspected of producing unruly children, it is also seen as socially irresponsible.

Babywearing is not perceived as a spiritual practice uniformly across cultures. Where babies are commonly carried, babywearing has no particular and separate spiritual dimension, although rituals might take place to mark the first time the child touches the ground or takes her first steps. However, where carrying babies is no longer the norm, media amplify advocacy narratives that exalt the maternal bond with the child or, conversely, the discourses–usually by male medical experts–that criticize this bond as too intense. Mainstream media and online platforms used by mothers themselves determine not only the spaces and forms of the discussion, but also their contents, especially when users and advocates of babywearing collectively moderate these spaces. They also set a tone for the discussion, either suspicious and accusatory or, at the opposite, apologetic. Such discourses reflect the difficulties that some users have in their practice of babywearing, but will rarely call into question the practice itself.

"Never alone with your wrap": Online communities

As noted, babywearing is much more than the purchase of an object; technical knowledge about its optimal use should be acquired. The following statement by JPMBB was posted in response to a debate about whether the group should remain visible and public on Facebook:

> It is part of the JPMBB experience to never be alone with one's wrap. There are the videos, this FB group, the detailed [user's] notice, the instructors (*monitrices*) [and] each one of these [has its own] specificity. Before being a brand, JPMBB is

an experience lived every day by parents, something strong, something useful, something that one wishes to share when one has lived it.[34]

This statement testifies to the mediation and mediatization of babywearing: the brand is present online, and so is the community of users and they reflect on their presence there. To users of the JPMBB wrap, this "experience lived every day" goes beyond the purely utilitarian. Mediation, here understood as the use of a variety of online platforms and social media, serves several interconnected purposes. Mainly, it allows the sharing of experience and knowledge concerning (1) the adult–child bond in parenting, and (2) the specific capacities that the wearer gains or regains through babywearing. More pragmatically, mediation is also used to transmit (3) technical skills necessary for using the wrap correctly, and finally it contributes to (4) the building of a fluctuant community of users willing to share "something strong": similar values, interests, and an attraction for a similar aesthetic. Such communities are constantly in the process of forming, dissolving, and reforming, migrating from one platform to another. Mediation plays an important role in the building of these "aesthetic formations,"[35] these heterogeneous "imagined communities"[36] of affinity that place a particular aesthetic and the embodied dimension of babywearing at the center of their common interests.

At the collective level, in addition to forming communities of users, online media is also integral to making babywearing visible and for the reclaiming of public space. For instance, babywearing flashmobs and strolls take place regularly in France, Switzerland, and Belgium. Other similar meetings in the public space such as breastfeeding sit-ins are held with the intent to make visible, normalize, and promote practices still considered marginal. Videos of babywearing choreographies performed in several cities in France during International Babywearing Week have been posted on YouTube. Successfully organizing such flashmobs would be difficult without using social media to advertise and recruit. For the babywearing choreography, participants could learn the steps of the dance ahead of time through video and join the group on the day of the event, without even having met the other babywearers-dancers ahead of time.

Media transmissions: Learning "from scratch" or "from screen"

In contrast to other types of baby carriers—which only require positioning the baby, clicking buckles, and adjusting the device—a wrap requires specific know-how in order to be tied correctly and securely. Advocates generally present babywearing as natural, necessary, instinctive, timeless, and universal. For instance, an author of the Feminist Breeder blog writes that babywearing is "what Mother Nature intended for us to do. Because of how we evolved as a species, we NEED to do it for our babies."[37] Such polysemic characterization of babywearing, relayed and amplified by media, conflicts with the reality that effective use of a wrap is not instinctive, but must be learned. Furthermore, the few paleoanthropological and historical studies about devices used to carry tiny humans insist on their technological or artificial dimension, as noted by Timothy Taylor in *The Artificial Ape*.[38] Baby carriers have evolved into fashionable—but still practical—artifacts the optimal use of which requires specific training that is often acquired through online media.

The website of the association Babywearing International states:

> Parents and caregivers often benefit from thinking of babywearing as a skill they can learn, rather than as the result of a product they can buy. Many babywearing techniques can be learned in just a few minutes. Some techniques, such as carrying a baby on your back, take more time and practice to master, but the extra effort is rewarded with liberation and increased comfort.[39]

This statement reflects the disjunction between owning a product and having the skills to use it. The complex tying of a wrap becomes easier with practice, and some people learn faster than others. Various media fill the gap between consumption and a learning process that requires "extra effort" but offers rewards including "liberation," not unlike progression on a spiritual path.

Mediation plays a key role in the transmission of these skills, in particular in contexts where they are no longer passed down within families as a mainstream cultural practice.[40] "Vanessa" runs an online boutique where she sells items related to babywearing. She also is an instructor certified by the JPMBB brand. When I interviewed her, she was enthusiastic about transmitting her knowledge and "passion" to new parents. She organizes workshops, offers private classes, and even gives a few basic tips, free of charge, to parents who purchase their first wrap from her. When asked what she thought of the rise in popularity of babywearing, she said she was happy about it, but identified as a problem that even though the *object*—the wrap or the carrier—was becoming more widely used in Switzerland, the *know-how* and skills necessary to its proper use were often missing. Some parents use the wraps suboptimally or even dangerously. Vanessa said that "large department stores," unlike her "small online boutique" (*petite boutique en ligne*), sell the wraps along with users' manuals, but do not offer a live demonstration nor the proper, accompanying training. They do not "care" for their customers, which is also part of the JPMBB retailers' philosophy.

When they do not attend workshops such as those organized by Vanessa, parents are left with several meters of fabric, a baby, and no technique. If they cannot "learn from scratch" by following the static illustrations and instructions in the owner's manual, and if they do not have an experienced friend to help them, their only alternative is to "learn from screen." New users seek to emulate moving images found on the many tutorial videos available on a variety of video-sharing platforms. Although JPMBB sells products for profit, the firm strives to make the know-how associated with them available for free, at least to some extent. The company provides many free tutorial videos on its website and through its YouTube channel[41] that featured 66 videos and had 2,588 subscribers at the time of submission of this chapter. The second most popular video, after the one for tying the basic knot, demonstrates a position that enables breastfeeding in the wrap. It has been watched more than 200,000 times. The demonstrators appear at ease during the manipulation, and the videos are carefully edited: potential failures, such as a baby fussing or the carrier dropping the baby, are edited out. A musical soundtrack is added, and visual clues are superimposed on the image.

JPMBB was founded in 2007, and Facebook was made available to the general public in 2006. Most mothers who are currently buying and using wraps are proficient media users, and the youngest among them even qualify as "digital natives." Social media and other online platforms (e.g., forums) constitute a primary source of information on child-rearing issues. When asked whom they turn to solve a nonlife-threatening emergency parenting issue, most parents I interviewed said they would first look online. Because a majority of their own mothers (and possibly even grandmothers) were not familiar with breastfeeding or babywearing, the mothers I interviewed generally ruled out older generations of women in their family as experts on such issues. Instead, they tended to turn to models outside of their immediate relatives, and their discourses emphasize this collective dimension of online communities of mothers constituted through and taking place mostly on mediated spaces. Online mediation thus is a key instrument in their reappropriating of these skills and in their reclaiming of babywearing as something they can feel good about in their mothering.

On videos posted by JMPBB and by authentic users of their products, some viewers post thanks for the tutorial while others bash babywearing in general and still others post precise criticisms of what they think is a poor performance of babywearing or a tutorial of low quality. Similarly, on the JPMBB Facebook group, many first-time users—almost exclusively women—post pictures of themselves with their baby in the JPMBB wrap, hoping for advice on how to achieve the perfect position. Posting a picture of a "perfect" *portage* gives a sense of achievement and pride. New users try to emulate this aesthetic orthodoxy. The insistence on the right technique is amplified by its media reproduction, helping to turn babywearing into a form of orthopraxy. Within the truncated context of these videos, pictures, and comments, the reasons for babywearing matter less than its correct performance. Whether a mother uses a wrap primarily to soothe her baby's colic or to regain the use of both her hands to make herself a sandwich is not important here. Examples of "bad babywearing practice" are publicly vilified online, even though most group participants would not likely confront a mother in the street about her erroneous tying of the wrap. Participants regularly announce that they are "leaving the group," irritated by critiques that they feel "tend [to be] on the verge of extremism."

The social and relational dynamics of a live babywearing workshop differ from those in the mediated space of the Facebook group, where some users ask for feedback and more experienced users give advice or criticism. At the live workshop, all participants are there to learn and give new parents a chance to socialize and interact. Workshops are advertised, often through social media, as an occasion to learn in a safe and relaxed environment with immediate, constructive feedback provided by the instructor, face to face. Although not all participants will engage in babywearing to the same extent after taking a workshop, it is likely that they all share, at least, an interest in safe and efficient practice, but maybe not enough to form a community of affinity.

Concluding remarks

Babywearing in the media age reflects some of the changing values that (re)define and express prevailing and culturally specific norms of "good mothering." Media, mediation, and mediatization directly affect the practice of parenting and the objects associated with it such as babywearing wraps. Parenting choices are framed as part of different lifestyles and broader conversations about society and about how to parent as mothers inserted in specific social and natural environments.

Because of their materiality, wraps, slings, and carriers serve as customizable media for expressing this maternal identity. Particular spaces of social media such as the JPMBB Facebook group enable the transformation of a practical object into a (fashion) statement of identity and values. In turn, social media extend such identity statements beyond offline practice by providing spaces where users can demonstrate their authenticity and authority in the matter of babywearing. Specific brands of babywearing devices such as JPMBB address their actual and potential consumers through these same media and encourage users to discuss their experience with their products and to solicit solutions to the issues they encounter.

While mainstream francophone media tend to present babywearing as harmful to children, mothers, and society, online social media that advocate for natural parenting and attachment parenting provide a friendly and safe space for users to discuss in their own terms the values that sustain their everyday practice and the benefits they achieve through or expect from it. Babywearing thus often is one element at the center of discussions that take place mostly online within communities of parents drawn to lifestyles that emphasize healthy living, sustainability, bonding with one's children, and practicality.

Whether practiced in public spaces or mediated through the online sharing of pictures and videos, babywearing can function as a statement of a maternal identity that is at odds with dominant conceptions of proper childrearing. Babywearing embodies proximity and intimacy with one's baby, whereas the dominant discourses in the particular contexts I surveyed emphasize early independence in children and generally recommend distantial parenting techniques. There, when babywearers account for their practice, they insist on the practicality and freedom that they regain through it, as mothers, women, and participants in society. This freedom of movement includes reinvesting public spaces and showing it through the performance of babywearing flashmobs, or gatherings, among others, that are then also mediated.

Now that parenting is discussed and debated online as much as—if not more than—it is offline, babywearing has turned into a mediated performance accompanied by proselytizing efforts. In addition to being "brand evangelists," some mothers become guardians and promoters of an "orthopraxy" of babywearing. In line with this religious analogy, babywearing can be a "profession" in a double sense: some babywearers start *professing* to other mothers, teaching them a gospel of babywearing, leading by example and convincingly passing on their knowledge, often through online media. Taken to the next level, this can become a *professional* activity for some of them who decide to become certified babywearing instructors (as in Vanessa's case) who actively use online media to publicize their activities, along with word-of-mouth advertising.

Babywearing workshops and social media play an important role in disseminating a new culture of babywearing in contexts where it is not part of mainstream parenting skills. Because properly tying a wrap is a kinaesthetic practice that involves two bodies and complex manipulations, video clips are one of the best media to demonstrate it. Social networks and video sharing websites are thus among the social media platforms used both by wrap retailers and manufacturers and by their users. Through shared images, video tutorials, narratives, and comments, new aesthetic and physiological orthodoxies are constituted online. Social media are used to transmit not only practical skills but also to model discursive strategies to justify going against the grain of conventional child-rearing modes in certain contexts. Further, they reinforce the users' convictions that they made the right choice in using the wrap, even if their immediate friends, relatives, and healthcare providers say they have not. Such sensibilities are enabled to emerge transnationally and to be expressed in a variety of ways, both individually and collectively.

Contemporary mediation contributes to the regeneration of babywearing, while attaching new meanings, identities, and markets to it. Manufacturers and retailers of babywearing devices address primarily a specific community of consumers and market the practices as a transformative experience that eases transition to parenthood. As claimed by its advocates, babywearing indeed is not a new practice. The need for devices to carry infants preexists its mediation. Although media did not create this market segment, they have amplified it and transformed it into a community, through, for instance, popularizing certain brands of wraps as fashion accessories or through promoting the idea of collecting and displaying pictures of wraps. Media have also given babywearers greater visibility and a place to form online communities. They have contributed to transforming an object of consumption into one that indicates status, identity, and belonging to a community of shared beliefs, values, and practice.

3

Spirituality at Work: Servant Leadership in the Western Workplace

RuthAnn Ritter and Jeffrey H. Mahan
Iliff School of Theology

Introduction: Spirituality in the Western workplace

This book brings reflections on spirituality in contemporary media culture into conversation with reflections on the stages of human life. This chapter addresses work as a rich and lasting stage of life and considers some examples of companies and business leaders who have intentionally made space for spirituality in the workplace. While we touch on the way that thinking about the workplace as a spiritual location reshapes the way employees think about their individual work, we focus on how it can encourage collaboration and on the role of business leaders and the way they think about and organize their businesses. Finally, we frame this discussion within suggestions of how the emerging digital media culture invites and provides metaphors for this change.

Finding satisfying and meaningful work is traditionally one of the threshold challenges of early adulthood, eliciting such questions as:

- What are my talents?
- What do I love to do?
- How will I balance work with relationship and recreation?
- What skills do I want to develop?
- How will a particular vocation shape my identity?

In an era when vocational change is the norm, these questions and issues are seldom resolved once and for all. Changing economies and life situations keep such issues before us through much of the life cycle. It is commonplace to observe how digital communications technologies are remaking work, creating new jobs, and making other forms of work obsolete. We examine something beyond the direct consequences of the malleability of digital texts, sounds, and the networked relationships they make possible by suggesting that these things create new metaphors through which people think about their lives, spirituality, and work. Digital data is composed of pixels that can easily be rearranged in new ways. Thus we think of ourselves as projects under construction integrating data from various sources that includes the multiple components of ourselves. Digital natives and adept immigrants bring a different set of values and priorities to work than their predecessors that emphasize creativity, adaptability, and unique experiences.

How and why are issues of work and workplace spiritual issues? Today, spiritual practices extend beyond the boundaries of organized religion. Living out of the digital metaphor, people see their personal and professional lives as part of one larger evolving project of spiritual identity construction. Thus, when spirituality is infused into everyday life so that people seek to integrate the personal and professional, spiritual practices emerge in new locations such as the workplace.

One way that spirituality is expressed in the workplace is by individual employees who bring their own spiritual practices to work. However, we are focused primarily on organizational cultures that reflect spiritual values. Although the workplace has been largely considered a secular space since the Industrial Revolution, this is changing. Today, the workplace is often understood as a location for the sacred. For example, organizations such as Ford Motor Company acknowledge the importance of compassion in the workplace and of community philanthropy and General Mills offers employees opportunities to attend mindfulness training and to practice yoga or meditation at work as a way to improve focus and productivity. As a result, these organizations are thought to benefit from happier employees.[1]

It is not an entirely new phenomenon for businesses to be shaped by spiritual values or practices. Some privately held businesses have long reflected the faith commitments of the owners. Examples include the American corporation Hobby Lobby that has resisted the US healthcare mandate because of the owner's conservative Christian resistance to providing birth control, kosher butcher shops where butchering standards are set by Jewish law, or Indian restaurants where a statue of a Hindu deity is displayed.

In this chapter, we are interested in a more recent phenomenon related to spirituality in the workplace that does not identify with any specific religion or spiritual tradition. One example is the discourse of spiritually grounded "servant leadership" focused on service to others that is articulated and modeled by companies such as Whole Foods Market, Starbucks, and Zappos. These companies embrace an openness to spirituality (only loosely connected to any particular religious tradition) as a key component of work life. While it can be expressed in various ways, servant leadership generally emphasizes social responsibility, employee empowerment, and transparent communication. Rather than being limited to specific spiritual practices such as philanthropy or mindfulness, servant leadership itself is understood as a spiritual practice that seeks to transform organizational performance and increase satisfaction for both the employee and leader.

In popular discourse the phrase "spiritual but not religious" seeks to distinguish a personal life open to spiritual feeling and practice drawn from multiple sources from one embedded in membership and participation in organized religion.[2] This aligns with mediated practices of consumption through which people access images, material, and ideas from a variety of sources and shifts the location of identity from organized religion to individual spirituality. This raises new questions about assumed distinctions between sacred and ordinary spaces and between spirituality and religion as private and public activities. Because building and articulating identity is a holistic project the spiritual-but-not-religious do not think of shaping their spiritual identities and practices as a purely private activity carried on apart from work. Rather, these practitioners make their belief and practice a public activity to be incorporated into their professional life and sometimes see work itself as a spiritual practice.

The work in contemporary media culture

We live in the midst of an emerging media culture, and many of the changes in spiritual practices that we find at various stages of the life cycle emerge out of the ways that people adapt to the unique possibilities and limitations of this particular media culture. Millennials are the first generation to grow up in the current world of technology and new media, and the way they and accomplished digital immigrants think about their lives and vocations as an integrated and evolving construction is shaping new work structures and practices, including the relationship between work and spirituality. These changes lead to new forms of community and networked relationships. This in turn requires new understandings of leadership.

Digital media technologies

Digital media technologies enable new models of work. Tools such as Google Docs, for example, make it easier to work collaboratively. Teleconferencing empowers people to work from distant offices or at home. Online resources are easily adapted, instantly available, and encourage an expectation of constant access as well as an attitude of constant change. In this discussion, we are less interested in these technological changes themselves and more so in the ways digital cultures' mediated relationships facilitate collaboration and creativity.

Because digital information (music, text, or image) is made up of pixels that are easily reorganized and reassembled in new ways, artists can sample, reposition, and comment on other's work. In a similar way a business plan or project can be easily remade to accommodate changing realities in the work sphere. Ready access to these products and projects allow more people to bring their own values and vision to bear on the project. Creative participants see their work as part of the performance of an integrated spiritual self.

Community

A second important change associated with the media age is a shift in relationships. Where once people identified primarily with a single lasting community, today they are likely to participate simultaneously in multiple networks of relationships. Not only are people in the United States and elsewhere relocating and changing jobs more frequently, perhaps having fewer lasting face-to-face relationships as a result, but also people are increasingly connecting through ephemeral online communities such as Facebook, Twitter, and LinkedIn. Some people experience anxiety over the changing nature of community relationships, perhaps feeling that these relationships reflect connections that are not as strong they once were or are substantially different in nature. As Heidi Campbell has shown, this new networked way of relating has implications for how people connect."[3] Online networking makes it possible for people to easily gather around shared spiritual and work-related interests creating shared visions.

Authority

A third cultural change might be described as a conversational model of authority. Web-based systems of communications such as wikis, blogs, and websites create the expectation that followers can participate in creating new information and question and debate those in authority. Indeed, in such systems followers often grant authority to leaders based on the quality and usefulness of their interactions. With the increased influence of collaborative and socially conscious Millennials, authority depends more on the leader's charisma and usefulness to the follower than on traditional hierarchical paradigms that increasingly seem ineffective and out of touch with emerging cultural realities.[4] Leaders must make it possible for followers to ask questions, make comments, and participate in decision-making.

Spirituality in media culture

People bring the expectations developed in contemporary media culture to their spiritual lives. They seek to develop and articulate individualized spiritual identities and practices, to come together in networks around shared values and creative projects, and to be engaged by leaders in less hierarchal and in more conversational ways. Organized religions have not always adapted well to these changes. A growing number of people in the United States do not identify with any religion. This doesn't mean that Americans have abandoned an interest in transcendent experiences or given up the search for higher meaning.[5] In fact, a discontent with organized religion inspires an increasing number of people to turn to spirituality to derive a sense of higher purpose and meaning. The people who consider themselves spiritual-but-not-religious are one of the fastest-growing demographics in the United States.[6] Generally, their spirituality is expressed individually through discourse, practices, and behavior that are expressed outside the boundaries of a particular religion.

As the West continues to transform its spiritual and religious practices, many people create their own spiritual traditions by borrowing practices from various religious and wisdom traditions. The flexibility inherent in traditions such as Zen and Tibetan Buddhism—which allows individuals to adopt and adapt particular elements to suit their spiritual needs and goals—is a particularly good fit for the way that spiritual beliefs and practices are consumed in America. The digital practice of sampling, often thought of in relationship to hip-hop, provides a way to think about this practice. Individuals draw from a range of traditions to create a personalized spirituality rather than adhering to a specific or inherited religion.[7]

This new movement toward self-actualized individual spiritualities raises new questions about work. An employee's measure of satisfaction may no longer be linked solely to pay and a key to the corner office. Instead, worker satisfaction is increasingly associated with intrinsic value and reflects an individual's search for deeper fulfillment. Myler says, "While a paycheck is important, even more engaging rewards include human connection, peer recognition, self-expression, a stimulating career path, personal growth, sense of community, and other intrinsic incentives."[8] Scholars who research organizational life validate that meaningful work, personal fulfillment, and social connections are among the qualities that are significant to individuals in an organization. Spirituality in the workplace provides ways for individuals to engage with the organization in deeper ways.[9] Thus, workers are drawn to workplaces that make room for an integration of the whole self and are drawn to servant leaders who engage workers more fully.

As part of a series of interviews about spirituality in the workplace, author RuthAnn Ritter spoke with "Glenn," a package handler with a large shipping company. Glenn is a regular meditator and yoga practitioner who sees these spiritual practices as relevant to his job, one that requires physical labor and monotonous tasks. He says,"When you connect your time at work in a space of deeper purpose, no matter how repetitive the job is, the results show in the work that you do, and the positivity you can share with your co-workers."[10] Glenn's spirituality constructed personal meaning around the job itself but went further, also creating meaningful connections with co-workers.

Companies, too, increasingly challenge old models of what is appropriate in public spaces. One reason for this shift is the deepening awareness around corporate social responsibility.[11] Linked to this is the transforming demographic of the American workforce—employee diversity is an important factor in organizational management today. To this, "Maggie," a team leader in a publishing company, openly described people's religious affiliations and spiritual practices that are evident in her workplace. "Everyone comes from a different tradition," she says. "There are crystal healers, a Zen Buddhist, Orthodox Catholics, non-believers, and people who practice yoga and T'ai Chi. Everybody is a seeker on a different path, and all paths are respected at my work."[12]

Organizations attend to employees' needs for connection with community, meaningful work, and personal fulfillment at work by infusing spirituality in the workplace in various ways. For example, some encourage employees to take breaks together in nature. Clothing retailer Patagonia calls this creative break "Let My People Go Surfing," believing that time in nature spurs breakthroughs in problem solving and product development.[13] Tom's of Maine, a personal care manufacturer, incorporates philanthropy by providing employees with twelve days off a year to volunteer in the community.[14] Clif Bar focuses on social responsibility and practices that encourage a sustainable, green environment. The company culture is based on the motto that "every day is an opportunity to do something that matters," echoing the deeper meaning that many individuals search for in the workplace.[15]

Some organizations offer individuals ways to connect to deeper personal fulfillment on intrinsic levels. Clothing retailer Zappos offers personal and professional coaching to its employees and encourages crossover between life inside and outside of work.[16] Sounds True and Green Mountain Coffee offer dedicated spaces in the workplace for quiet time. Google provides an on-site training called "Search Inside Yourself" in which participants are trained in Buddhist practices such as mindfulness and meditation, often thought to develop concentration, compassion, and wisdom in followers.[17] However, such practices in the workplace are typically stripped of specific religious associations.

The ways in which organizations engage employees through external shared activities and internal practices that cultivate purposeful work for individuals also inform how leaders engage in conscious-business practices. That is, while leaders influence the organizational culture, the culture shapes their leadership practices in return. Not only do spiritual practices such as philanthropy and meditation connect employees and organizations in new ways, but also they inform a new relationship between leaders and followers. Senior executives such as Bill Ford of Ford Motor Company and Renata M. Black of the Seven Bar Foundation seek professional guidance from spiritual teachers such as Jack Kornfield and Deepak Chopra, suggesting an interest in an awakened consciousness that moves beyond the common external concerns of market position and financial results.[18] Much as individuals seek a deeper meaning and purpose in the workplace, many leaders, too, are negotiating new boundaries between business motivators such as competition and profits and between spiritual motivators such as individual and social well-being. As the workplace becomes a location for the spiritual, transformation can occur at all levels of the organization.

We have focused on underlying assumptions about the self, networks, and community, and styles of leadership and authority in cultures shaped by what we describe as the digital metaphor. Yet the technologies of a digitally networked society are more than a metaphor. They make possible the practices that inform this way of thinking about self, human connection, and authority. Further, digital communication makes possible the spread of these ideas and encourages networked connections.

Leadership as spiritual practice

The business practice of servant leadership is a contemporary leadership model conceived in the 1970s by AT&T executive Robert Greenleaf.[19] Inspired by Herman Hesse's story about a spiritual pilgrimage, *Journey to the East*, Greenleaf proposed a new relationship between leaders and followers that mirrors spiritual characteristics such as trust, compassion, and altruistic love—those characteristics common to many religious wisdom traditions. In essence Greenleaf invited business audiences to think of leadership as a spiritual practice.

In Greenleaf's theory a spiritually inspired model of leadership crosses into the secular boundaries of the workplace. Servant leaders may hold personal beliefs that align with various religious and spiritual sources such as Christianity, Buddhism, or Islam. However, the emphasis is less on identifying with personal faith traditions and instead more on how leaders carry out the spiritual practice of selfless service to others. This section explores the spiritual framework of servant leadership and examines how industry-leading companies and senior executives model traits of servant leadership. We examine how servant leadership distinguishes itself from traditional organizational models in the workplace in four significant areas: (1) Organizational hierarchy and power; (2) organizational space and schedules; (3) interactions between leaders and followers; and (4) the transformation of leadership as a spiritual practice.

Hierarchy and power

Traditional leadership models encourage a fixed organizational model in which managers practice autocratic decision-making and give orders to subordinates. In this framework, companies are generally organized in hierarchical structures with singular or group power at the top followed by subsequent levels of subordinates. Often, the primary focus is on maximizing profits and fulfilling self-interests.[20] Typically, there is a clear demarcation between those performing the work and those who manage and assign the tasks thereby creating emotional and physical distance among people and restraining how people interact with each other and find meaning at work. In many companies, there is a "distinct class system when it comes to benefits. Executives are given an array of special perks unavailable to everyone else."[21] Power might be designated, for example, by where people sit in the office and in what type of space. Often, people in positions of power have offices with doors while others sit in cubicles with little privacy. As organizations compete for market share and as the workforce presses for a purposeful identity in the workplace, these old structures are being challenged. Management scholar Louis W. Fry explains the significance of the transformation of conventional organizational models: "The creation of work environments that provide a sense of challenge and meaningfulness for employees has become a priority. The creation of such a work environment may very well be the strategic imperative of the new millennium."[22]

Conceptually, the pyramid organizational structure discussed above is bureaucratic, where lower ranked employees follow the commands of top-level executives. Companies that promote servant leadership, however, follow a different organizational paradigm—a flatter organizational structure that is conducive to workplace spirituality. Thinking digitally, servant leaders see the corporation itself as something that can be remade to better align with emerging values. Because servant leaders make a conscious choice to place the needs, aspirations, and interests of others above their own, the work environment is egalitarian in nature.[23] That is, the workplace places less emphasis on self-interests and privileges for the few and more on collaboration and growth of the community. This echoes spiritual practices such as Buddhism that values the needs of individuals in the *sangha* (community) rather than the power of individual leaders.[24]

Servant leader John Mackey, co-CEO of Whole Foods Market, describes the benefits system in the company as egalitarian, saying "a cashier who has worked for the company for several years enjoys the same benefits enjoyed by the two co-CEOs of the company. It's very powerful to be able to tell people about this practice. It creates a sense of solidarity throughout the organization."[25] Employees, or "team members," as they are called, vote for the benefits packages they deem most valuable. Similarly, former Starbucks president Howard Behar explains that in servant-led organizations the power is in the hands of the employees. He describes a key tenant of servant leadership as empowering all people across the organization: "At its most basic, 'It's all about the people' has always meant it's not about me. It's about us and what we can do together."[26] Servant leaders encourage the expression of individual talents and promote a sense of belonging in the organization. The inverted hierarchical model under servant leadership expands traditional organizational borders so that "servant leaders are influential in a non-traditional manner that allows more freedom for followers to exercise their own abilities."[27] This freedom affords individuals opportunities to construct a meaningful identity in the workplace.

Servant leader Tony Hsieh, CEO of Zappos avoids traditional titles or boundaries in the workplace that may obstruct individual expression or growth opportunities. Hsieh does not use his title to distinguish himself and sits with other employees rather than in the traditional corner office. He explains: "We don't like the term 'executive.' So, we went with 'monkeys' instead. Monkey Row is where myself and some of my co-workers sit."[28] Demonstrating a sense of community rather than emphasizing a power hierarchy enables conversations to occur throughout the organization. The openness and feeling of connection in all levels of the organization empowers individuals and the organization. Although servant leaders like Hsieh organize the workplace and interact with people in ways that are not bound by rigid hierarchies, the hierarchy does not disappear completely. Their empowering leadership remains important to the development of the business.

Space and schedules

Not only do servant leaders distinguish themselves by mediating new organizational structures and constructing innovative relational opportunities among employees, they also impact the patterns of work space and work schedules. New media allows spatial changes in the workplace that alter the physical relationship of workers bringing them in closer proximity with leaders while also providing greater autonomy in configuring personal workspaces. Personal workspaces may even mirror virtual spaces like Facebook where people freely and simultaneously display aspects of their family, recreational, and spiritual lives. For example, "Maggie" notes that the publishing company where she works has adopted components of Eastern spirituality through material objects of Buddhism such as Tibetan prayer flags, Zafu meditation cushions, Zen Buddhist wall hangings, and Tibetan singing bowls. While she contends that the company and leaders do not openly associate with Buddhism, the embrace of Eastern spirituality is clearly significant. However, Maggie asserts that the organization respects the broad range of spiritual seekers on her team such that individuals are free to personalize their office spaces and include objects of their choosing which may or may not reflect Eastern traditions.[29] By borrowing practices and objects from faith traditions and placing them into the public space of the workplace, organizations continue to negotiate with the larger conversation of consumer capitalism that helps people make sense of reality and connect with personal meaning.

As part of servant leadership's practice of transparent communication and expression of trust and compassion, their organizations may be especially open to work alternatives such as virtual teams where employees are in charge of their own time and work schedules. Digital communication has made it possible to work from home or elsewhere and to interact with team members from a distance. With the option to perform work in alternative locations, individuals' schedules may be better able to accommodate time for meditation in the workday and provide for greater flextime in order to accommodate family responsibilities as well as provide for release time for public service. Servant leaders believe that these practices contribute to human flourishing and that this flourishing contributes to both the business's success and the civic good. Work becomes an expression of deep values and commitments where life integrates aspects of work, recreation, family, and even spirituality.

Servant leadership: Leaders and followers

By channeling their power through service to others, servant leaders sacrifice self-interests for others' growth. In the context of the workplace, these leaders often offer emotional support, provide opportunities for educational and personal development, and create other opportunities to empower employees. Selfless service takes on a spiritual dimension when the servant leader and followers join together in transforming the purpose of the organization. Service "becomes a source from which leaders derive meaning and purpose" as well as a way for others in the workplace to connect to something higher.[30] In this way, there is an interdependent rather than hierarchical relationship between leaders and followers where everyone in the organization is valued for their contributions.

Behar describes the relationship between the leaders and followers at Starbucks in the spirit of philanthropy: "I like to think of a business as a group of volunteers who lease their creativity for the good of the organization. When any of us, from staff to managers to the CEO, think of ourselves and our colleagues as people—not workers or assets—we discover a wealth of knowledge and talent."[31] In this way, the workplace models purposeful collaboration within all levels of the organization.

Because they approach their leadership positions with the purpose to serve others, servant leaders are often considered organizational stewards who advocate for their organizations to create value for the whole community.[32] For Mackey, the notion of community not only includes Whole Foods employees but also is inclusive of all stakeholders—investors, customers, and suppliers. Together, leaders and followers that are internal to the organization and external stakeholders co-create a workplace culture infused with spirituality.

Through their example of service to others, servant leaders empower the organization to be innovative and serve a higher purpose. According to Mackey, "Conscious businesses use an approach to management that is consistent with their culture and is based on decentralization, empowerment, and collaboration. This amplifies the organization's ability to innovate continually and create multiple kinds of value for all stakeholders."[33] Starbucks holds that the firm is in the human-service business rather than the customer-service business. While the company happens to serve coffee, "the vision has to be inspiring and meaningful to our partners, the communities we're a part of, and all the people we serve."[34] In order to serve the external followers at Whole Foods, Mackey says "the relationship between customers and team members is crucial, especially in a service business like retailing. For Whole Foods Market, it is impossible for us to create value for customers except through our team members."[35]

Servant leaders seek to support their followers with empathy and make a positive impact in their lives, and at Zappos, the brand is "powered by service" that is available to both employees and customers.[36] The Zappos team strives to offer similar values to its customers by selling "happiness in a box" rather than focusing on specific material goods.[37] In this case, happiness is more than a trite marketing slogan but signifies that employees in the organization are empowered to make decisions that positively impact the customer-service experience. By leveling the hierarchy, employees become decision-makers that serve others with care and compassion. Hsieh says:

> We just care about whether the rep goes above and beyond for every customer. We don't have scripts because we trust our employees to use their best judgment when dealing with each and every customer. We want our reps to let their true personalities shine during each phone call so that they can develop a personal emotional connection with the customer.[38]

The vision of some servant leaders—such as that held by Mackey of Whole Foods—includes a workplace that invests in love and care rather than provoking fear and stress.[39] Fred Kofman, a scholar of leadership and organizational development, explains that love in the context of the workplace relates to a specific kind of love—*agape*—that refers to a commitment in the mind rather than to emotions in the heart. Agape, he writes, is "the noblest form of love . . .

a commitment to the other's well-being."[40] Such love can be a transformative ingredient in the workplace that is embedded into servant-led cultures.

Some contemporary spiritual leaders such as Marc Gafni, of the Center for World Spirituality, even suggest that the workplace is the new spiritual center of the modern age:

> The world of business is becoming one of the great cathedrals of spirit. Businesses are becoming places in which meaning can be created, in which mutuality begins to happen. Business is the force in the world that is fulfilling every major value of the great spiritual traditions: intimacy, trust, a shared vision, cooperation, collaboration, friendship, and ultimately love.[41]

Still, can qualities of servant leadership like love really coexist with profits in a high-performing company? Recent empirical studies have shown that while servant leadership functions in accordance with spiritual values such as altruistic love, vision, and hope/faith, there are also measurable outcomes for the organization associated with these.[42] That is, these leaders do not demonstrate spiritual values out of abstract altruism but instead believe that these activities produce creative and higher-performing corporations. They believe that commitment to spiritual values actually builds stronger and more flexible businesses that work more efficiently than do those run according to older hierarchical models.

Generally, servant leaders demonstrate core spiritual values in the workplace rather than basing their leadership on specific personal spiritual practices or religious beliefs.[43] That is, servant leaders are collectively known to demonstrate spiritual values such as compassion, empathy, and altruism in the ways in which they communicate with employees and create organizational cultures. Some servant leaders report that awakenings achieved on their personal journeys are the impetus for their focus on spirituality in the workplace. For example, Whole Foods' John Mackey describes his life-changing experience as a young entrepreneur: "Almost everything I had believed in about business was proven to be wrong. The most important thing I learned in my first year at Safer Way was that business isn't based on exploitation or coercion at all. Instead, I discovered that business is based on cooperation and voluntary exchange."[44] By realizing that there were alternative ways to growing a business and leading others, Mackey started to listen to and lead from his heart.

For some servant leaders, spiritual practices also encourage self-awareness. Mackey, for example, recognizes the value of constant personal growth: He says, "We should be willing to embrace wisdom of all kinds and can find great value studying any of the great philosophical and spiritual traditions."[45] The spiritual practices of servant leaders positively influence their followers and the organization as a whole.

Conclusion: Care of communities, persons, and the bottom line

In cultures shaped by contemporary media's possibilities, spirituality is infused into aspects of everyday life in ways that invite opportunities for spiritual practices to emerge in new locations such as the workplace. Whole Foods co-CEO Mackey speaks to work as a "calling" and says that this is an opportunity for the individual to align with life inside and outside of the workplace. According to Mackey, a calling ensures that "we feel most alive, most ourselves, when doing that work."[46] This may bring rewards to both the leader and the follower. Servant leader Colleen Barrett, former President of Southwest Airlines, highlights the shared rewards between leaders and followers: "It's pretty remarkable in the overall scheme of things if you can say that whatever you do for a living, that you enjoy it, that you contributed in some way and made the world a better place. . . we've helped people achieve dreams."[47] As servant leaders are called to transform the work environment and stimulate growth in others, followers are also called to meaningful work that is in alignment with their personal values inside and outside of the workplace.

As more people live out the digital metaphor—that is, thinking of their lives as a construct under constant editing—they are drawn to organizations with values that align to personal values. Along with this, individuals are interested in other types of work-related rewards different from the traditional focus on external rewards such as profitability: "Servant leadership does not emphasize tangible outcomes . . . but rather emphasizes the need to create a positive impact throughout the organization and in the community."[48] This suggests that incentives in organizations with servant leaders are sparked through intrinsic or spiritual motivators.

In these organizations, servant leaders place spiritual values such as compassion, altruism, and meaningful work in conversation with traditional business objectives such as the bottom line, so that servant leaders and their followers connect with their work community in new ways. Servant leadership and the resulting organizational culture might not focus on external practices and material displays of spirituality. Rather, servant leaders focus on intrinsic practices that become embedded in the organizational culture. This is likely closely tied to the manner in which consumer capitalism is influenced by what some management scholars refer to as "spiritual capitalism"—wealth that is generated through a life devoted to a higher purpose and service to others rather than through external practices.[49] Leadership educator and servant leader Danah Zohar recognizes the intrinsic nature of this model: "I envisage business raising its sights above the bottom line. I envisage businesses becoming a vocation like the higher professions. . .eliminating the assumed natural distinction between private enterprise and public institutions."[50] As servant leaders influence spirituality in the workplace, many of the old distinctions between private and public institutions, sacred and secular, and leaders and followers will likely continue to evolve.

These changes in leadership style and business practices happen in the context of an emerging media culture that influences how individuals navigate the traditionally secular space of work and the new business models discussed in this chapter. As individuals search for meaning and purpose in their work and seek to bridge the separation between their work and personal lives, the workplace increasingly becomes a location for the sacred. Spiritual values such as compassion, altruism, and community are practiced in the workplace without necessarily being tied to specific religious traditions. These new models may be particularly appealing and effective among digital natives and others who have embraced this media culture and its digital metaphor. These changes recognize that people increasingly think about identity as an integrated assemblage that crosses over traditional distinctions between public and private, sacred and secular, work and personal life.

Innovative servant leaders are reconsidering hierarchy and authority and are implementing changes in their organizations—such as encouraging networked relationships within companies and between businesses and their customers—that reshape position descriptions, lines of accountability, and even physical spaces and work schedules. These leaders share power so that people across the organization have creative voice to assist in articulating and embodying a shared company vision. In sharing power, these leaders are guided by three key values: (1) an openness to multiple and assembled spiritualities; (2) care of and respect for employees as creative contributors; and (3) a commitment to contributing to the common good through their products and services.

4

"Helping Glastonbury to Come into Its Own": Practical Spirituality, Materiality, and Community Cohesion in Glastonbury

Marion Bowman
Open University

Introduction

This chapter explores materiality, commodification, consumption, and community in relation to practical spirituality in the context of Glastonbury, the small but internationally significant town in the South West of England in which I have conducted long-term fieldwork.[1] As I have commented frequently elsewhere,[2] Glastonbury is by no means typical, but it is indicative of trends such as spiritual entrepreneurship, "materialising" worldviews and praxis, operationalizing relativism, and negotiating new forms of community that are also taking place in less obviously concentrated form in other parts of the UK and Europe. A locus in which both traditional and contemporary forms and modes of "doing religion" coexist, Glastonbury highlights the importance of examining vernacular religion, material culture, and relationality in practical spiritual life.

A number of trends in the study of religion are contributing currently to a more nuanced understanding of practical spirituality, and indeed religion per se. There has been an increasing interest in the study of religion in everyday life,[3] or, in the terminology of pioneering vernacular religion scholar Leonard Primiano, "religion as it is lived: as human beings encounter, understand, interpret, and practice it."[4] "The study of vernacular religion," Primiano claims, "like the study of folklore, appreciates religion as an historic, as well as contemporary, process and marks religion in everyday life as a construction of mental, verbal, and material expressions."[5] While the significance of materiality was never absent from folkloristic, ethnographic, and anthropological engagement with religion,[6] as Engelke observes, "Within religious studies and the human sciences more broadly, there has been a growing interest in what the study of materiality offers for our understanding of the lived experience and practices of religion . . . Approaching 'religion' as 'material religion' allows us to consider the material as part and parcel of our interests and of the religious worlds of the people we study."[7] It is clearly not simply productive but necessary, as Morgan counsels, "to study the response to objects as they are displayed, exchanged, destroyed, and circulated in order to determine what they mean to people, that is to say, how they build and maintain life-worlds."[8] These trends encourage a more nuanced approach to the creativity, consumption, commodification, and community-building potential of "material religion" and its role in relation to practical spirituality.

Gauthier, Woodhead, and Martikainen assert that "consumption and consumerism are driving forces of globalisation, hand in hand with the hyper-mediatisation of culture. Together, they have profound consequences on religious practices, beliefs, expressions, and institutions worldwide, and as such deserve more scholarly attention."[9] They claim, for example, that there may be gender implications in some treatments of contemporary religiosity, suggesting that consumption "has been deemed trivial, superficial, feminine, and debased, and therefore not a serious and worthy object of scientific interest,"[10] with current trends "critiqued as signifying some kind of degradation of religion in comparison with its 'serious,' traditional, male-dominated forms."[11] Gauthier et al. also draw on the work of anthropologist Mary Douglas and economist Baron Isherwood, *The World of Goods*,[12] stressing their insight that "consumption is a social fact as well as an economic one," that consumption's essential function has to do with "meaning, value, and communication" and that "consumer goods are not acquired in order to satisfy (individual) needs, as they are markers of social relations and socially constructed meanings."[13] Stressing that markets are market*places*: "loci for complex social interactions and social re-formations,"[14] Gauthier et al. insist that "[t]he social constitution of markets and economic exchange in general is important, as it supports the argument that consumption is a web of practices that involve not only the satisfaction of needs but also social functions, and that these practices carry and express values."[15] These are significant insights for the Glastonbury context.

Contra Carrette and King,[16] Dawson regards contemporary society as being in continuity with what has gone before, not "a fundamental break with established processes of modernity but rather a series of variations on the modern theme," observing "more a difference in degree than a difference in kind."[17] Within the holistic worldview, collapsing the distinction between the material and the spiritual, material goods are not regarded as "potential impediments to spiritual realization but are instead regarded as expressive of, if not intrinsic to, the success of the spiritual quest."[18] It is important to remember that for billions of people "doing religion," past and present, these are not new insights; we have to keep contemporary phenomena in perspective. As Gilhus remarks:

> "New-Age" phenomena are frequently seen as a peculiar type of religion. This impression is misleading. These phenomena include astrology, divination, healing, magic, communication with superhuman beings and a lot of other practices that have much in common with the oldest and most durable forms of religion that we know. They are basic forms of religion, and not something that is strange and anomalous. Not least because of medicalization and the market, these phenomena are now "all over the place."[19]

Such insights and approaches are pertinent to Glastonbury, a site within which materiality, commodification, and consumption are understood as positive, desirable, and integrated in practical spiritual life, and where spiritual seekership, diversity of lifestyles, and multiple spiritual paths and praxis are seen neither as inherently selfish nor inimical to community building. This chapter raises the frequently neglected issues of philanthropy and community building within contemporary spirituality and the creative, constructive employment of an item of material culture, the Glastonbury Candle, in that mediatized milieu.

Glastonbury: a brief introduction

Throughout the twentieth century, Glastonbury attracted cultural creatives, visionaries, spiritual seekers, pilgrims, and visitors simply curious to see what was unfolding culturally, spiritually, and materially in this small English market town.[20] The vernacular Christian myths that Christianity had been brought to Glastonbury by St Joseph of Arimathea, and that Jesus himself may have spent time in Glastonbury prior to his ministry, appeared to attract new interest and speculation at the start of the twentieth century. A new wave of Christianity-related activity and interest in the town was heralded by a number of disparate events and characters. The first large-scale, post-Reformation Roman Catholic Pilgrimage to Glastonbury occurred in 1895 to celebrate the beatification of Abbot Richard

Whiting and two monks, John Thorne and Roger James, who had been hanged as traitors on Glastonbury Tor at the brutal dissolution of Glastonbury Abbey in 1539. In 1908 the ruined Glastonbury Abbey was acquired by the Anglican Bath and Wells Diocesan Trust, to be followed by the revelation in 1918, in *The Gate of Remembrance*, that Frederick Bligh Bond had used psychic methods to guide his excavations of the Abbey grounds, in particular channeling information from former monks of Glastonbury via automatic writing received by a medium.[21] Clearly, new ideas, visions, and practices were being envisaged which moved beyond and could engender tensions with and between institutional forms of Christianity.[22] This was but a taste of things to come.

By the latter part of the twentieth century, the extent of visions, lifestyle experimentation, spiritual praxis, and claims made in relation to Glastonbury had increased exponentially, and myriad versions of Glastonbury's past, present, and future significance were envisaged, narrated, and contested. This increasingly drew people to Glastonbury and/or caused them to see it in new ways.[23]

Glastonbury's identification with the Isle of Avalon, where according to legend King Arthur was taken for healing after his last battle, had been "materialised" in the twelfth century with the alleged discovery by monks of Arthur's body in the Abbey grounds. There has been renewed interest in and reinterpretation of Arthurian legend from Dion Fortune's *Avalon of the Heart*,[24] Geoffrey Ashes's *Avalonian Quest*,[25] and Marion Bradley's *Mists of Avalon*[26] to Arthur's metamorphosis into New Age spiritual quester and the "rediscovery" of the Glastonbury Zodiac (a huge landscape planisphere).[27] The upsurge of interest in Celtic spirituality, either as indigenous paganism or an enlightened, inclusive, "pure" form of Christianity, increasingly brought people to Glastonbury. Many now come to celebrate and create rituals around the eightfold calendar[28] popularly believed to have been observed by Celts, feeling a sense of continuity with pagan and Druidic ancestors. The widespread belief that Glastonbury hosted a great center of Druidic learning and Bardic activity adds further to its appeal. The establishment of the annual Glastonbury Goddess Conference in 1996, followed in 2002 by Britain's first officially registered Goddess Temple (where legally recognized marriages can now be conducted) reflects the passion with which Glastonbury has been promoted and embraced as an ancient center of Goddess devotion and a site where her presence is felt by many to be particularly strong. The contentions of geomancer John Mitchell in *The New View Over Atlantis*[29] that interconnected grids of "ley lines" link ancient sacred places worldwide, with a single unit of measurement used in the construction of everything from Stonehenge and Avebury to Egyptian and Mayan pyramids, proved popular and influential in Glastonbury, contributing to much subsequent speculation and dowsing activity in relation to the lines of earth energies that are said to converge there, and which some believe generate powerful forces for healing and personal transformation. A variety of religious groups and individuals (including Baha'is, ISKCON, Buddhists, Sufis), assorted gurus and at least three claimants to be Buddha Maitreya have been drawn to Glastonbury. Conferences focused on crop circles, megaliths, and earth mysteries have been held, and contact with extraterrestrials, angels, and myriad other than human beings have been pursued in Glastonbury, in keeping with its reputed status as a "thin" place, close to other worlds and realities. As Ivakhiv puts it, people can come to Glastonbury (as other New Age destinations) with "a multitude of desires: To heal the sores and imbalances of a society perceived to be broken, to feel strange energies and open mysterious portals into the unknown, to map out the alternative universes exposed by New Age theories and Gnostic impulses."[30] A number of experimental lifestyles (spiritual, communal, counter-cultural, ecological, traveler) were developed with varying degrees of success and longevity, and there has been a strong tradition of art, music, drama, and community arts projects in the town.[31]

This brief account only scratches the surface of the lifestyle and spiritual experimentation, experience, and diversity in late twentieth-century Glastonbury, much of which has either continued into or has been influential on twenty-first century Glastonbury. Some of the very real fears, prejudices, tensions, and social problems faced by Glastonbury in its transition from the 1970s from a small, conservative market town with an agricultural hinterland and leather-processing industry to a largely post-industrial, post-agricultural tourist-and service-based economy and contested sacred site left difficult legacies.

As the claims for Glastonbury's past, present, and future status and significance have grown ever more varied and encompassing, from "cradle of English Christianity" to "heart chakra of planet earth,"[32] and as it has appealed to a progressively wider range of visitors, a unique spiritual-service industry has arisen, which includes specialist bookshops; spiritually oriented workshops, conferences, and courses; a huge variety of healing; bed and breakfasts offering meditation and assorted therapies; and shops selling goods intended to enhance and expand people's spiritual lifestyles and practices. Part of Glastonbury's importance and value to a variety of people is as a site of spiritual consumption.[33] As one shop owner put it, "People often come without fixed purpose, but find themselves finding something."

Glastonbury's development as a multivalent pilgrimage destination and spiritual center has been spearheaded for the most part by incomers, comfortable with the concept of fair payment for spiritual services, for whom material goods are "expressive of, if not intrinsic to, the success of the spiritual quest."[34] As the owner of a pagan lifestyle shop put it, "What I'm saying is 'Evolving is what you should be doing, I can supply these things, but you have to pay x amount so that this roof can be here so that I can provide it.'" These incomers, often referred to by Glastonians as "alternatives," and sometimes self-identified as Avalonians, frequently narrate a sense of being called or drawn to Glastonbury, and feel that they are engaging in business with a purpose, with spiritually informed values. One Glastonbury therapist expressed it thus: "I suppose one would hope that values such as integrity and honesty and compassion, you know, some of those values would not be left at the door when you go into the market place, you know, that those were actually integrated into everything that we do."

A number of Glastonbury residents see themselves as part of a timely coalescence of disparate talents, spiritual insights, and visions working toward Glastonbury's restoration as a sacred site of religious and spiritual seeking, instruction, healing, experience, and consumption. The plethora of "spiritual" goods and services and the presence of people who might be described as "spiritual entrepreneurs" is seen as integral to that renewal. Just as early in the twentieth century Frederick Bligh Bond became convinced that he was in psychic contact with the Company of Avalon, perceived as a group of souls of Glastonbury monks committed to help with the re-emergence of Glastonbury as a great spiritual center,[35] a number of people involved in various aspects of Glastonbury's contemporary spiritual and economic revival feel that they have been led to Glastonbury by, and are working in the service of, the Company of Avalon. An idea that has been expressed on a number of occasions is that many people have been called to Glastonbury as part of a great jigsaw, but initially they may be incapable of seeing beyond their own piece. As individuals often come to Glastonbury seeking personal renewal, they can be disinclined to cooperate, construing cooperation as compromise. Nevertheless, various people among the "alternatives" and incomers have worked together to bring about change of various sorts in Glastonbury.

Glastonbury as "intermediary" space

With around 40 percent of the High Street now occupied by "alternative" shops, and a hinterland of spiritually related businesses, healing practitioners of many sorts, specialized bed and breakfasts, diverse devotional communities, and myriad spiritually inspired events and activities, there is a clear impact on the economy and population as a whole. Guy Redden, having studied Body, Mind, Spirit Fairs where "products are presented side-by side and the activities of many otherwise independent actors are interwoven," refers to the Fairs as "intermediary spaces" on account of "their function of catalysing networked relationships between diverse actors (both providers and participants) through presentation of multiple options for belief and practice."[36] Glastonbury itself, it could now be argued, functions as an "intermediary space." The goods and services on offer in Glastonbury are similar in kind to those found at Body, Mind, Spirit Fairs (crystals, "esoteric" books, pagan paraphernalia, healing goods and experiences, yoga and meditation requisites, and so on), but in Glastonbury they are a permanent part of the fabric of everyday life, woven in among the cafes, post office, newsagents, pubs, butcher, banks, supermarkets, churches, library, doctors' surgeries of an otherwise ordinary small town. While there are undoubtedly strongly held, sometimes exclusivist, beliefs among the religious groups and individuals who visit and live in Glastonbury, on a day-to-day basis value-relativism is the modus operandi. Because of this locational interweaving of "otherwise independent actors," it is an environment that can embrace, accommodate, and affirm an immense spectrum of belief and praxis. As I have argued elsewhere,[37] there is contestation, certainly, but there is also often a consensus built on the act of spiritual seeking—regardless of what is being sought, found, or experienced.

Numerous people attracted to Glastonbury have donated time, skills, and resources to community initiatives and philanthropic pursuits beyond their own spiritual paths and enterprises, considering this helpful in enhancing quality of life and enabling Glastonbury to fulfill its mission as a nationally and internationally significant spiritual resource. A strong ethos of "selfless service" has emerged in the many interviews I have conducted since the early 1990s, such as is frequently found at pilgrimage sites.[38]

In the late 1970s a Dutch couple, Willem and Helene Koppejan (Dutch Israelites drawn to Glastonbury in part on account of the legend of Jesus in Glastonbury) purchased a collection of buildings at the intersection of the High Street and the Market Place, an area collectively known as The Glastonbury Experience.[39] Functioning as a significant "alternative" enclave, over the following decades, The Glastonbury Experience has accommodated arts and crafts shops; the town's first vegetarian restaurant; the Bridget Healing Centre; the Library of Avalon (a myth- and spiritually focused library envisaged as the modern successor of the once great Abbey library); the Isle of Avalon Foundation (originally known as the University of Avalon, to continue Glastonbury's tradition of providing spiritual education); Bridget's Chapel (no longer functioning but for thirteen years a nonaligned site for prayer and meditation); the Goddess Temple; and shops such as Stone Age, Starchild, and Courtyard Books.

Barry Taylor, a spiritually inspired philanthropist and former businessman who felt "called" to Glastonbury in the mid 1980s, assisted the widowed Helene Koppejan to sort out the considerable financial difficulties the Glastonbury Experience had by then accrued.[40] Thanks to Taylor's efforts and financial acumen, since 1998 the Glastonbury Experience has been owned by The Glastonbury Trust:

> A charity that works with individuals and community groups to promote emotional well-being, citizenship, environmental improvement and spiritual growth, supporting projects which have community cohesion and inclusion at their heart.[41]

The Isle of Avalon Foundation, the Library of Avalon, the Goddess Temple, and the Glaston Centre (which runs the Glastonbury Reception Centre) all benefit from subsidized rents within the Glastonbury Experience, supported by the income from the shops in the complex. The Glastonbury Experience is emblematic of the varied levels of business skills, the mixture of inspirations and aspirations, services and commodities to be found in Glastonbury, and ways in which Glastonbury is (re)developing as a pilgrimage site. Not simply by directly running businesses geared to the pilgrim economy, but as volunteers or Trustees for Chalice Well,[42] The Glastonbury Trust, The Libray of Avalon, and numerous other ventures, people feel that they are helping to restore Glastonbury's spiritual infrastructure. Since 2000, the increasing participation of 'alternative' business people in the Chamber of Commerce, and the presence of Green Party councilors on Glastonbury Town Council have been indicative of changing patterns of working and interaction between erstwhile seemingly irreconcilable Glastonians and Avalonians. In 2015, Denise Michell (Druid and widow of John Michell) was elected Mayor.

Naturally the "globalizing mediasphere that has exploded since the advent of the Internet, email and social networking sites"[43] has had an impact on how Glastonbury is presented, perceived, and experienced by spiritual seekers and residents alike. Any Internet search on "Glastonbury" will reveal a large number of websites offering different theories about and claims for Glastonbury; accounts of individual and group experiences there; details of religious groups, events, tours, workshops, goods, and services; and opportunities to participate in virtual pilgrimages. The Internet has also been the vehicle for a form of social bridging in Glastonbury. Realizing that for the most part it was the "alternatives" who were making best use of the Internet to boost business or publicize events, a not-for-profit company Glastonbury Online Ltd was created to assist "the development of Internet use amongst Glastonbury businesses, community groups & people: Glastonbury Online was formed out of a loose collection of local webworkers and eventually became a Company Limited by Guarantee. We are proud of our good relationships with other webworkers in the town and continue to promote co-operation rather than competition in our community."[44]

It is important to acknowledge, however, that it is not only the "alternatives" who have been outgoing in relation to encouraging dialogue, embracing diversity, and creatively employing religious materiality. One of the most remarkable developments is the very distinctive Shining Branches Festival of Trees hosted by St John's Anglican Church since 2005, in the run up to Christmas. It provides trees within the church, which are then 'adopted' and decorated by different groups. From 2006, these trees have been decorated not only by different Christian denominations, youth groups, and local businesses, but also by the Goddess Temple, local Druids, Glastonbury Festival, and shops such as The Magick Box. Confident in its own position, even the Anglican Church in Glastonbury is functioning as an "intermediary" space.

Unity in diversity: The Glastonbury candle

A number of people who came to Glastonbury originally as pilgrims felt they had to stay. Now residents, they feel that they are not simply living (and making a living) in Glastonbury, but are helping to develop a new phase of Glastonbury's destiny as a pilgrimage site—"Helping Glastonbury to come into its own."[45] The Glaston Group, formed in 2004, wanted "to explore and listen to how the town could provide better services for pilgrim visitors and become more cohesive for those living in Glastonbury."[46] In 2007 the Glastonbury Pilgrim Reception Centre (commonly known as PRC) was established, and eventually settled in premises just off the High Street beside the Assembly Rooms (itself an iconic Glastonbury building with a complex history[47]).

Operating with the definition of pilgrim simply as "One who makes a journey to a sacred place," the PRC's stated objectives were twofold: "To actively help in building Glastonbury as a centre of pilgrimage for people of all faiths and beliefs" and "To offer a range of services to pilgrims, visitors, residents and researchers including information, teaching and support." The PRC website explained:

> Glastonbury reached its peak as a centre of pilgrimage in the Middle Ages with the needs of pilgrims being met by the monks of the Benedictine Abbey. With the destruction of the monastery, pilgrimage lapsed. Today in the twenty-first century, there has been a huge resurgence of interest in the town as a centre of pilgrimage. But now, instead of a centre of Christian pilgrimage, Glastonbury has fully emerged as a place that recognises and honours all faiths and beliefs and all those on a sacred journey.
>
> The increasing number of visitors, interested in the spiritual and healing aspects of the town, led to an awareness that a centre specialising in informing and supporting "pilgrim" visitors would be of value to both visitors and the community alike.[48]

A not-for-profit company, the PRC attracted volunteers from a variety of spiritual backgrounds and provided the sort of specialist information, publications, and artifacts that are not found in ordinary Tourist Information Centres, such as information on the various religious and spiritual groups in Glastonbury, and the activities, services, workshops, and rituals held by them throughout the year; maps showing the location of earth energy lines; PRC products such as publications including advice on "spiritual crisis"; and fundraising artifacts featuring the PRC's distinctive logo. From the start it maintained a very informative and visually attractive website, providing information on various aspects of Glastonbury, giving the opportunity to purchase things online, and very much in line with the importance of healing at many pilgrimage sites, the PRC undertook the gargantuan task of compiling and providing details of the many forms of therapies and healing found in Glastonbury.[49] The PRC also promoted links with a number of scholars, encouraging academic research on Glastonbury, and increasingly acting as the first point of contact for people coming as individual researchers or those wishing to organize student trips to the town. In a financially creative manner, in 2014 the Centre worked out that 500 individual pledges of £25 could sustain it for twelve months; "The Glastonbury 500" who donate £25 each year have the opportunity to have a "pledge pebble" on which their name is painted at the Centre, "particularly welcomed by those not resident here" letting them sense "a deep connection, allowing them to become part of the actual fabric of our beautiful town."[50] This underlines a particular understanding of the role of materiality in the building and maintenance of life-worlds and the connectivity that consumption and materiality can convey.

The most significant example of materiality, commodification, and community building pioneered by the PRC has been the Glastonbury Candle. In 2010, the Glastonbury Candle was developed in conjunction with Starchild, a long-standing business located in The Glastonbury Experience. In the "spiritually significant" color blue (representing "faith, devotion, peace, inner knowledge, love, tranquillity and harmony") and "infused with herbs, trees and flowers, including the Glastonbury Thorn that have been gathered in and around Glastonbury," it was described as "an excellent representation of the Whole that is Glastonbury and also goes some small way in helping to celebrate our ethos of honouring all paths."[51]

While at one level it is unremarkable (there being many candles for sale and on display in Glastonbury), the Glastonbury Candle became emblematic of a new emphasis on cooperation and consensus-building around the concept of Glastonbury as an all-embracing pilgrimage site and sacred center, through the "Glastonbury Candle Journey." The candle was "activated" by being lit and blessed in a ceremony at the PRC in July 2010, since which time:

> The candle, held in a large glass lantern, is passed around the town to different community groups/organisations to light and bless in what ever way is appropriate for them. This might be a ceremony, activity, meditation, meeting or simply holding the energy of it during a typical day in the office. . . The candle arrives at its destination unlit. This permits those lighting it to focus on the flame itself, allowing them to feel they are actively involved in the process of "awakening the light."[52]

The Glastonbury Candle I purchased in 2013 came with a double-sided leaflet explaining about the candle being passed around in this way, declaring that the PRC feels that this "brings the town together into the energy of the candle." Furthermore, stapled into the leaflet was a taper "lit from the activated candle so that you might light it and use it to light your own and thus perpetuate the energy: Lighting it and focusing on the flame will connect you to the energies of Glastonbury /Avalon and remind you of your own inner flame and the Divine Spark that resides in us all." The leaflet thus encapsulates a number of significant assumptions about the nature of the individual, the nature of "energy," the nature of Glastonbury, and the properties of the material as conduit to, and for, the immaterial and spiritual. Furthermore, the leaflet pointed out that the candle's "Pilgrimage" round Glastonbury could be followed on the Glastonbury Candle page of the online shop, or through the candle's Facebook page.

The meticulous documentation of the candle's journey has both recorded and promoted its success, revealing that the Glastonbury Candle in its lantern has spent time at ever more diverse venues and occasions. These have included the United Reformed Church, the Goddess Conference, the Anglican-led Holy Thorn Ceremony, Glastonbury Natural Health Centre, Archangel Michael Healing Centre, and shops such as Yin Yang and Starchild. It has been present at rituals at the White Spring and Chalice Well, an Earth Day ceremony on Wearyall Hill, and a handfasting rite on Glastonbury Tor, and has been lit by Sufis, Buddhists, Anthroposophists, Pagans, and Sai Baba devotees. Not only did the Glastonbury Candle become a fixture of Glaston Group and PRC meetings and events, it started to appear at the monthly Town Council meeting in the Town Hall, at the weekly indoor market, and in pubs and cafes (Figure 4.1).

In April 2012 A Celebration of Harmony and Healing organized by Morgana West of the PRC was held at Chalice Well, led by the Mayor, to mark and celebrate the significance of "Unity through Diversity." The renamed Glastonbury Unity Candle was a focal point, being lit at 8.30 a.m., then "carried in its lantern on a flower-bedecked bier throughout the town by more than fifty representatives of different Glastonbury faith organisations and beliefs":

> Starting at the Pilgrim Reception Centre, its journey throughout the town saw it calling in at thirty different places, including temples, churches and sacred sites, until reaching its final destination at Chalice Well Gardens, where more than fifty different faith and belief representatives had gathered for a simple ceremony beneath the two ancient yew trees. Each representative was given a half-sized Glastonbury Unity Candle and had brought with them a small blue glass bottle containing water which had been gathered from many places in and around Glastonbury.
>
> Each individual was invited to come into the circle and pour the water into a glass bowl, specially engraved with the words Glastonbury 2012, Harmony and Healing. Each one lit their own Glastonbury Unity Candle from the flame that had journeyed around the town and, following a declaration of their faith, their path or their beliefs, they offered their own blessings on Glastonbury, its people and on out into the wider world.[53]

This event deftly used the candle to address a number of issues and motifs relating to division and diversity within Glastonbury. Using the candle as focal point of a procession, it both referred to and deflected from the use made of processions in Glastonbury to carry particular images (whether the Virgin Mary during Roman Catholic pilgrimages or a form of the Goddess in the Goddess Conference processions) to stake claims to the town by and for particular

Figure 4.1 Morgana West of the Glastonbury Pilgrim Reception Centre with the Glastonbury Candle after the 2013 Holy Thorn Ceremony. She is standing beside the tree sponsored by the PRC at that year's "Shining Branches" event in St John's Anglican Church. Christmas trees are sponsored not simply by other churches and youth groups, but also by PRC, The Goddess Temple, and some shops. Photograph by Marion Bowman.

groups.[54] Stopping at places special or relating to a number of groups and individuals (including private houses) the procession was inclusive, and while representatives of different groups participated in the central ritual of candle lighting they were able to make distinctive but nonconfrontational declarations of their worldviews, and the focus was on blessing Glastonbury as a whole.

In 2014, the Glastonbury Pilgrim Reception Centre changed its name to Glastonbury Reception Centre, although pilgrimage still features prominently throughout the website. The URL of the Centre's website has become www.unitythroughdiversity.org, and the banner of the Centre's homepage is now "Inspiring Unity through Diversity":

> Our Centre has an ethos of *Unity through Diversity* but this is not to suggest we feel all faiths and paths are the same, or that they should be. It is an expression

> which has been in use for thousands of years and in essence, can be seen to imply the working together of all aspects of a community without losing the special personality and beliefs of the individual projects and people involved and we acknowledge that diverse beliefs and practices can present complex and difficult challenges creating chasms that often-times are difficult to bridge. However, rather than focus on the discordant differences, our goals are to create 'living spaces' where tolerance, understanding and co-existence can be found, demonstrating how together, we can live well, whilst remaining different. [55]

Many within and beyond Glastonbury see the Glastonbury Candle Journey and the activities of the PRC/GRC as remarkable breakthroughs in creating a new level of interaction among the town's varied factions, fostering an acknowledgment of difference in worldviews and lifestyles that need not rule out cooperation and respectful coexistence.

Conclusion

Folklorist Henry Glassie claims, "We live in material culture, depend upon it, take it for granted, and realize through it our grandest aspirations."[56] Examining materiality, commodification, and consumption in Glastonbury highlights the extent to which "consumption is a social fact as well as an economic one" and demonstrates that consumption can be very intimately connected with "meaning, value, and communication."[57]

There has been a growing awareness that Glastonbury is faring better than many other small Somerset towns and that the plethora of goods, services, venues, and events offered year round in Glastonbury benefits traditional as well as nontraditional businesses. Markets, as Gauthier et al. suggest, can be seen as "networked and hyper-mediatised arenas of mutual exposure,"[58] and if brands can be seen as the symbols around which social relations form themselves, and commoditization functions as the circulation of these symbols to produce and reproduce meaning and value,[59] Glastonbury can truly be seen as a powerful and successful brand.

In the Glastonbury Candle, we see the importance of the material in creating, expressing, and actualizing the relativism, which is the town's modus operandi. Through the PRC/GRC site and the Candle's Facebook page, its involvement in a variety of ritual contexts and sojourns at a great range of venues has reinforced visions of inclusivity and cohesion in a highly disparate setting. Not simply (though in fact) a means of raising funds, for those returning home from

Glastonbury and so minded, the candle can act as a conduit of Glastonbury energies. The Candle is used as a metaphor, as a vehicle, as the material expression of relationality, unity, and the aspiration of community building and cohesion in a spiritually diverse context.

Operating as an intermediary space, "catalysing networked relationships between diverse actors (both providers and participants) through presentation of multiple options for belief and practice,"[60] Glastonbury has developed an infrastructure that includes a Goddess Temple, the spiritually focused Library of Avalon, numerous opportunities for healing and spiritual education, and both charities and not-for-profit organizations that aim to improve the physical, social, and spiritual well-being of those who reside and work in Glastonbury, as well as visitors to it. This has been brought about through a mixture of entrepreneurial and philanthropic activities, by people who do not share a single vision, but who hold in common a sense of purpose, which might be summed up as "helping Glastonbury to come into its own." This is practical spirituality *par excellence.*

5

Hula Hoop Spiritualities: Social Media, Embodied Experience, and Communities of Practice

Jenna Gray-Hildenbrand
Middle Tennessee State University

Martha Smith Roberts
University of California, Santa Barbara

Introduction: Hooping as practical spirituality

The Hula Hoop has been resurrected in American culture during the past two decades. No longer just a children's toy, hooping is an adult trend, and hooping classes exist around the country and world. Often advertised as a "fun" way to exercise, hoop fitness is only one small part of the larger hoop movement. Like many hoopers, we (the authors) started going to "hoop classes" with friends for the fun and exercise it promised. We began noticing that our instructor, KiT, was ending classes with "manifestation" exercises and referring to hoops as "powerful manifestation tools." As we continued to attend classes and other hoop gatherings, we discovered that this type of manifestation language was quite common. We also found that it was quite common for hoopers to have had an unexpected experience of transformation (mental, emotional, and/or physical) while hooping, and they were happy to share their stories with us.

In these stories, hoopers often utilized religious or spiritual language to describe their experiences and their motivation to continue hooping. The prevalence of spiritual language and transformation stories made us curious about what was happening in the hoop community, and we set out to try and understand the broader significance of "Hula Hoop spiritualities" for the study of religion. In the process, we found a thriving hoop community that attributes meaning to their hoop practice in diverse and compelling ways: some who draw upon traditional religious language and symbols, others who draw upon metaphysical teachings, and still others who create their own unique spiritual narrative.

Over the course of two months (from December 30, 2010 to March 1, 2011), we conducted an anonymous online survey of over 500 hoopers.[1] When asked to describe their hooping practice, 69.1 percent of hoopers described it as "meditative," 43 percent described hooping as spiritual, and 8.1 percent described their practice as "religious." Their descriptions of hooping experiences in all of these categories are highly personal and individual. And, as might be expected, their descriptions of community are pluralistic, diverse, and inclusive enough to embrace all of these individual interpretations. However, the dynamics of personal and communal spiritualities in hooping are quite sophisticated. Using plastic hoops and social media, these primarily Generation X hoopers have developed and shared complex spiritual narratives and practices that reveal the intersectionality of the material and virtual worlds.

Our chapter draws on large-scale survey data, in-depth interviews with hoopers, and participant observation at workshops, retreats, and in the online community. We also utilize hoopers' self-generated media as data—videos, photos, and texts from their websites and social media—to develop a nuanced understanding of this spiritual community.

This chapter investigates how the Hula Hoop has become both an empowering tool for embodied practical spirituality rooted in metaphysical religiosity and a basis for a thriving community connected not by a shared dogma but by a common practice. We argue that the growth of the hooping subculture lies in its ability to nurture the diverse spiritual experiences of individual hoopers and to build an inclusive hooping community (composed of both spiritually and recreationally motivated hoopers). Through social media, hoopers connect virtually; share spiritual testimonies through dance, spoken, and written word; and teach various hooping techniques intended to help others develop their spiritual practice and flow. Social media is second only to the hoop as the means to accomplishing these goals. To better understand the nature of hoop dance as a spiritual practice, three intersecting themes must be engaged: the characteristics of metaphysical religion in the American context, the generational specificity of hoop spiritualities, and the use of media in cultivating personal practice of hoop dance and creating community.

Metaphysical context

Meaning-making

The emergence of hoop spiritualities is not anomalous in US religious history. Rather, hoop spiritualities fit well within the long tradition of metaphysical religion in the United States. As Catherine Albanese demonstrates in her work on American religion, an exploration of what she calls "metaphysical religiosity" helps us to better understand "what is *American* about American religion."[2] Metaphysical religiosity transcends religious institutional boundaries, appearing both within and outside of established religious traditions.[3] This long tradition of metaphysical religion has been recognized in contemporary American incarnations as well. Scholars continue to be captivated by the "spirituality" present in a variety of contexts, including the combinative nature of lived religious practices, as well as those who define themselves outside of traditional religious frameworks, calling them "spiritual, but not religious," "unchurched," or "nones."[4] In the midst of diversity, Albanese's four characteristics of metaphysical religion—mind, correspondence, energy, and salvation—remain apt descriptors of hoop spiritualities. These attributes continue to pervade American notions of what constitutes a "spiritual experience."

Figure 5.1 Hoopers gather in Carrboro, North Carolina, for "Sangha" the seventh annual national HP Retreat (June 20–23, 2013).

First, Albanese describes "a preoccupation with mind and its powers."[5] The emphasis on the mind includes a privileging of reason as well as an exploration of the things the mind can do through intuition, clairvoyance, telepathy, trance, and meditation, to name a few examples.[6] The impact of hooping on the state of the hooper's mind was a constant theme in survey results. As one hooper explained:

> I first started hooping for exercise purposes, but then I quickly learned that it was more fun than anything, and if I can have fun while working out—awesome! Then I started to see the meditative qualities of it. I began to notice my *mind state* before, during, and after. I could tell that it was a positive thing in my life. Then I began to grow as a hooper, and in a lot of ways, as a person. I started feeling like I was becoming the person I had wanted to be my whole life. I started changing my life more to resemble my ideal "me." This is when the journey became spiritual. [Emphasis added]

Another hooper described her/his practice this way, "Hooping is my church . . . Hooping is where I commune with God. It's my quiet space where I can quiet my *mind* and just be . . . I stopped going to church about 6–7 years ago and use my hoop time as my spiritual haven . . . my place to find/meet God and be gracious for what He provides, and I usually become overwhelmed with my gratitude of movement." The quieting of one's mind is seen as a necessary catalyst to reach a state of peace, meditation, spirituality, and transcendence. The hoop is a tool in achieving this desired state.

Second, metaphysical religions typically contain a theory of correspondence between worlds.[7] Albanese explains, "The human world and mind replicate—either ideally, formerly, or actually—a larger, often more whole and integrated universe, so that the material world is organically linked to a spiritual one."[8] According to Albanese, "In these traditions, the human mind—often acting out its imaginative grasp of the world through the body and thus through ritual—has operated as a transformative agent, taking advantage of the secret symmetries and connections for its own purposes. Religion thus is above all a work of the practical imagination."[9] For those hoopers surveyed for whom hooping was a meditative or spiritual practice, the clearing of their minds allowed them to feel a profound connection to their bodies and to a more authentic self or higher power. One hooper described her/his experience this way, "Hooping helps me center within myself, to remember who I am, to feel my body and listen to my body like I never have before. It has taught me to love my body and what it can do. . . Hooping is the first thing in my life that has tapped into my insides, into my soul and find a light and a joy that I never knew was there and had never found with any other activity."

Third, Albanese observes that movement and energy characterize both mind and correspondence: "metaphysicians find a stream of energy flowing from above to below—so powerful that they discover themselves to be, in some sense, made of the same 'stuff.'"[10] The correspondences between mind/body and human/divine are energetically formed; they are not static or fixed relationships. For Albanese, this prompts a search to better understand the energy that makes these cosmic connections along with "notions of proper and correct motion."[11] The movement and action that are central to hoop dance as an embodied practice become the energetic pathways for metaphysical correspondence. This experience is recognized and cultivated in many hoopers' personal practices, and often referred to as "flow."

Flow is described as an alignment of body and mind in the hoop, though it means different things to every hooper. The experience of flow is thus another instance of diversity and plurality that is accepted as a part of hooping itself, as each hooper must find his or her own flow. Hoopers's descriptions of flow rely on the feelings generated by the energy and motion of a fluid state of hoop dance and often contain references to being "one with the hoop," "a state of bliss," or "a loss of time." Albanese's observation that utilizing "proper and correct motion" is important to metaphysical practitioners also applies to hoopers. Hooping involves the acquisition of a basic set of movement skills. Mastering and utilizing these skills is a necessary tool for hoopers to achieve a flow state. Hoopers clearly connect feeling and practiced movement in their descriptions of spiritual experience: "Getting centered in my own body, gaining muscle memory when I learn new tricks, feels very spiritual to me." Others directly connect the acquisition of hooping skill with finding flow: "My skill level has increased and I am finding more of a flow to my practice." "Being able to do skills without as much thinking has helped to build it more into a meditative practice." In hoop dance, the energy and motion of the hoop allows for alignment and correspondence that cultivates what many hoopers call a spiritual experience or flow state.

According to Albanese, the energetic quality of metaphysical practice is where "the practical imagination joins forces with will. We enter the realm of what properly may be described as magic, but—and this is important—magic read in a healing mode."[12] The experience of energetic motion and correspondence with mind has an important practical application, a salvific quality. This brings us to the fourth and final quality of Albanese's metaphysical religion, which emerges out of "a yearning for salvation understood as solace, comfort, therapy, and healing."[13] The spirituality of hoop dance also relies on the efficacy of the practice, and while the transformative effects of hooping vary for each hooper there is a sense of progress that pervades the discourse of hoop dance more broadly. In addition, the hoop is a conduit for psychological and physical healing: overcoming depression, losing weight, and recovering from injury are some of the benefits that hoopers attribute to their hooping practice.

Narratives of transformation and healing abound in the hoopers surveyed. "I started hooping when I was very ill, mentally and physically," one hooper explained, "I was able to detox from all of my medications for depression, anxiety and epilepsy by hooping daily for a year. Hoop dance literally allowed me to maintain my sanity and ease the physical and emotional withdrawal symptoms I was experiencing." Another hooper expressed a similar sentiment, "Hooping has refined, enriched, and blessed my life. It saved me from the darkest place I have ever been . . . It helped my mind, body, and heart reconnect after they were severed from abuse in my late teens. The more I hooped, the less I had stress-induced seizures, the fewer nightmares I had . . . It balances my mind and body more completely than any therapy session or medication ever has." There are many more testimonies like the above. In addition to relief from physical pain and mental anguish, hoopers testified to increased self-esteem, improvements in their sex lives, and recovery from addiction. These narratives of hooping salvation cover a multiplicity of ailments, physical and emotional, but all share a sense of progress toward a better state of being.

Community

Albanese characterizes metaphysical groups as pluralistic and diverse, privileging individual conscience over group cohesion. As a result, metaphysical communities are often "ad hoc and flexible, and authoritarian voices and concerns have not gotten very far."[14] In order to study metaphysical communities, she tells us, we must examine their diversity. This approach "begins to ask questions about new and distinctive forms of community—less organized from the top down, more fluid and egalitarian."[15] Wade Clark Roof comes to a similar conclusion in his analysis of seeker spirituality. The religious seeker's concentration on the development of an authentic self does not mean that they have an aversion to commitment to community formation and engagement. Spiritual seekers search for a spirituality which is "all-encompassing, reaching to the very depths of people's lives and giving birth to new forms of community."[16] This relationship between the personal, individual search for an authentic spiritual self, and a commitment to community may seem contradictory. There is a sense that the two—individualism and a sense of belonging—are antagonistic to one another. Roof argues that this conclusion is too simplistic: "Americans not only pick and choose what to believe, by and large they also set the terms governing involvement in religious communities. Especially in a time of heightened spiritual activity, we would expect a more rampant subjectivity, but also the possibility of new, emerging forms of community giving expression to personal enhancement."[17] Robert Wuthnow makes a similar observation of post-Boomer spirituality, which he defines as "pieced together . . . from materials at hand."[18] For the researcher this means investigating manifestations of religiosity in unconventional places.

The hooping community shares many of the characteristics of metaphysical, seeker, post-Boomer spiritual communities. Having a physical, emotional, and spiritual transformation while hula hooping is certainly an example of finding religiosity in an unconventional place, and many hoopers (who often describe their transformation in the hoop as unexpected) would agree. Their practical, embodied spirituality arises independent of any religious authority or institution, consequently it is expected within the larger hoop community that there will be a variety of interpretations of that hooping experience. The hooper is free to peruse a variety of hoop approaches (focused on meditation, spirituality, exercise, performance, etc.) and utilize what works for them in their hoop practice. The growing number of hooping retreats and workshops that feature a diverse range of hooping instructors with very different approaches further illustrates the variety of tools at hand.

There are also many examples of hoopers drawing upon their own reservoir of religious symbols and language to describe their experience. While a full 33.6 percent of hoopers in our survey identified as a "member or practitioner" of Buddhism, Christianity, Hinduism, Islam, Judaism, or Paganism, 55.9 percent of hoopers claimed no religious tradition, and 21.6 percent chose "other" and defined their own tradition outside of institutional affiliations. Usually these "others" described themselves as "spiritual" or an eclectic blend of traditions. One hooper told us, "I choose not to label, but feel great spiritual connection expressed through work, music, and hooping." Another hooper explained, "I tread my own personal spiritual path, which includes elements of many of the aforementioned religions, though I do not consider myself to be a practicing member of any organized religion." And some had come up with their own titles for their spiritual practices: one hooper chose the description "Secular Humanist Transcendentalist Existentialist," another clarified, "I practice earth-based magickal Judaism . . . one might call me a Jewitch. I am not pagan, though." All of these descriptions of religion tend to be inclusive of other views, no matter what the individual's own tradition might be. While hoopers might find spirituality outside of an institution best for themselves, their pluralist frameworks are also present, and they see religion as an individual choice for themselves and others. Many hoopers expressed this sentiment of respect for individual faith. "I respect every religion for what it's worth," one hooper explained, "but I'm not extremely religious." Another hooper surveyed explained, "I respect every religion and the people following a religion different from mine."

Traditional means of delineating the boundaries of a community based on believers (insiders) and nonbelievers (outsiders) are not adequate in exploring hoop spiritualities. For instance, in our survey there were many "non-believer" quotes like this one: "I think hula hooping is a fun activity! I don't feel like hooping will heal depression as some have claimed! I don't find it spiritual or meditating either! I feel ppl take that part to the extremes!" [*sic*]. This hooper and others like him/her are still accepted members of the community even though hooping is not spiritual or religious for them. Likewise these hoopers are not saying that those who do find hooping spiritual should leave the community. The boundaries of the community are built around the shared practice of hooping. One survey participant explained, "[Hooping] is a conduit to a larger community of people that share the same sorts of experiences in their hoop." Articulated another way by another hooper, "If I see someone walking down the street carrying a hoop, I know they understand something that I get as well." "Everyone who hoops knows that someone else who also hoops just 'gets it.'" Again and again, hoopers note that it is the practice (not one particular interpretation or belief) that unites the community.[19]

In fact, the practice and the hoop itself are the only two stable markers of the hoop community, which in other ways sees itself as very diverse. The hooping community, which contains those who find hooping spiritual, religious, or meditative as well as those who see it purely as recreation or exercise, constructs the boundaries of the community around the object of the hoop and the acquisition of hooping skills. As one hooper noted, "There is nothing unique about the hooping community that differentiates itself [*sic*] from any other community . . . except that they come together for the hoop." From this shared *practice*, hoopers recognize each other as part of a unique community.

It is important to highlight that many of our hoopers fit into the Generation X category (born roughly from early 1960s to early 1980s), and while the number of millennial hoopers (born from early 1980s to early 2000s) will likely continue to grow in numbers, our data shows that a high percentage of hoopers (64% of our survey) and almost all of those who founded and remain important figures in the movement come from Generation X. Steeped in pluralism, the Generation X emphasis on individualism and subjectivity are not a barrier to community. In fact, for hoopers, they have become the marker of the community. "Open," "diverse," "non-judgemental," "respect for individual choices," "accepting"—these are all common ways in which hoopers characterize their community.

The multiplicity of possible interpretations of hooping reveals the importance of tolerance, diversity, and inclusivity in creating community. The fluidity in content also hints at fluidity in form. The ways in which members communicate, form friendships, share tools, and support one another happens in multiple spaces, both virtual and nonvirtual. The beginnings of the hoop community, which was more sprawling than dense, demanded alternatives to face-to-face encounters. New media has been an essential part of the formation and spread of the hooping movement. Community happens online, and virtual exchanges are an authentic way to for hoopers to connect. The hoop community thus offers a space where individual, embodied practices combine with virtual encounters to cultivate a truly practical spirituality.

Generation X spirituality

Generation Xers share much with their metaphysical foremothers and forefathers; one distinguishing factor, however, is that Gen Xers spent their entire lives in the presence of new media and technology and have drawn upon these sources for meaning-making throughout their lifetime. Tom Beaudoin notes that "although the Internet (as a popular communications medium) and the World Wide Web gained prominence in the 1980s and early 1990s, involvement with these media can be seen as continuations of two older technological developments: the computer and the video game. Generation X grew up on intimate terms with these machines, and [their] smooth entry into the nether reaches of cyberspace is directly linked to this technologized upbringing."[20] The media that bombarded Generation X during their formative years underwent a transformation that left them thoroughly familiar with technology, but also wary of its incarnations. Much as Generation X's absorption of popular culture is both self-aware and critical, their use of technology is as well.[21] A participatory culture of sharing and critique punctuates hoopers use of new media.

Figure 5.2 Hoopers "sway" during the warm-up at the HP7 Retreat.

Hoop spiritualities are a mediated form of meaning-making and community building. While the practice of hooping is often a solitary endeavor for hoopers, hoopers reach out through various forms of media to connect with others in order to sustain and reinvigorate their personal practice. In our survey, 87.4 percent of hoopers use YouTube, 43.5 percent use Online Forums, and 15.3 percent purchase online classes to support their hoop practice. When asked how they participate in the hooping community, 72.2 percent noted that they participate in online hooping social networking sites. Even more, 93.5 percent said that hooping alone (by themselves) was one way that they participate in the community. Many hoopers live in locations that have no other hoopers. Therefore, online connections are a way for them to share their personal experiences and develop hooping skills. When describing the community, many hoopers mention the Internet as an important space. "The closest hooper that I know lives about an hour away," one survey participant explained, "I do feel like I have a strong online hooping community, and for that I am grateful." Another hooper expressed a similar sentiment, "Where I live, the hooping community is very small and it has been difficult to organize people . . . When I interact with hoopers on hoopcity.ca, hooping.org, and at music festivals and raves, it is generally a very outgoing, fun, and playful experience."

The use of media in hooping has dominated the community since its earliest incarnations. As early as 2003, hoopers were forming an online community at Tribe.net, an early chat and message board site where hoopers could converse and share video. The Tribe.net site became unstable in 2006, and hoopers migrated to other sites for community and support.[22] In addition to Facebook, Hooping.org and HoopCity.ca are now some of the most popular networking sites for hoopers. In a larger sense, online social spaces are a fundamental part of how the hooping community has always communicated. The early discussion forums set the stage for the hoop community. Individuals would share ideas, techniques, instructions on how to make hoops, and more.

The YouTube revolution is an extension of this basic format. The addition of easily accessible visual and audio components have broadened the community, allowing those unfamiliar with hoop dance to experience it outside of the festivals, concerts, and raves that spread the early movement. Because hooping is an embodied practice, seeing the movement of hooping is crucial to understanding, mimicking, and creating a hoop dance of one's own. In order to do that, one must first have a basic set of skills that allow a style to emerge. This is where technology is critical. "There is such a focus on teaching others" one appreciative hooper explained, "there are so many free videos on the internet to help me learn it is great." The sharing on social media does not end with posting videos. Hoopers ask one another questions and respond promptly. When so many hoopers are separated by distance, they are often eager to share and help one another grow in their practice. As one survey participant put it, "We are a tribe, a social network." Media directly supports the development of individual hooping skills, yet it is only through a context of a sharing community that this is possible.

For hoopers there exists a kind of dialectic between the construction of a meaningful self and the construction of a supportive, pluralistic community. While the individual hooper may have come to hooping individually, experienced a spiritual transformation unexpectedly, and primarily hoops alone, the hooping experience is not a solitary one. Hoopers reach out to the community, primarily through social media, to both share and receive different tools, skills, and techniques to expand and deepen their personal practice. The community, then, grows in depth and numbers when more individuals participate and claim membership, thus creating an increasingly diverse depository of symbolic tools for meaning-making for individuals to draw upon. None of this is possible without media.

Media and spirituality

How do we understand the role of media in the lived embodied spiritual/religious experience of hoopers—not only as they generate individual meaning and cultivate self but also as they build a hooping community? To answer this, we will now shift our focus (1) to articulate our approach to media, which is informed by the work of Stewart Hoover and (2) to illustrate the insights which can be drawn through the application of the framework we have outlined to a specific case study: Jonathan Baxter, founder of HoopPath, and one of the most well-known hoop teachers in the community.

Stewart Hoover's ground-breaking work on media, religion, and culture is informative as it marks a significant departure from the ways previous scholars analyzed media. Traditional approaches understood media merely as tools for information distribution and consumption. This traditional "'effects'-oriented media theory," according to Hoover, focused on media institutions and texts as ideological constructions that impact human behavior in a variety of cultural, social, and psychological ways.[23] Furthermore, this effects-oriented approach tended to see media and religion as two separate social institutions, often competing to influence human behavior.[24]

Hoover proposes a shift away from investigating media in terms of their effects on daily life and rather an investigation of media's *integration* into the lived daily experiences of spiritual actors. From this perspective, one must investigate media from the perspective of media audiences. How do individuals and communities engage media as a symbolic reservoir of meaning-making and the construction of selves? How are the production, distribution, and reception of mediated communication integrated into individuals' religious/spiritual lives? In this way, religion and media are not seen as competing institutions. Rather, this approach shines a light on the previously overlooked possibility that media could both ignite and sustain religion/spirituality.[25] When one begins to think of media as practices, and not merely institutions, texts, and objects, the scholar is open to a more complete view of both media and religion.[26]

Hoover draws upon Jesus Martin-Barbero in his critique of effects-oriented media theories. Rather than acting upon and influencing culture, media mediates between the individual and his/her culture. Hoover explains, "In fact, a series of 'mediations' enable individuals to locate themselves in social and cultural space and time. We assume that such things as language, ideology, received history, social and cultural values, mythology, and consciousness of location serve to enculturate us and provide means of solidarity, binding us to our place and time.

These shared ideas mediate our experience of the physical world, enabling us to interact, develop psychologically and socially, learn, and achieve the kind of social autonomy that is at the base of human-ness and freedom."[27] This further illustrates the vital role media have, not as a distinct from one's everyday social, cultural, and religious life, but as an integral part of it. As Hoover explains, media are "a part of the fabric of social consciousness, not just an influence on that consciousness."[28] Applying mediation to the social media utilized by hoopers means taking seriously their claims that it is integral to community meaning-making, that one can authentically participate in the community online.

The theory of mediation does not explain, however, how individuals experience this mediation in the contexts of their daily lives and personal spiritual experiences in a construction of a sense of self, identity, and community. This information must come from the individuals themselves, by engaging "in conversations with real people about the way they use media, about the way they think about religion and spirituality, and about the relationships between these things in their lives."[29] Hoover acknowledges the limitations of his approach; however, the advantages outweigh these limitations.[30] According to Hoover:

> Looking at things in this 'lived' way gives us a perspective that at the same time reflects emerging trends in religion and media, and enables us to get past some of the problematic ways the interaction between media and religion has been looked at in the past. It radically centers the question on three related parts. First is the question of what *symbols* or *scripts* are available in the media environment, what we might call the '*symbolic inventory*' out of which individuals make religious or spiritual meaning. Second is the *practices of consumption, interaction, and articulation* through which those meanings are accessed, understood, and used. And third is the centering of this in *the experiences of the individuals* who are doing the consuming and the meaning-making.[31]

The firsthand accounts of hoopers evidence the larger trends in hooping spirituality and community: individual embodied experiences, diversely interpreted and shared in a pluralistic, accepting community that convenes in person and online. For the hoop community, some scripts of media exchange can include tutorials, testimonials, performances, and discussions that are created, uploaded, and consumed in various formats (videos, photos, texts) utilizing the group's articulation of their acceptance of diverse beliefs around a shared practice. The experiences of individuals in the community reveal their investment in media as a way to experience authentic meaning-making in relation to hoop dance.

To add specificity to this broad survey data, we will examine the particular history of the HoopPath, a hooping community based in Carrboro, North Carolina, and founded and led by Jonathan Baxter (known simply as "Baxter"). The story of Baxter and HoopPath serves as a significant case study for a variety of reasons. Our survey of hoopers found that HoopPath had the highest workshop attendance rate, with 44 percent having participated. HoopPath has also been awarded Hooping.org's "Community of the Year" award (2008). And Baxter has been inducted into their "Hooper Hall of Fame" (2013) and won the "Male Hooper of the Year" (2012) award. HoopPath is a well-known and respected group within the hoop community, and a fitting case study for the mediation of hooping spirituality because of their metaphysical framework and use of social media. Baxter's own narrative of media and practice, as both a hooper and a teacher, illustrates the lived realities of a mediated spirituality.

HoopPath

The teachings of HoopPath emerged out of Baxter's personal practice. Baxter began hooping regularly in 2002, while he was healing from a broken collarbone. "That's when my own hoop story began" he explains, "as an exercise for an atrophied shoulder."[32] Baxter soon discovered benefits beyond his physical rehabilitation. His depression was slowly and surely dissolving, his self-consciousness fading, and his confidence and happiness were growing. Using a blindfold to avoid the stares of neighbors as he hooped in his backyard, he had to feel the hoop through the darkness, and "he made a simple and transformative discovery: his body could communicate directly with the hoop."[33] One of the most profound experiences to come out of Baxter's backyard blindfold hooping sessions was the intuited story of the Maidan (pronounced "myDAN"). As he hooped, their story developed. The Maidan are "the ancient order of holy women who connected to their ancestral energy, the Spirit Wind, through Hoop Meditation."[34] Their story is an epic myth of the lives of the Maidan, one that tells the story of the tribe and the individuals in it. Each of the Maidan's lives represents a story of individual struggle, tragedy, and victory.

Baxter describes the way in which the story developed:

> Almost every time I would hoop I began to collect pieces of a narrative. Small bits of a story trapped in a world's past. Every day with my hoop I would visit and commune with the characters of the story until over time it felt as real to me

Figure 5.3 Jonathan Baxter leads a workshop on hoop techniques at the HP7 Retreat.

> as any of the stories of my childhood. This story was teaching me how to hoop, but it also was teaching me how to be. It was revealing to me again and again that happiness was not a destination that we one day arrive at in this world, but rather it was the way we walked through this world. This story that taught me how to hoop is the story of the Maidan.[35]

For Baxter, the HoopPath practices were the vessel that brought the narrative of the Maidan to his consciousness, and that narrative then began to guide his practice; the language of that narrative became a part of the symbolic inventory of the community. The power of intuition, mind, and myth-making are fundamental to HoopPath spirituality, and they also clearly correspond with the embodied practice.[36] In fact, sustained and disciplined practice are essential to the efficacy of hooping. Hours logged in a hooping practice are referred to as "flight time," which becomes a source of credibility and legitimacy in the community. The more flight time one has logged, the more time they have spent building physical and mental skills. Baxter's website notes that he has over 10,000 hours of personal flight time and 6,000 hours of teaching flight time.[37]

While many of the metaphysical and spiritual practices of HoopPath are rooted in the symbolic inventory of the Maidan narrative, the narrative is not an exclusive source of spirituality. Spiritual diversity and pluralism are important in the community. Baxter is a practicing Quaker who sees Ram Das as an important spiritual guide. His own spirituality is fully combinative, utilizing a variety of philosophies and practices to complement the ritual practice of hooping. These other influences are also discernable in Baxter's teachings, particularly his YouTube channel, which has become an especially powerful medium for communicating his philosophy.

Cultivating community online

"I started talking about 'community' before I could really see one. But once you give a name to something, it helps to shape it," Baxter explained.[38] For Baxter, as well as other hoopers in our survey, a transformative experience in the hoop engenders a desire to find people with whom one can nurture and develop one's hoop practice and with whom one can share his/her hoop experience. Individual, physical experience in the hoop is an authentic way to participate in a broader community of practice. Spirituality is thus embodied and individual; sharing those personal experiences both creates community and invigorates and expands individual meaning-making and practice. This is where media serves as a crucial conduit of community participation. Baxter's own use of media to communicate spirituality highlights the combinativeness and plurality of a community where individual authority is key, geographic distance is the norm, and social media is second nature.

The ways Baxter engages media are central to who he is as a hooper and teacher—one is not without the other. As he stated in a 2014 interview:

> Ever since I was a little kid, I have taught—my little sister things or my friends things. It seems that [this] is [an] aspect of my nature because it has been consistent through all the modes and forms of me that I, for whatever reason, like to teach. I like to communicate with the public . . . And, over the course of my life the universe has told me that one of my talents and gifts is talking to people . . . So, its like, my talking at times, and I don't mean [only] about life issues, but how I would teach you how to chest hoop or whatever, it tends to work ya know, and it tends to help bridge people to things. And, then my spiritual seeking, has a nurture in it . . . And this is not necessarily a motivation but a result, is that it helps me deal with my ego. Service is a great way to deal with your ego. To feel like you are in service, and I do.[39]

Baxter's practices of communication, articulation, and utilization of media are geared purposefully not only to teach and nurture others on their individual hoop journeys but also to develop his own gifts, talents, and spiritual journey as well as to discipline his ego.

Social media is Baxter's principal means of communicating with the hoop community. This mediated form of communication is more than "advertising" for Baxter. Although it is certainly the primary means through which hoopers find out about Baxter's classes and workshops, it is also the means through which he nurtures his own hoop practice and personal spiritual development. Baxter posts comments on Facebook, tweets on Twitter, and very rarely writes a blog on his website; however, he primarily uses these forms of media to share videos he has created. It is clear that communicating through video has been the most consistent means of media use for Jonathan Baxter.[40] Since 2006, Baxter has posted more than forty videos on YouTube. These videos include clips of his hooping (both to music and to spoken word) and video blogs in which he shares his thoughts with the hoop community.

In a 2014 interview, I asked Baxter to comment on his use of social media. He explained that he originally posted videos on YouTube to "flag a technique." In other words, he wanted to produce evidence on social media that he was the first to develop a new hooping technique or style. As his own teaching evolved, so too did his use of social media. His own hooping practice and teaching has slowly matured over the years. "It is almost like the more you practice the better feel you have for what your practice is . . . It becomes a much more living thing . . . And sometimes my practice is spiritual sometimes, and physical sometimes, and work related sometimes." The difference among these types of hooping practice, for Baxter, has to do with awareness, discipline, and focus. These are qualities he has worked to cultivate throughout his years of hooping—not through a guilt-ridden rigor but by being fully present in the moment and allowing the creative energy within him emerge naturally through hooping.

Baxter recognizes that this creative space is often a vulnerable emotional one for hoopers, including himself.

> The hoop community just exposes all the insecurities that we have. It puts you through the whole gamut of things . . . I really think it is because you have to be vulnerable . . . That is the connective tissue of the hoop community. We have to be vulnerable. We have to look around and be "alright, we are willing to look stupid, right?" Because you have to! . . . And, I think that is why we bond. I can't speak to other workshops because I don't attend them that much, but I think what happens in the HoopPath, and what helps create the learning container,

> is that we start off so vulnerable in the beginning and we do the most awkward thing in the world which is sway. And once we sway up, people have gone to the land of awkward, and now they are ready, it is like jumping into cold water.

Baxter understands this sense of insecurity and vulnerability and shares his own personal struggles with his students. The reason he started using a blindfold in his personal hoop practice was to overcome the insecurities he felt hooping in his own backyard. When he could not see his neighbors watching him with curiosity, he could focus on his own practice. He continues to use this tool in his own personal hoop practice and as a teaching tool in his workshops.

Baxter acknowledges that his teaching techniques have changed over the years. These changes include the ways he engages with media. He explains:

> Part of how I choose to connect has been through trial and error because when I first started teaching in the hoop community I opened up some powerful boxes. I was really raw. And some of my earlier workshops, in some ways they were probably some of my best, because I was super raw. I was like completely uncensored and we would go deep. And it was like there was nothing I was afraid to talk about or say. We put it all out there and we would go to some deep places . . . What happened was that I started realizing that I was conjuring up and dealing with and processing powerful emotions and energy and psychologies in people that I did not know how to handle.

According to Baxter, the power and emotion behind the HoopPath approach to hooping is the openness of the community.

He very consciously works to cultivate a nonjudgmental space where hoopers can be completely vulnerable and open with themselves and with others. The practice of hooping is an indispensable part of this process. As a physical, embodied, meditative tool, it is difficult to both focus one's mind on hooping while simultaneously focusing on the stress of the day, the answer to a current personal trouble, or the insecurity of how one looks. Baxter's ongoing encouragement throughout a workshop or in a video to let go and fully experience the hoop practice helps students to transcend daily mental chatter and to process what one is feeling. According to Baxter, we store these stresses in our bodies. Humans have a fundamental need to process these stored pressures and experience relief. This is an empowering experience for hoopers.

Social media helps Baxter to introduce hoopers to the HoopPath approach to hooping as well as to reach hoopers who may never attend one of his workshops. In his videos, like in his workshops, Baxter aims to keep people curious and inspired in their hoop practice by presenting inquiries—a question, idea, or technique to set the hooper on an individual meditative hoop path and to expand her/his practice. This is a technique Baxter uses in his own practice, and one he attributes to his longevity and position in the larger hoop community. He sees his spoken word videos as "pep talks." He explains:

> Pep talks are not just for people who are down. They are for everybody . . . Trying to push you to that intangible place . . . To help inspire people. Because we all need a push. And I am inspired by speakers, so many of them, and usually what really makes an inspiration inspiring, is when the speaker says something that you believe but you did not have words for it yet . . . When I speak to groups that is kinda what I am trying to do. Not like, sell them on some technique or ask them to change their life, but I make these observations and people are like 'exactly.' I help them find their own feeling. Not convincing them to take mine.

Baxter is careful to avoid making people feel that they must share his spiritual worldview in order to participate in his workshops. He states, "I am making a conscious effort actually to not sell but to share." He is not trying to "convert" anyone, and this is why he would not categorize HoopPath as a religion. Baxter clarifies, "When I do preach, I am trying to preach more in the uplifting way . . . The people who come to HoopPath are usually not lost sheep . . . They are sort of already on a path that is why they are there. Or they want to be there."

YouTube and Facebook are ways for Baxter to convey his message to those outside the HoopPath community. An audience he feels particularly drawn to is the "spiritually abused." Baxter describes this group as:

> People who try church and for good reason have scars. And have, because of that, tuned out all things . . . spiritual . . . and become emotionally protected by this shroud of cynicism . . . If they only experience negative impacts of religion, the moment you say spirit they go off into religion land . . . Well, my sort of feeling of spirit is right now to try and help the non-spirit person understand the context of the spiritual person. And, not that they become spiritual, but that they respect them.

Baxter wants to be an interlocutor between these individuals and the spiritual path he finds fulfilling in his own life. What he feels the nonspiritual person does not understand is that the spiritual person is not clinging to a superstition or a dogma, but is rather feeling and experiencing something transcendent, life-changing, and empowering. For HoopPath and Jonathon Baxter, that transformation happens in the hoop.

Conclusions

The story of Baxter's experiences as a hooper and a teacher shed light on the larger phenomenon of hooping spirituality. His practices continue the long history of metaphysical religiosity in the United States. A focus on mind, correspondence, energy, and healing are all present in his spiritual quest to overcome physical and mental injury and to develop an energetic connection to the Maidan narrative and experience. He also clearly identifies with the Generation X emphases on spirituality as individual, plural, and virtual. However, Baxter's *practice* is not isolated, nor limited to cultivating his own spiritual journey. His drive to share this experience with the community through shared practices—techniques, workshops, retreats, and social media—is what has informed his hooping identity. His YouTube videos and Facebook posts are practices in the community, not simply means of transmission. When Baxter shares a flow set to music or spoken word, when he speaks directly to the camera and talks about how the universe doesn't make mistakes, and when he demonstrates a technique with spoken or written descriptions, he is participating in the community, and his contributions are received and responded to as authentic exchanges.

Hoover's mediation theory exposes the vital role of media in creating, maintaining, interpreting, and representing the hoop community. The personal

Figure 5.4 Baxter teaching at the HP7 Retreat.

spirituality and experiences that are so important to the hoop community are not distinct from the virtual mechanisms of the community. These experiences support each other; the embodied practices of hoop dance are very much tied to the embodied practices of community sharing, and both rely on a pluralistic and accepting environment. Hoop community is deeply invested in sharing, openness, personal insight, and support, and technology is a way to *practice* this, a way to make meaning. The symbolic inventory of the community thus seamlessly incorporates practices from physical and virtual worlds.

This chapter has examined some of the ways in which hoop dance is both a tool for embodied spirituality and a basis for a thriving community connected not by a shared dogma but by a common practice. To return to one of our survey participant's quotes from earlier in the chapter: "Hooping is my church . . . Hooping is where I commune with God. It's my quiet space where I can quiet my mind and just be . . . I stopped going to church years ago and use my hoop time as my spiritual haven." Her statement replaces church with hooping. But "hooping" is more than the time spent in the hoop; it is mediated by all of the practices of social sharing that create the new space of the hoop and the community where hoopers feel that they can be their authentic selves.

Hoop dance, at first glance, might seem like a solitary activity, or even an exercise trend, and in fact, it can be both of these. In a recent essay discussing Hoopnotica, a Los Angeles-based hoop company, Kelly Moore evaluates the neoliberal techniques of bodily discipline that play out in their rhetoric of hooping as a "fun exercise" that actually replaces play with discipline. Moore's point is an important one. Most hoopers do begin hooping for fun and/or exercise. So what differentiates a spiritual hoop community such as HoopPath from the neoliberal individualist etiologies of self-care espoused by hoop exercise enthusiasts? Perhaps community meaning-making offers a space for hoopers to overturn these expectations, to replace the prescriptions of exercise with their own interpretations, and to find new meanings through the self-generated, shared media of others. When we shift our framework of what constitutes the practice of hooping to include the mediations of real and virtual actions, and of both nonspiritual and spiritual interpretations, we can begin to see the multiple possibilities that the hoop offers practitioners.

6

"Another Way": Modernist Artists, Media, and the Desire for Spiritual Community

Jeremy Garber

We are wrong to believe in facts; there are only signs. We are wrong to believe in truth; there are only interpretations.

Gilles Deleuze, *Proust and Signs*[1]

Introduction

A substantial amount of work has been done on researching how individuals interpret media in their own religious frameworks, but comparatively little qualitative research has been done on the process of group interpretation of media. Likewise, popular distinctions between "religion" and "spirituality" place these terms in opposition, but a deep qualitative reading aids interpreters of religion and media in understanding the philosophical implications of this popular split. In this chapter, my fieldwork with "Another Way," an original Mennonite-inspired conversational community, will be placed in conversation with the media theories of Stanley Fish, Jeremy Stolow, and Thomas Lindlof to explore a contemporary manifestation of the tension of a minoritarian community with surrounding semiotic societal pressures.[2] The struggle of the participants in Another Way to cohesively perceive themselves as part of a community results from their difficult negotiation of the tensions between minoritarian meaning-making and the peculiar tensions of the twentieth- and twenty-first-century perception of religion, spirituality, art, and artists.

Another Way: Art, spirituality, and interpretation in Denver, Colorado

Another Way was founded by a former Mennonite pastor (hereafter referred to as John) as an intentional gathering to discuss the intersection of art and spirituality. The group began meeting on November 2, 2008, in an art gallery that was the home of a community of artists in one of the art districts of Denver, Colorado. John met the owner, who he described as an artist and "fabulous philosopher, theologian, discussionist," and suggested the idea of a discussion group primarily for artists to discuss the spiritual aspect of their own creativity and work. The group met for about six months in the art gallery/coffee shop's original location, designed to attract practicing artists to become part of the conversation by displaying their original works and then offering them to the group for discussion of the works' connections to participants' self-defined spirituality.

However, this initial intention for Another Way to provide artists a forum to discuss the spiritual ramifications of their work did not last long. As described in interviews, the artists quietly drifted away from participation, and the coffee shop decided to stop hosting the gatherings. The remaining participants moved into a stable group, composed almost exclusively of persons from Mennonite-associated backgrounds. Rather than contributing and discussing the spiritual import of their own creative work, the participants in the newly structured group instead brought media artifacts such as poems, film clips, and musical tracks created by others. The remainder of this chapter will explore how the subtle change of the early primary work-of-art model to a second-order analytical discussion, as well as their self-perceived difficulty in creating community, resulted from Another Way participants' perceptions of themselves as subjective individuals and their rejection of structured community as "religious" and "oppressive."

Media theories of communal interpretation—such as those of Stanley Fish, Jeremy Stolow, and Thomas Lindlof—provide a complementary interpretive strand that underlines the reality that meaning is created within an interpretive web of social relations rather than from within an individual's subjectivity. Following this strand of communal versus individualist interpretation, interviews and participant-observation of Another Way gatherings also reveal the inherent tension of subjectivist individuals attempting to define themselves as a minoritarian community within what Deleuze and Guattari define as the capitalist semiotic regime. Another Way's stories provide important implications for the study and self-perception of groups defining themselves as art- or media-focused, as "spiritual but not religious," and as minoritarian (or defining themselves differently from majority conceptions of social, moral, and epistemological obligations). Study of Another Way reveals three specific tensions in such groups:

1. The tension between majoritarian and minoritarian modes of community, particularly religious or spiritual community;
2. the tension between the desire for community (and the presence of communal interpretation) and modern artists' sense of self as subjective individuals in possession of the right to create their own individual meanings; and
3. the continuing interpretation of "religion" as an oppressive oedipal construct and "spirituality" as a liberating yet still individualist subjective mode of religiosity.

The voices of the participants of Another Way, and the observation of their connections as they gather together, reveal the ongoing negotiation of all of these tensions as they seek to be alternatives to prevailing discourses of self, religion, and art—as all minoritarian communities have negotiated their own tensions in their own particular semiotic regimes.

A typical Another Way Gathering

When participants are asked to describe a typical Another Way Gathering, the first (and most commonly mentioned) response was alcohol—with the associated food a close second. Fred, a pastor in an associated Anabaptist tradition, keenly observed the intercommunal workings of the group—sedimentary tendencies that both reinforce the group's own perceived identity and also subtly exclude outsiders, despite its mandate:

> We eat. We drink wine. We chat. There is a good core of people who are in the Mennonite family, and so they're all very happy with each other, because of that connection. And I'm not. And I'm very sensitive to that issue, having not been part of the Brethren family and having given myself to that family all these years. Umm . . . so it's, there's an underlying social reality and social commonality. That I think is bigger than the commonality over art.

After the communal discussion and meal time, the more formalized ritual part of Another Way begins. Typically, the pattern begins with John's toast to the Creator, in which John will use words such as "To the Creator whose spirit of creativity lives on in the universe and in us." John describes the importance of the toast as an invocatory ritual with characteristic humor: "And then there's . . . yeah, the toast, I think, is something important, to the Creator. No, it's important to *us*, but the toast to the Creator is important. It's not important to the Creator [laughs]." Even this seemingly self-deprecatory statement reveals an implicit commitment both to an immanent theology and to a perceived status as rebellious outsiders combined with a desired minoritarian communal existence. Participants privately express that this portion of the gathering, along with the benediction, feels the most "religious," but that they participate in order to honor John's sense of ritual stemming from his ministerial training.

Members of the group arrange themselves on the couches and easy chairs scattered around John's house, festooned with Nora's textile work and John's extensive collection of LPs and CDs. Following the toast, there is typically a thematic discussion that John sends out via email and Facebook three to five days before the meeting time to all persons associated with the group. This theme usually is described in one word, either abstract or figurative; some examples of recent themes include "faith," "darkness," and "aliens." John often opens with a mini-homily expressing his thoughts about the theme, often pertaining to some biographical event during the week. He then opens up free-form discussions to other persons, who follow a particular thread of the conversation to inject their own observations or meanings either on the theme or on John's own reflections. This free discussion time can last from ten to thirty minutes.

John then invites people to share the cultural artifacts that they have brought that connect to the theme of the evening. Group members are invited to bring either a creative piece of their own to share or an artifact created by another person that bears both relevance to the theme and some personal meaning for themselves. Self-created pieces brought by artists in the past vary from formal professional photography to self-written comedy skits to poetry; artifacts created by others include song tracks from popular music albums, excerpts from novels, even birthday cards that have some meaning for the presenter. The presenter will present the piece, sometimes explaining the significance of it as it pertains to the theme or of their lives, or sometimes simply offering it to the group and awaiting their response in silence. Then a second round of free discussion follows, others offering stories or comments about each particular piece that resonate with their own individual experiences. Finally, John offers a sort of benediction, usually mentioning the Creator and tying in the theme of the week, often instructing the participants to go and create in the image of the God who is a Creator and created us.

Another Way is an explicitly hermeneutical gathering. The focus of the group is on presenting pieces of media and works of art, whether self-created or created by others, and then engaging in a communal conversation about how those works are significant in the participants' lives, particularly related to questions of self-worth, belonging, and ultimate meaning—otherwise known as questions of religion and spirituality. The challenge for Another Way as a coalescing group is how to enable a dialogue that moves from a series of individualist monologues to recognize the communal nature of meaning-making (in the theories of Fish, Lindlof, and Stolow). The next section briefly outlines Thomas R. Lindlof's markers of community from his studies of communal media use as a supplemental theoretical framework to partially investigate Another Way's longing for community—and the difficulty in achieving the reality that would satisfy that longing.

Another Way and the longing for community

The description of community-building versus the talents (or enunciatory input) of individual artists in Another Way plays out in different ways in different interviews and transcripts. Thomas R. Lindlof, in his helpful overviews of media studies and religion,[3] offers a provisional definition of "community" that aids in exploring the tensions expressed by Another Way participants between their desire for community and its perceived absence in their group. Lindlof outlines four features common to established communities: (1) possessing a "unity" (not necessarily consensus) of shared circumstances, interests, customs, and purposes; (2) defining moral obligations that the community must share; (3) possessing stability over time, usually aided by the establishment of symbolic nexuses (in the case of religious communities, doctrines of belief and practice); and (4) communicative occasions and codes that enable social coordination and definition.[4]

According to Lindlof's insightful definition, Another Way already possesses a unity of shared interests and purposes as a group coalescing around the spiritual interpretation of art and media. Its stability over time is being developed, aided (and hindered) by the establishment of its own symbolic nexuses and communicative codes. Finally, parallel to other religious groups developed in opposition to traditional religious structures, Another Way participants emphatically reject (at least in their own words) the notion of defining moral obligations.

The participants of Another Way, by virtue of its stated intentions, all share a common shared nexus of interest in the production and reception of various forms of art and media. Many of the participants are practicing artists themselves, from sculptors to photographers to actors. They also share a commitment to some form of spirituality or religion—although, as we will see, these definitions vary widely from participant to participant, and are often in direct contrast to the participant's expressed desire to be part of a community. An excerpt from my interview with Dan illustrates the intersection between art, spirituality, and interpretation that form the Another Way "assemblage":

> Yeah, yeah, and [Amy] was, she took pictures of open spaces through an awning or metal or whatever, and just . . . I should back up and just say that I am *so* intrigued by the creative process. By other people's creative processes. That . . . I love listening to DVD commentary about a movie, or I love hearing, going to a talk-back after a show where a director will talk about his or her vision for a theatrical play, or a lecture about a particular musical piece. I love that sort of thing. So, when Another Way allows insight into that creative process, that is a draw to me. And, going back to that particular time, hearing her talk about her wanting to explore the basically wide-open spaces through confined spaces, I loved hearing about her inspiration and that kind of juxtaposition. I mean, it's kind of a . . . an anomaly, or a non sequitur, not a non sequitur, what's the right word, a paradox! To take a picture of something as wide open as the sky through a very confined space. That was just, it was fascinating to me. And then to relate it spiritually. And, you know, I don't know if I can exactly recount all of the reflections that were made upon it from a spiritual sense, I wouldn't be doing it justice, but it was a special moment for me.

As Another Way continues to meet semimonthly, the stability over time continues to increase—particularly as participants offer the circumstances of their particular lives together in a shared group setting, as they participate in the discussion about art and spirituality, and as they engage in extra-gathering activities such as attending Jazz in the Park concerts or camping together. Nora expresses her sense of the developing stability of the group in its regular gathering times:

> Community for me is more of a continuity of interaction with a core of people. And then certainly people coming in and out. So for me, as that core develops, then I begin to see it more as a community. So the more I see your family, you know, they're sort of more on my radar, wondering how your wife is this week, wondering how your daughter likes school, blah blah blah, you know. Just kind of in the back of your mind. Certainly more interaction with [other members of the community]. So that's kind of the continuous interaction for me makes a community.

However, the symbolic nexuses of the group are also in flux—as in any assemblage, different emphases and concepts create blockages in establishing those shared nexuses. What initially began as a place for artists to present their own artistic works and the connection of spirituality to creativity has become a place for a second-level discussion of other works already created, as Nora again articulates:

> I would like to see . . . a little bit more art pieces. Whatever the art. Being explored and discussed. And reacted to and experienced. That was the beginning theme, and it's become less. But it's a difficult thing to do. Also. Because I think people are reluctant to bring in pieces. And I think one thing that happened early on is, and that's what John said, is that he invited people who he knew were artists, and they came and presented their piece and have never come again. And so, the number of people there who would consider themselves artists, I'm not sure how many would. And so that may influence that a little bit. Or if people would just choose a piece of art and bring that and focus on that. At least once in a while, I think.

Finally, the group shares a vision of shared moral obligation—but only in a negative sense. Another key marker of Another Way's determination to create a minoritarian identity—minoritarian both in larger American society and in the microcosm of the Mennonite-related world—is the perceived rejection of majoritarian moral obligations. Participants articulated (as in the seemingly transgressive references to alcohol consumption above) that what was attractive to them was particularly the *lack* of a shared moral obligation within the group, a kind of shared moral obligation that was a lack of a stated moral code (even though acceptance of difference was the unifying negative factor).

> Jeremy: How does Another Way compare with other religious or spiritual experiences that you've had?
> Bert: Probably there's nothing there that you could do that's unacceptable. So maybe that would be the biggest difference.
> Jeremy: Whereas there are definitely unacceptable behaviors . . .
> Bert: In most other religious/spiritual experiences.

John articulated that his vision for the formation of the group was specifically to invite people who did not feel that they had been accepted into a "church community" or Christian community because they were "too far out" or "because they think outside the box." Although John was not aware of Lindlof's definition of community, John's vision was for Another Way to include persons who did not fit Lindlof's definitions. That is, Another Way was to be a community for persons who did not find unity in previously existing religious communities primarily because they did not share the moral obligation, the symbolic nexuses, and/or the communicative codes of those communities.

However, participants almost uniformly expressed the sense that Another Way was a community that was in flux but not yet forming, almost five years into the establishment of the group. Bert provides a representative sample of participants' hesitation about naming Another Way as a community because of the lack of commitment from the members and the still-coalescing nature of Another Way's symbolic nexuses:

> I think it's getting there. And I think what I'm seeing is that there's different relationships among the people. That are very community-oriented. And part of that is because different people have known each other for various lengths of time. But I think new ones are growing. And I think again, community is a process. It's not gonna happen in a year. But I think it's on its way. And part of the sorting out of what Another Way is gonna be is gonna take several years. And it's gonna be a different thing than it is now. Or than it was envisioned to be at the beginning.

I suggest that Another Way's desire for community but difficulty in enacting that desire, and the nature of its developing symbolic nexuses (including the resistance to sharing those nexuses), can also be explained as characteristic of individuals in the capitalist semiotic regime—particularly individuals who understand themselves as artists or artistic in an individualistic and subjective sense. This tendency to lock the self as a stable pattern rather than a communally negotiated process also exacerbates the tension between privileging individuality as "spiritual" and denigrating community—the actual focus of meaning-making—as "religious." If the self reigns supreme, and the self is spiritual, then it proves difficult for selves to engage in communal meaning-making—as the next section of data demonstrates.

"Spiritual but not religious"

Spiritual good, religious bad

Much has been made of the modern distinction between "religion" and "spirituality," religion often being compared with rigid, hierarchical, oedipal structures, and "spirituality" being associated with fluid, individualized, productive flow. Almost universally, with a few qualified exceptions among those persons actively involved in institutional religion, these associations were echoed during the interview process. Participants in Another Way equate "spirituality" with the liberation of desire, the flow of creativity, and the possibility of something new:

> I find it spiritual because it's . . . we're using . . . it seems very open. Very . . . it seems intentional, like we're seeking something greater than ourselves. And it seems very spiritual because we haven't created this very narrow definition of what it is. It allows spirit to move maybe more freely, and let it become what it would become at any given session that we would have.

Bert, the sculptor, describes his creative process in a manner that suggests a Deleuzean following of the rhizome. He expresses a desire for his works of art to communicate his feeling of connection with his larger environment—his existence on the planomenon of artistic creation, what he describes as spirituality. His works are almost exclusively a connection of wood, stone, and worked metal, his attempt to blur the distinctions between so-called natural materials with an explicitly human technological product. So, at least on his own understanding, Bert is most artistically creative and most connected when he allows the flow of desire to express the nonhuman becomings of humanity and the nonhuman landscapes of nature.

When asked to describe spiritual experiences, a majority of participants describe individual experiences but connected to natural surroundings. Contrasted with "spirituality" as a self-directed and solitary act, interviewees almost uniformly equate "religion" with structure, dogma, hierarchy, and oppression:

> "It's negative. And, um, for me it has to do with a tradition that is applied poorly to the particular context of a time."
>
> "Church. Structure. A little bit top down," And spirituality, "The opposite. [Laughs] It's very much open to each person's experience and interpretation. You know, there's no right or wrong kind of thing."

Another Way participants generally reject the orthodox view of God as an omniscient, omnipotent, eternal person. God is often described in terms of a force or a tendency—understandings compatible both with modern theological movements such as process theology and with Deleuzean understandings of flow and sedimentation. God, then, becomes less a "person" with whom the respondent has a "relationship" and more a recognition of the movement of things and meaning around them in society and in their interpersonal relationships. In a sense, the repeatedly expressed longing for a community that is still in the process of becoming, a community that struggles to connect itself through artistic creation and second-order connection of art with their circumstances of their own lives, the participants of Another Way are seeking another way to connect themselves to God.

Media and minoritarian identity

When discussing "media" as a concept, interviewees recognize both the potential of media to be both a liberative and connective "medium" (in Jeremy Stolow's sense)[5] and a reinforcement of majoritarian modes of Oedipal control. However, they almost always associate the latter tendencies with those religious communities whose central modes of interpretation and moral cohesions they reject. Participants express a desire for their use of media and art to be minoritarian and creative in explicit opposition to the use of media for purposes of oppression, as in this interview excerpt with Charles, another professional clergy member:

> Yeah. Well . . . I'm not enamored by the religious folks who use the media. That's not something that I think is . . . When I was a kid growing up, you know, you had people like Kenneth Copeland and Kenneth Hague and some of these evangelists, you know, James Dobson, Jimmy Swaggart. I mean, yeah, they used the media. It wasn't impressive to me at all. It didn't feel like, it felt like Hewlett Packard, it was about the bottom line. Trying to get money.

For Another Way participants, media and art can either reinforce majoritarian facelessness and anonymity, or unleash the flows of desire that blur the distinctions between human and environment and allow the recognition of the connectedness and fluidity of reality. These are their understandings of the theology and spirituality of art, the center around which all participants are drawn to and remain within the group.

As the theoretical conversation partner in this particular chapter, the communal interpretation theories of Stanley Fish, Jeremy Stolow, and Lindlof remind us that the individual interpretation to which Another Way participants unconsciously subscribe is a modernist myth. Instead, these theorists maintain that meaning is created in verbal and physical interchange between the constituents of various social groups, including those that identify themselves as creative and as religious or spiritual. The final section of this chapter describes these theories of communal interpretation in order to converse with how Another Way participants' individual subjectivism interferes with their desire to create an alternative minoritarian meaning-making community.

Theories of interpretive community

Stanley Fish and the authority of interpretive communities

Media and interpretive theories of scholars such as Fish, Lindlof, and Stolow argue that meaning is not something that resides statically in an object or other person for individuals to discover using their own subjective rationality. Rather, meaning is an ongoing process of symbolic negotiation between individuals and the social web in which they are embedded. A summary of these theorists explains the workings and blockages of Another Way's attempted explication of the spirituality of art and media. Stanley Fish is perhaps the best-known theorist of interpretive community, particularly as it applies to textual analysis, and thus provides a helpful lens into how meaning is created as a communal endeavor rather than discovered as an individual project. Fish begins his classic *Is There a Text in This Class?*[6] with the observation, "The field of inquiry is *constituted* by the questions we are able to ask because the entities that populate it come into being as the presuppositions—they are discourse-specific entities—of those questions." To put it in more theological terms, the cosmology that we bring to a particular intellectual endeavor determines the epistemology that we use to investigate that very cosmology—and often predetermines the answers we receive. Moreover (and more radically), the group process of interpretation—what we might call ecclesiological hermeneutics—is a key factor in creating meaning in the texts themselves, not merely uncovering a kind of mining deposit of hidden meaning that pre-existed the community's interaction with that text.

Fish rejects the assumption that either the text or the reader is a stable entity; shifting focus to the reader as determiner of meaning still privileges the text as a stable entity.[7] Instead, he suggests a theoretical move to investigating the interpretive community.[8] Rather than seeing one's subjective interpretation from a particular time and place as being a hazard to "authentically" interpreting a text, Fish sees subjectivity as an essential and practically indispensable part of the interpretive process. If one sees textual interpretation as the nexus of a larger, ever-shifting community across both time and space, the observer can investigate the way that texts work in connection with the particularities of the persons who are connected with them.

An interpretive community is neither objective nor subjective but an assemblage, a "bundle of interests, of particular purposes and goals," that consumes and produces (or enunciates) driven by particular motivated interests (or desire).[9] This produces a certain "stability" of interpretation for Fish because the similarities of desire and enunciation are present in a given moment of assemblage. Obviously, then, there is no "correct" or "truthful" reading in a Fish-driven perspective, only a way of reading that is an extension of the community perspective. For Fish, therefore, criticism is not "to determine a correct way of reading but to determine from which of a number of possible perspectives reading will proceed."[10] The choice for any given interpretive community is which reading strategy it will choose to use.

Fish observes that communities are relatively stable not because of the texts around which they gather (think of the almost inexhaustible possible definitions of the word "biblical" here), but a (temporary) stability in the makeup of the interpretive communities and even in the opposing positions those communities make possible.[11] This observation also stresses that particular individuals employ different interpretive strategies, even on the same text, because they belong to different interpretive communities.

How does Stanley Fish help us understand the communal hermeneutic process of Another Way? First, Fish's observations about the epistemological boundaries of a given group springing from its particular cosmology suggest that Another Way participants' understanding of spirituality and art shape their conversations in particular directions before those conversations even begin. As the interview data illustrate, the participants' notions of themselves as creative individuals rather than part of a larger hermeneutic community limit their ability to engage in self-aware participatory discourse. Although the participants' backgrounds and sense of themselves as subversive outsiders shape the possibility of their conversations, they describe themselves as bringing their own unique insights on other people's creativity to the process—a set of ready-made individual meaning statements that other participants are expected to digest. This self-perception contrasts with Fish's demonstration that neither subjects nor texts are stable entities, reinforcing the participants' own self-perceived separation from the group rather than allowing them to acknowledge that both participants and conversations are constantly negotiated shifting processes.

Fish's theories of literature also help us understand how Another Way participants sort their categories of spirituality, religion, art, and media into accepted and rejected shared communal texts, as discussed above. Another Way participants see "authentically spiritual" art and media as privately created, and media created for communal consumption as capitalistic and inauthentic. This tacit agreement about what counts as authentic art comes from the participants' cosmology of individualism. The stability of Another Way came from the relative temporal stability of the group's commitment to individual creativity in the face of majoritarian exploitation. There is some fragile community in the refusal to abandon individualism—and it is this interpretive stance that shapes Another Way's consumption and discussion of media, both allowing and blocking the flow of group members' desire to become truly creatively minoritarian. The theories of Jeremy Stolow and Thomas Lindlof will round out the exploration of the tensions of majoritarian/minoritarian interpretation, of the desire for community versus the sense of self as individual, and the tension between the perception of religion as oppressive and spirituality as liberating yet still individualistic.

Theoretical models of the semiotic study of media and religious studies

Another Way participants are explicitly engaged in exploring the permutations of religion/spirituality and media/art. Jeremy Stolow, in his intriguing article "Religion and/as Media,"[12] examines the assumed distinction between "religion" and "media," questioning the modern myth that media play a key role in disembedding religion from popular life on both sides, either as the loss of moral meaning or as the triumph of social groups over repressive institutions. Stolow observes that traditional communities still use contemporary communication methods, even to the extent that their religious symbols and practices have been extended through the religious "colonizing" of those methods.[13] Stolow rejects the evaluation of the "success" or "failure" of religious communities to transmit their message (an "instrumentalist" approach), noting the grassroots role of interpretation and an interpretation not of "religion and media" but of "religion as media".[14] He suggests that religion and media are not ontologically different entities, but subjectively similar structural mechanisms; that is, in a ritualistic understanding of communication, religion and media both provide *forms* for the cultural transmission of meaning in structurally similar ways. Stolow provides this tantalizing question for further researchers, based on Derrida and Walter Benjamin's observations: "What happens to sacred presence once it is mediated, and re-mediated, through an ever-thickening raiment of technological apparatuses and in ever-widening circuits of exchange? Can mediation actually bring 'the sacred' closer to us, and if so, with what 'effect'?"[15] Another Way's example suggests that mediation can either facilitate "exchange" or can reinforce the sedimentation of subjectivist individualism characteristic of the modernist semiotic regime. Whether as religion as or interpretation of "media" as classically defined (i.e., art, music, literature, YouTube videos, etc.), mediation either aids the minoritarian community in navigating its way through majoritarian culture—or aids its absorption into that majoritarian culture instead.

Aiding a religious community in examining its understanding of mass media requires understanding how that community prepares its members to interpret the meaning of media texts. Thomas R. Lindlof, in his already mentioned articles, integrates broader semiotic understandings and the "interpretive community" model in his study of media and religion. Lindlof observes that there is a consensus among mass communication scholars that media consumers use some interpreting activity, but that not much study exists on how this process actually happens. People interpret media not only on the individual but also the social level. In a semiotic move, Lindlof describes this process as "explicitly hermeneutic," rooted in a communal understanding that may be incommensurable with other interpretive communities. He rejects the understanding of meaning as *presented meaning*, objectively presented content designed by the agencies that produce it, in favor of an observed process of *constructed meaning*, controlled by the persons who engage in mediated communication.[16] This process of construction does not happen on a merely individual (and therefore ungeneralizable level), however; the interpreter comes to a media artifact with a "virtual text," an understanding of how media are to be interpreted in regards to daily belief and practice, that is given by the interpreter's chosen interpretive community. For example, a fundamentalist Christian from Appalachia will read the Creation narrative in Genesis with a "virtual text" very different from that of an atheist student of neurobiology trained in the scientific method. The participants of Another Way similarly bring their virtual texts of alternative identity, individual artistic creation, and individualist spirituality to their interpretation of media artifacts. The scholarly goal for Lindlof, then, is first for the researcher to acknowledge the messiness of the interpretive culture that he or she is investigating and also the world of meanings in which he or she is already enveloped,[17] and then to trace the interaction of the interpretive community that is being studied through a semiotic explication of the community's "virtual texts" and tactical readings of particular media artifacts.[18]

Conclusion

When I set out on the research project described in this chapter, I had intended to use the Another Way group to explain how the creation of meaning happens as a communal process when the conversation is centered on the intersection of art/media and religion/spirituality. In this chapter's analysis of Another Way, I found instead a mostly individualist interpretation of spirituality and self in tandem with a fragile but ever-evolving sense of minoritarian community. This tension arises from a historic understanding of artists as minoritarian individuals, without the corresponding communal understanding that often accompanied such minoritarian creation, such as the salons of Paris and those in which Schleiermacher participated, for which these poets, sculptors, administrators, and intellectuals long.

Two themes in the Another Way interviews and transcripts recur repetitively: (1) the dichotomy between "religion" and "spirituality," and (2) the longing for community without being precisely clear about how to define what that notion of community is or how to enact it. Since "spirituality" is positive but individualistic, and "religion" is communal but negative, an inherent tension presents itself in the conceptual framework of most Another Way participants. It is significant that Another Way individuals express a desire for community, but attach their notions of both the creation of the work of art and their expression of spirituality to privatized individual experiences. Conversely, although they view religion as structured, outdated, and oppressive, they also express that the times when they feel most like community are through shared life experiences and practices. So Another Way participants display the tension between wanting to be traditional liberal individualist artists on the one hand and part of a radical minoritarian creative community on the other, displaying a desire for interconnection while insisting on being active subjects completely in charge of their own creative output. This ongoing tension between the desire for communal connection and the sedimentation of the Oedipal subject is displayed both in transcripts of the Another Way gatherings and in the enunciation of the interview subjects themselves.

Throughout the interviews, the reflective nature of theological analysis is not primary to the identity of Another Way. In a group centered on the discussion and experience of works of art, the attempt has always been to focus on describing the impressions of the affects and percepts of the work—which interestingly is itself a second-order discourse. This tension between the intersection of the planes of philosophy and art is reflected in the tension articulated by members of the group—both in the desire to connect with each other, which is not evidenced in second-order discourse or articulation, and in the temptation to resort to enunciation in order to capture the dangerous flow of desire that can be liberated by experiencing the work of art. Only when those flows of desire are liberated from the second-order level of discourse, when the participants become other-than-gender, other-than-human, and most importantly other-than-self, do they describe a feeling of connection or wholeness, both with other members of the group and, significantly, with their own theological perceptions of God.

7

"Dancing Our Prayers": Material Culture and Practical Spiritualities of the Jam Band Scene*

Lucas F. Johnston
Wake Forest University

Miracles are a regular occurrence in the jam band scene. The term "miracles" is widely used to refer to what some perceive as incredibly fortuitous circumstances—which these people often describe in terms of the intervention of cosmic or supernatural forces that manifest their deepest desires. It is not unusual to see dozens and sometimes hundreds of people (depending on the show) outside performance venues with a finger in the air asking "who's got my miracle?"—and what they mean by miracle is "extra ticket." An example will be illustrative. One jam band enthusiast described his miracle this way:

> We all had tickets except Max. He couldn't find shit in the lot. I was coming down off a great acid trip and was in a super, skippy mood. So, in my homemade tie-dye I walked the lot with a finger in the air offering cash. After missing out for a while, I changed my tune to needing a miracle for my birthday show (it was not my birthday—it [had been] a couple of weeks later). After only a few short moments, a hottie came up hugged me, kissed my mouth, told me happy birthday and gave me a free ticket. It was up in the high seats, but Max was in. I felt a little bad for the birthday thing, but hey—a lion's gotta eat. Max had to suffer the Karma bite. Some hippie puddled his palm with some good liquid and he tripped his fucking face off so hard by himself that he had to leave [the] show early. When I got out, he talked me into driving him home . . . through the night. So I guess karma bit me too.[1]

This was a miracle, if not of biblical proportions, at least significant for a couple of people at the time. That religious terms are used to describe such moments of convergence is no accident, but instead reflects the ways in which people manufacture meaning through the appropriation of religious symbols, metaphors, and tropes to navigate the worlds they find themselves thrown into. Increasingly, such meaning-making occurs outside the boundaries of what we might consider traditional religious structures. Focusing specifically on participants in improvisational rock music subcultures, I highlight the historical tributaries to these movements and the ways in which various media shape and help to broadcast alternative, improvisational spiritualities.

Performance-oriented subcultures offer a provocative case that illustrates the ways in which alternative cultural mores have flourished and spread and that also highlights some of the shortcomings that have hampered the scholarly analysis of practical forms of religious meaning-making. In what follows I consider people who self-identify as "spiritual but not religious" to be engaging in religious meaning-making. If we define religion broadly—as related to both ordinary and extraordinary experiences and the ways in which people embody their values in everyday life—then these subcultures and the forms of cultural production in which they engage are certainly religious.[2] Such spiritualities, which often contain green if not dark green themes, are becoming more common and socially impactful. But questions remain as to whether they will continue to grow in size and efficacy or whether they will, like some of their precursor movements in the late 1960s in the United States, fade away.

Such social movements can be fruitfully analyzed by considering modes of cultural transmission first recognized by the philosopher Colin Campbell in his influential arguments about the cultic milieu, which he characterized as a system of countercultural social movements that seem to rather freely exchange metaphors and tropes, although the core values of these groups, and their ultimate aims, may differ significantly.[3] Later work extended this argument to environmentalist[4] and sustainability milieus[5] specifically tracing the ways in which such motivational metaphors and tropes were exchanged between grassroots and international organizations, countercultural and mainstream groups, and between religious and secular movements. At play within the performance-oriented subcultures I examine here a similar sort of exchange, though I will focus on material culture, the pragmatic and situational spiritualities that underlie these expressions, and the ways in which they express core values of these constituencies. In important ways the religious expressions I will explore and analyze illustrate a concern for performance and embodiment that nuance if not challenge some frequently exercised definitions of religions.

For instance, many scholars have argued that worldviews—that is, ideas about religious belonging and the tenets of specific religious groups—guide real-world behaviors.[6] If people change their minds about their worldviews, so this reasoning goes, their behaviors might follow.[7] My ethnographic work and historical analysis of performance-oriented subcultures says otherwise: interpersonal interactions, and specific behaviors and practices, exercise significant influence on the shape of worldviews, not the other way round. Moreover, a "worldviews" approach misses the ways in which such practices are enshrined—and re-broadcast in various media—overturning conventional artistic sensibilities in a fusion of folk art and "high" art to project specific spiritual values into the public sphere. Music festivals provide a good example. Attending the now ubiquitous jam festivals is both expensive and requires significant preparation and effort.[8] Often a physical pilgrimage is required, and the travel and anticipated musical events become a central focus of social media communication that begins months prior to the event itself. In interviews and surveys and through social media, participants consistently refer to these experiences as formative for values that are articulated in terms of interdependence or fellow-feeling and as generative of spiritual well-being. Experience, then, can prime individuals to be receptive to certain facets of particular worldviews, but, in such cases, worldviews are often derivative of embodied, affective experiences of belonging and participation. Often participants indicate that these infrequent but highly affective experiences sustain them until the next big happening. In this analysis I focus specifically on the religious dimensions of these movements as revealed in both material culture (popular forms of ritual engagement evident in performance venues), and media dissemination, noting how they shape and express varied spiritualities. It may be helpful to offer some historical background about the emergence of improvisational rock music subcultures, to provide a better understanding of what material practices characterize this milieu and how these shape and express varied religious practices and identities.

The genesis and rising popularity of improvisational rock music subcultures

As 1965 drew to a close, the critically acclaimed author Ken Kesey and his friends (referred to as the Merry Pranksters) held the first Acid Test in Soquel, California, a multi-media event fueled by still-legal LSD (lysergic acid diethylamide), a powerful entheogen.[9] Although not a concert in the usual sense, the Warlocks, a band which shortly thereafter renamed themselves the Grateful Dead, performed there, and their music was significantly impacted by the countercultural ethos and performance sensibilities of this and later Acid Tests. The Pranksters' Acid Tests were designed to push the boundaries of both individual and collective exploration beyond the burgeoning hippie movement, to help people recognize and challenge the presuppositions behind their everyday perceptions, and to experiment with ostensibly more authentic, embodied forms of community. The spiritual sensibilities of this countercultural scene were more performative than intellectual or rational, influenced by non-Abrahamic religious traditions, and they exhibited a normative concern for tightly knit community. For many, these were highly affective experiments in religious meaning-making, embodying alternative values based on public expression, community, and a critique of "straight" mainstream America.[10]

These trends arguably reach back to the post-World War II period when younger generations in particular began to exhibit strong distrust in traditional sources of economic, political, and religious authority.[11] Most of the social movements that the sociologists Charles Glock and Robert Bellah identified as exemplars of the "new consciousness" included a focus on alternative living arrangements or lifestyles.[12] These often included forms of spiritually grounded practice such as meditation, vegetarianism, and pacifism. These practices could be imagined as micro-level enactments of the public discontent evidenced in public image events[13] such as the 1967 Human Be-In, the 1967 demonstrations against Army recruiting in Berkeley, arson attacks on Reserve Officers' Training Corps (ROTC) buildings and other buildings in the San Francisco Bay Area (1968), and the occupation of Alcatraz by members of the American Indian Movement (AIM) and their allies (1969–71). Such countercultures were often inspired by the valorization of Eastern philosophies and religions (especially Buddhism and Daoism) or of indigenous lifeways and practices. These political and religious trends converged as expressions of this new consciousness, the era of radical politics that emerged in the United States in the 1960s, but that had by the 1970s largely lost its political teeth. Although it has been argued that there were important divergences among the more politically concerned Berkeley New Left,[14] the socially focused San Francisco hippie movements, and the perhaps even more radical Acid Test counterculture, each of these contributed to the cultic milieu a rejection of traditional political, social, and religious norms and helped translate into improvisational rock subcultures forms of cultural expression that included a concern for communalism, psychedelic experimentation, and an experience-based spiritual sensibility.

The Grateful Dead epitomized the experimental ethos of this period, along with other bands such as Santana, Jefferson Airplane, Hot Tuna, and Big Brother and the Holding Company. Characteristic of this growing scene was an emphasis on live musical experimentation, including unpredictable set lists and unstructured jamming, which often developed into songs that were much longer than the typical three-minute forms that were popular at that time. The Great Human Be-In in San Francisco included many of the most influential San Francisco bands as well as notable writers of the Beat generation such as Allen Ginsberg and Louis Ferlinghetti and figures such as former Harvard professors Timothy Leary and Richard Alpert who were themselves engineering psychedelic experiments on the East Coast.[15] The title of the event, reminiscent of the sit-ins that were formative for the US civil rights movement, hinted at the contemplative and experimental habitat created there. Drawing on strategies pioneered by the Pranksters, who had advertised their Acid Tests with wildly experimental poster art, the Human Be-In poster was reflective of much of this cultic milieu's admiration for indigenous and Eastern philosophies and metaphysics, invoking American Indian images and advertising that the Buddha would be among the attendees. The Grateful Dead and other related improvisational rock acts popularized the psychedelic rock poster, which became a crucial piece of the material culture of improvisational rock scenes.

These countercultural movements were engineering new forms of expression that paralleled their new ways of being-in-the-world—they were practical spiritualities manufactured in a rich *bricolage* of cultural elements including experimentation with entheogens, and indigenous, Eastern, and other sets of values, which provided some anchor in an era characterized by what some perceived to be an evacuation of meaningful forms of interpersonal engagement. In some respects, such perceptions of disconnectedness were motivated by the rise of suburban consumer culture in the postwar period as well as from the supposed secularization of American culture. America was in a liminal phase, between the unifying values that buttressed the Allies during World War II, and the hyper-individualism that characterized the postwar period. The countercultures under analysis here were not only participants in this transitional phase of American culture, but also intentionally manufactured liminal modes of being that rejected the still emerging postmodern social structures and the firmly entrenched military-industrial system of the second half of the twentieth century.

Liminoid cultures and secularization

Liminal states were characterized by the anthropologist Victor Turner as initiating a "subjunctive mood," one in which participants "express desires, hypotheses, suppositions, [and] possibilities"—they engage in performing the world-as-it-could be.[16] This state can be dangerous, overturning certain social conventions and understandings. But this uncertain state is also capable of generating a sense of *communitas*, a relatively undifferentiated group that experiences through this erasure of structure a sense of effervescence.[17] These terms, however, were used by Turner to describe highly ritualized lifeways that were typically observed among smaller, more ethnically and ethically homogenous groups.

In contrast, the postmodern cultures in which improvisational rock subcultures came of age were more heterogeneous, characterized by divergent ethical perspectives, differing cultural backgrounds, as well as by radical socioeconomic disparities. Turner viewed such cultures as "liminoid," places where liminality was no longer expressed in social rites of passage or ritual forms but instead sought by participants through recreational or other pursuits that allowed them to divest from the structured modes of culture that characterized modern and postmodern capitalist societies or at least to engage in performances "as though" they were removed from them. Importantly, hybrid spiritualities, cobbled together from multiple sources and largely customizable, grew in popularity in this milieu, with participants eschewing what they perceived as empty rituals and hierarchical structures. Ritualization did not disappear but rather took on new contextual forms. Many individuals have preconcert rituals—or believe that specific drugs should be ingested at particular places or types of events—and some friend-groups that gather at concerts and festivals fashion large flags or other symbols, which are raised over camping or parking areas prior to shows. In most cases such rituals involve much improvisation if not spontaneity, and provide cognitive anchors that hold fast threads of memory from these highly affective events. These are contextual and embodied practices, rather than the intellectualized or rationalized theologies that scene participants often reject.

Events such as the Human Be-In, the Monterrey Pop Music Festival (1967), and Woodstock (1969) became the quintessential exemplars of this modern manifestation of *communitas*, where people performed new modes of religious meaning-making and later recalled these moments as spiritually formative events. To illustrate, at Woodstock an Asian Indian guru named Swami Satchidananda gave the opening prayer and referred to music as the "the celestial sound that controls the whole universe."[18] He encouraged the gathered youth to promote a spiritual awakening for the good of the world: "America is becoming whole. America is helping everybody in the material field, but the time has come for America to help the whole world with spirituality also."[19] The group yoga sessions at the festival were also unique sites of spiritual improvisation, with the teacher (unnamed in the film) comparing Kundalini yoga to the "same energy that drugs give you . . . [It's] the same channels, only drugs do it *for* you and this way you can do it yourself . . . I learned it in Los Angeles. It would be groovy to experiment with it, like these guys who've been experimenting with it for at least 6,000 years, and getting very high behind it."[20] The teacher later compared the sensations that could be cultivated through proper yoga practice with what happened when he smoked DMT.[21] Yoga, in this interpretation, is a spiritual practice for achieving altered states, parallel to the ritualized intake of strongly entheogenic compounds. At one point during Woodstock, a large-scale neotribal chant and drumming ritual commenced as a storm descended on the concert-grounds, including improvised drumming with instruments such as sticks and empty beer cans.[22] These illustrate the sort of spiritual *briocolage* that characterized these milieus, but Woodstock is merely one pivotal illustration of a transitional cultural moment when, as the festival organizer Michael Lang said, the youth were moving away from the "previous generation," and it was possible to see what the younger generation does "on their own, without cops, without guns, without clothes, without hassles. Everybody pulls together, everybody helps each other, and it works."[23]

Interestingly, the form of Kundalini the Woodstock yogi employed included instructions that led the practitioners to hyperventilate, a practice that is now common in forms of New Age ritualization such as holotropic breathwork.[24],[25] Yoga remains a common practice across North America and is frequently included as a free event at contemporary rock festivals. Pagan and neotribal practices such as ecstatic and group drumming, fire spinning, and face painting are increasingly commonplace and many, particularly at festival scenes, are reminiscent of this countercultural foment in the late 1960s. One common cultural narrative supposes that these hybrid spiritual practices emerged during this time as a result of an increasing secularization. Two things are clear, however: green religious practices have much deeper roots that reach back before the onset of secularization,[26] and syncretism—the combination and re-combination of religious dimensions of human life (from food customs to dress to doctrine)—has been the rule rather than the exception.[27] The developments in the late 1960s, however, were colored by the unique cultural upheavals of that time. Let us turn back now to that pivotal phase to illustrate some of the ways in which these hybrid spiritualities were disseminated in various media through popular culture.

The material culture of the improvisational rock milieu and the failure of progressivism

Important popular works, both literary and artistic (e.g., the poster art of these scenes), were expressions of what had become, for those who participated in it, new spiritualities that better fit the rapidly and radically changing cultural circumstances of the 1960s and early 1970s. Some examples of how such themes and tropes manifested in the material culture of these movements will be illustrative here.

The Grateful Dead archivist at the University of California, Santa Cruz, Nicholas Meriweather, wrote that "For the Dead, the Tests showed how an artistic event could be a transformative community ritual, a sensory alembic that could redefine the idea of performance by making everyone an artist of the experience. The audience became participants, participants became co-creators, and everyone left transformed."[28] If he is right, then the art that accompanied these events was more than mere visual representation. It was, rather, first, an expression of an upcoming moment of *communitas* and, thereafter, a cognitive trigger for a highly affective experience of fellow-feeling and meaning-making. Many of the artists who created official show posters for the Grateful Dead and other bands from the burgeoning psychedelic music scene on the West Coast embodied these new modes of art. For instance, artist Lee Conklin was well known for amazingly intricate, fluid images where faces, creatures, and other images were embedded within the larger, more obvious portraits. His art, according to Meriweather, suggested "boundaries between forms could blur just as the limits of ego could dissolve under psychedelics."[29] Psychedelic art celebrated some of the key elements of the new practices of this scene, by attempting to capture some of the visual experiences of entheogenic states by implying a sense of interconnectedness and invoking religious imagery.

Well-known artist Bob Fried noted that he designed his posters to convey a sense of "dimensional space. . .a kind of space network, rushing, floating . . . through time . . . the sense of discovery that I myself was experiencing [under the influence of entheogens]."[30] Some of artist David Singer's most important works likewise projected a sense of pilgrimage. His posters for the final Fillmore West series (1970) shows featuring the Grateful Dead, Taj Mahal, and Bigfoot depicted two prominent mushrooms framed by a series of receding arches. There are steps leading up to the arches and, within them, behind the mushrooms in the foreground, contributing to the sense of journey, a picture of deep space lit by a nebula. Running up the cap of one of the mushrooms is a silver, cosmic hominid creature. Meriweather elaborated that the poster was a "depiction of the loneliness of the human journey in the cosmos," and, as he noted, "it is hard not to see in it something of a parable for the Dead's own journey, as they navigated the end of the sixties."[31] As with the music, the material culture of these improvisational rock scenes was intended to mimic the intrepidity, the danger, and sometimes even the solitude of the psychedelic journey. Psychonauts in the scene typically imbibed entheogens with friends and fellow concert-goers, but the psychedelic experience was also always an intensely personal experience variously characterized by feelings of unease, isolation, empowerment, a sense of belongingness, and sometimes even feelings of deep interconnection and fellow-feeling. These new experiential and highly participatory art forms had birthed a new consciousness widespread among these subcultures: a great hopefulness and a desire to restore, or better yet, to recapture a sense of the American Dream. But the dream lost steam and revolutionary sensibilities and community experiments did not move into the mainstream.

The sociologists Charles Glock and Robert Bellah, along with doctoral students from the University of California at Berkeley and the Graduate Theological Union in Berkeley, launched a research program that explored various manifestations of this new consciousness, which emerged in the 1960s.[32] Although the countercultural milieu that drove the radical movements—from violent anti-war and racial equality movements to psychedelic experimentations paired with improvisational rock music (that had by the late 1960s grown far beyond the Grateful Dead)—had lost its political traction by 1970, the strong focus on alternative lifestyles articulated within these subcultures persisted.[33] Such countercultures were characterized by a rich hybridization of cultural elements from indigenous lifeways and Eastern philosophies and religions (especially Buddhism and Daoism), which were ostensibly both more holistic in orientation and more environmentally friendly in prescriptions. In other words, while the possibility of political revolution seemed to have dissipated, countercultural emphases on communalism and a new spirituality continued to evolve if not flourish.

The material culture of contemporary improvisational rock subcultures still exhibits similar themes and performs many of the same functions. Popular and scholarly interest in Asian cultures and attendant philosophies and religions had percolated in the cultural background since the late 1800s, as anthropologists and linguists explored these through scholarly lenses. But interest in the East flourished in the 1950s as Beat authors discovered the work of such authors as D. T. Suzuki and as books such as Jack Keroauc's *The Dharma Bums* (2006 [1958]) became more popular. Gary Snyder, the real-life referent for Japhy Ryder, the protagonist of *The Dharma Bums*, wrote his Pulitzer Prize-winning *Turtle Island* in 1974 and was a frequent participant in the subcultures that popularized improvisational rock music; he was a purveyor of both indigenous and Buddhist philosophies and religions. Similar to the case with Asian traditions and cultures, indigenous North American cultures were also popularly imagined as offering holistic, alternative ethical foundations and spiritual orientations grounded in respect for nature. There continues to be a strong presence of imagery drawn from dharmic traditions and cultures (especially from Buddhism and Hinduism) as well as indigenous cultures. To illustrate, consider the recent triptych of posters by the artist Jeff Wood commemorating the 2013 Christmas Jam sponsored by Conscious Alliance and depicting what he refers to as a "neo-Tribal, Pagan Yule Priestess" summoning companion animals.[34] Although the main body of the portrait is a woman that is clearly Native American in appearance, the colors and style are distinctly psychedelic in form and color with fluid lines and boundaries. It clearly invokes dark green animistic themes[35] by depicting a theriomorphic being who summons the animals through the manipulation of elemental forces like fire.[36]

In addition, as it did among the Grateful Dead scene, fan art remains an important accompaniment to the mobile improvisational rock scene. For those unfamiliar with improvisational rock scenes, it is important to note that much of the cultivation of *communitas* occurs in parking lots and other areas near the venue before and after shows, sharing stories, music, fellowship, and making cottage industry purchases to take home as "relics" that remind participants of the spiritual happening. This material aspect of the spiritual community is most associated with the 1980s and 1990s Grateful Dead shows where it was not uncommon to find crowds upward of 300,000 people on stadium properties participating in a homemade "church" experience. Still today improvisational rock fans create artwork depicting favorite songs, lyrics, or other representations; embellish shirts, hats, pins, and posters with them; and sell them at live venues and online.[37] This small cottage industry—along with the sale of food, alcohol, and various drugs among these subcultures—generates a small but significant alternative economy based in both cash and trade.

Other experiential curiosities are also on display as in the case of the "rocket ship" available to brave travelers at the Lock'n Festival in 2014. Several women—dressed in garments both vaguely animistic (at least one of them wore an animal "tail") and indigenously inspired—beckoned passersby to climb aboard the spacecraft for a trip "out of this world." Those intrepid explorers that boarded the craft sat in a circle inside the ring of gongs (pictured), as the women, now the pilots

Figure 7.1 "Plastic Jesus."

of the craft, pounded the gongs with varying ferocity to generate the vibratory and sonic impression of "blasting off." In general, the festival grounds were arranged to provide a sense of both vacation and adventure, with guided hikes, mountain bike rentals, and various food vendors available throughout. The grounds provide a *liminoid* sensation, a temporary reprieve from the "real world," though ironically they were oriented to maximize the consumer experience. Festival-goers are never far from concessions (both alcohol and food), though access to the quantity and quality of such goods is conspicuously on display in the physical segregation of the general admission, VIP, and Super-VIP constituencies.

At many festivals, where many if not most of the participants stay on the premises for several days, activities that reflect a concern for self-reliance and spiritual practices remain common. At one of the newer but still high-profile festivals, Lock'n Festival, there was a yoga session each morning. Although this was a free activity in this particular instance, outside the festival world it is largely practiced by middle- and upper-middle-class Americans, and it is a service for which they pay. Other organizations such as Backyard Revolution, a historical society that promotes self-sufficiency and the renewal of sustainable

Figure 7.2 "Blast Off."

living practices of early pioneer culture, also have large interactive displays and activities.[38] These organizations teach woodworking and demonstrate blacksmith skills, archery, canning, and other largely lost skills.

One interesting connection between the material culture of the Acid Tests and contemporary improvisational rock subcultures is the presence of the "Furthur" bus at several summer and fall festivals in 2014. This was the infamous rig that transported the Merry Pranksters through the Acid Tests of the late 1960s in their wide-ranging cultural experiments (Wolfe 1968),[39] painted in bright Day-Glo colors and fueled by speed and acid-heads. Long inoperable and stranded in Oregon, the bus was eventually restored by Ken Kesey's son Zane and made several festival appearances. Although taking pictures and walking on the bus is free, Zane also sells posters and t-shirts along with small, handpainted toy busses with psychedelic colors and other wares to support the bus's maintenance and transportation. The intense interest demonstrated by contemporary festival-goers in this relic, which according to some retains some spiritual significance, demonstrates both a knowledge of and endorsement of at least some foundational aspects of contemporary rock subcultures, including their countercultural roots and anti-authoritarian ethos.

Figure 7.3 Yoga at Lock'n Festival 2014, Arrington, Virginia.

In short, the material culture of contemporary improvisational rock scenes invokes several of the key ideological and normative features of the late 1960s counterculture and psychedelic rock subcultures. First, much of the art of improvisational rock scenes continues to invoke indigenous and dharmic traditions, which were embraced as US youth searched for alternative sources of authority in the post-World War II period. Second, the material culture exhibits affinity with philosophies or practices, often spiritualized, that attempt to tap into another realm of experience or reality whether through the ingestion of entheogens (epitomized by the continuing popularity of the Furthur bus, which is emblematic of psychedelic experimentation) or which question received societal norms and values. The presence of local food vendors—even small-scale barter and cash economies outside of concert and festival venues—begin to indicate an interest in divesting from the dominant consumer paradigm, even if the capitalist, consumerist paradigm structures the whole experience in significant ways. Nonetheless, people still find within these constrained spaces opportunities to express practical, if improvisational, modes of religiosity that challenge both traditional mores and classifications prevalent in religious studies.

Figure 7.4 Ken Kesey and the Merry Pranksters' "Furthur" bus.

Practical, improvisational spiritualities

The press release from the Rock and Roll Hall of Fame induction ceremony in 2014 said, "Much about the Grateful Dead was improvised or left to chance. Theirs was a laissez-faire anarchy that assumed things would work out as the cosmos intended. This faith in a universal order, gleaned from the start at Kesey's Acid Tests, freed them to pursue music without the usual constraints."[40] Interestingly, this anarchistic approach was grounded in a "faith" in a universal order. More often than not, the ultimate order was imagined to be grounded in forces or relationships that were very this-worldly, immanent rather than existing in some transcendent realm. In many cases this seems to manifest in a sort of normative improvisation, as individual mores are scrutinized, questioned, and sometimes overturned. Such situational ethics also seem to overlay a metaphysic of interconnection that underpins many of the moral pronouncements that derive from the scene.

Dark green modes of religiosity—those that have in common a perception, grounded in emotive experience, that living things or even the biosphere itself are sacred and that there is an ethical obligation to engage in behaviors that protect or enhance ecosystem fecundity[41]—are relatively common within improvisational rock subcultures, even among those who identify with a specific institutionalized religious group. Over 75 percent of the respondents ($n = 651$) to the survey on which this chapter is based expressed some sense of obligation to care for or protect nonhuman nature, and well over one-fifth (23%) assented to the idea that "there is no such thing as an 'environment' separate from humans"

($n = 651$); these sentiments are clearly present in predecessor movements. Some sentiments expressed by fans of the Grateful Dead will be illustrative. One fan wrote:

> I grew to love the Grateful Dead because they sang more songs about love, happiness, hope, sharing, helping, and caring than any other band I've ever listened to. Jerry Garcia lived his life this way and taught others to do the same. It is kind of ironic that this is considered the "counterculture." . . . I grew to love the Grateful Dead because they passionately care about our fragile planet. Our precious plants, animals, land, water and air are for our compassionate use—not abuse. The Dead encouraged people to become actively involved in protecting and wisely using our resources . . . I grew to love the Grateful Dead because they were about higher consciousness. They wanted you to break beyond the "conventional" norms of society—to live your life by your own values, beliefs and desires. I grew to love the Grateful Dead because they never wanted you to hurt or harm any living creature . . . They showed us the way we ought to live—in a loving, caring, compassionate and gentle manner.

Or, in the words of another:

> We just wanted you to know that we have gone out and done something with our lives as a result of seeing the Grateful Dead in the late '70s through the '80s and into the '90s . . . We left our urban life five years ago and we now live in a solar powered log cabin in the hills of S.W. Wisconsin. We garden organically and we sell organic sprouts of all kinds wholesale and at the Dane Co. Farmer's Market (in Madison, WI). We also sell home sprouting kits like the one enclosed in the hopes that people who don't grow their own food and/or live life on a treadmill might become inspired to change. We actively oppose things like the current marketing of Bt engineered crops, BGH in the milk supply and the proposed expansion of low level military flyovers of F16s, B52s, you name it, in our area of SW Wisconsin. We are part of a larger community in this area composed of homesteaders, artists, craftspeople, musicians, and alternative people of all kinds. . ..We just wanted you to know, since we could not be there [Jerry's memorial], that the Grateful Dead and Jerry Garcia in particular have made a great difference in the life of our family; how we conduct ourselves and what we do for the world.[42]

There are hundreds of folders full of letters in the official archives, many of which convey religious themes or deploy religious imagery, and in many cases condolence cards themselves carry religious imagery, often related to dharmic or indigenous traditions. The continuing influence of such non-Western philosophical and religious symbols and themes is clearly a continuation of the flourishing of countercultural interest in these traditions in the 1950s and 1960s, and they continue to represent a holism and interconnectivity supposedly absent from Western religions. Environmental and social issues were often and easily connected to other countercultural forms in the late 1960s and early 1970s, and some of these letters illustrate the continuing influence of these dark green and countercultural values into the end of the twentieth century, and likely beyond.

An important question however is whether, and to what extent, these experiences are translated into consistent action. The above quotes from Grateful Dead fans were written in 1995 by fans attempting to make sense of their grief over the death of Jerry Garcia, the frontman for the Grateful Dead. Many expressed nostalgia for a way of life that was presumed to be going extinct with Jerry's death. "Going on tour"—leaving behind jobs, daily routines, and oftentimes family—emerged during the 1970s and 1980s as the Dead and other jam bands with heavy tour schedules gathered a following, and it remains an important part of the scene. Today, among fans of Phish, Widespread Panic, moe., String Cheese Incident, and others the number of shows attended—and especially the number of concerts per tour attended—demonstrates the "headiness" or level of commitment to the band of individuals.[43] In the 1960s and 1970s many were able to go on the road following a band for an entire tour, often funding their journey by selling food, drugs, or other bootleg merchandise in the parking lots near concert venues. This is still a feature of the jam band scene, although my conversations and interviews suggest that it is much rarer than it once was.

As improvisational rock became a powerful cultural force in the 1960s and 1970s, some discovered how to commodify such movements, radically changing the communal feel. For instance, on the thirty-year anniversary of Woodstock another festival was held, this time televised on MTV and funded by corporate sponsors. It erupted into riots and violence, a scene opposite in significant ways from the first festival. Some venues have actively discouraged the sale of unlicensed merchandise. Festivals almost always include a selection of both food and alcohol, licensed by the festival organizers, and the competition with professionalized food vendors has significantly reduced the number of people who make and sell food in lots surrounding the venues. In addition, today nearly all tickets are handled through Ticketmaster, or LiveNation, two companies that merged in 2010 and, according to many fans, have a monopoly over the industry, which allows the companies to charge exorbitant fees. Fans frequently note that "Ticketbastard," as the firm is often called, now also owns Stub Hub, the leading secondary resale venue for tickets for sold-out events, illustrating the corporatization of such events. But fans have responded by exploiting social media to generate alternative economies for goods. At least a few bands have social media pages that provide a place to re-sell tickets at face value, and fans sell bootleg merchandise on various webpages and social media sites. Improvisational rock subcultures have adapted to this corporatization and media commodification by building extended online communities, but the physical scenes around improvisational rock performances began exhibiting distinct participant hierarchies beginning in the early 1990s, gaining momentum in the early twenty-first century.

There is some continuity between the *liminoid* experimentations of the 1960s and contemporary improvisational rock subcultures—at least in their adaptability and in their use of non-Western symbols, metaphors, and tropes to characterize their often spiritualized vision of community. The generation and spread of positive energies and the dharmic notion of karma are frequently invoked to explain morally charged events. A sense of interconnectedness is further illustrated by noting that 54 percent of my survey respondents (n = 587) assented to the statement "I have a strong affinity, spiritual reverence, or ethical concern for nature," indicating that for these individuals nonhuman nature holds some spiritual (inherent, rather than utility) value. Several respondents added further comments regarding their spirituality by expressing animistic or pantheistic spiritual sentiments. To provide just a handful of illustrations, one of my respondents said s/he "no longer attend[ed] church—[I] find spirit in [the] natural world," while another opined, "Nature is my deity." One person claimed to be "extremely spiritual" and to "see the divine everywhere, in everything and everyone," a distinctly pantheistic sentiment. In an invocation of Gaia theory, the notion that the Earth is a self-regulating organism, one person said "the world is a living being and human[s] should be helping her/him live and prosper," and one respondent even stated that they were a "fan of james lovelocks . . . gaia hypothesis [*sic*]."[44] In my experience these animistic and pantheistic metaphysics, and concomitant ethical obligations, are fairly common among performance-oriented subcultures.

One of the largest festivals, Bonnaroo, advertises the "Bonnaroovian Code," which asks participants to "play as a team," "radiate positivity," and recycle and reduce waste, and invites them to "apply what you do on The Farm [the festival location] to improving you and the world beyond 'Roo.'"[45] Although the Code exhorts people to continue their positive behaviors beyond the festival grounds, it is clear that there is a special normative dimension to performance events that does not obtain in all facets of participants' lives. For instance, one fan declared on a social media outlet that he enjoyed going to shows because it allowed him to re-embody his "real self," something his occupational endeavors did not foster. Many others also expressed this disconnect between their work life and a more authentic way of being, epitomized by the fellow-feeling and communalism experienced at performance events. Moreover, these normative expressions of the subjunctive mood are frequently expressed in religious language or imagery, for instance by one concert-goer who posted that he was "Heading to Church [:] 6pm Sermon with the boys [Widespread Panic]."[46] Too, consider the woman who expressed that she was on the way to the show to "Dance my prayers." One informant who self-identified as a Pentecostal stated "I often feel God @ Panic shows. I do the same as I meet him every time . . . I dance & sing with praise . . . I am so grateful for the experiences I get to have with 1000's of my best friends all feeling good!! Perfect place to dance your prayers!!!"[47]

An artist called The Polish Ambassador stated on his social media site the following description of a performance:

> For an hour and a half friends, family, and extended tribe made their way around the table and dance floor: smiles beaming, hearts bursting open, tears welling up, people dancing their prayers.
>
> It felt more real, more connected than any performance I've ever played. Fully immersed in the crowd. Fully tapped into the collective movement and consciousness that was that dance floor. It felt like a ceremony, a hive mind movement meditation with a continuous exchange of giving and receiving, both ways by audience and performer. For me, there was no clear separation. At the end of my set, a flood of tears spilled forth.[48]

John Bell (JB), lead singer and rhythm guitarist for Widespread Panic recollected his experience at a Grateful Dead show, saying:

> Jerry Garcia's talking Guitar and vocal approach together painted images that let me experience the music on both a personal and what I believed to be a universal level. Jerry and the Band were playing and singing, but it also seemed that they were letting the songs play them (the musicians), as well—creating a kind of "musical sincerity." That "letting the song play you" impression has since played a part in the way I try to apply myself to a tune—be it an original, or someone else's."[49]

JB was expressing the notion that music has agency that flows from some universal force or source and helps to shape these transitory but highly affective experiences, an idea echoed by both movement participants and other musicians.

My ethnographic work, in-depth interviews, and participation in social media groups indicate that such sentiments, and their expression in religious imagery and language, is commonplace. Yet these spiritual sentiments, though consistent across time, have proved to be radically adaptable, infiltrating the Web and social media to generate new forms of cultural production. There are now virtual venues that act as news sources about improvisational rock bands, some that act as trading posts for bootleg recordings of favorite artists, and others that are closed chat pages where fans interact. Live audio streaming of many performances now offers a mediated means of participation for people to listen to concerts from the comfort of their homes, often chatting online with others who are on "couch tour," as it is often called. Even when fans go to shows, social media and smartphones make it much easier for people to reconnect in person, facilitating social exchange, something not possible even twenty years ago. These are improvisational, practical, and often transitory spiritualities.

The above examples illustrate that at least some of the spiritualities that sprout from these subcultures are about recognizing and embracing some affective experience in the present moment, not about some transcendent or rational religious experience. Moreover, these are hybrid spiritualities that cobble together both traditional religious imagery and practice with indigenous, dharmic, and sometimes biocentric forms of religious expression, some measure of moral flexibility, and the importance of belongingness and fellow-feeling. It is clear that some of the normative and spiritual components of improvisational rock subcultures persist, though the cultural geographies in which they are expressed has shifted dramatically. It remains to be seen whether there will be another cultural "moment" like the late 1960s where such fellow-feeling and community experimentation can gain traction.

Conclusions

Conversations and experiences with participants in rock subcultures revealed spiritual sensibilities that often exhibited a metaphysics of interconnection, an ethical stance primarily informed by emotively rich experiences of fellow-feeling and a desire for communitarian or egalitarian living arrangements or experiences. In some cases, however, such desires and ethical orientations are manifested only temporarily—*liminoid* departures from a real-world where many occupational habitats do not promote feelings of interdependence—and where many scene participants enjoy their ability to live at relatively high standards.

My ethnographic and survey data illuminate two important points about these unique religious formations. First, many of them express such a metaphysics of interconnection and mutual dependence, and ethical norms related to fellow-feeling and care, while also expressing at least nominal adherence to one of the so-called world religions. A hypothesis in need of further study, then, is that the multiple religious belonging exhibited by many of these participants in improvisational rock subcultures is also characteristic of broader populations. There are few if any survey tools that adequately tease out the multiple communities of accountability to which various individuals belong, including their multifarious and sometimes contradictory religious commitments. Second, it is clear that the embodied experiences related to improvisational rock scenes are formative for individuals' religious and ethical sentiments, sometimes providing a language for expressing deeply affective experiences or a framework for understanding them. This points toward the poverty of analyses that uncritically posit that it is some vaguely defined idealized worldview that shapes and constrain behaviors. Instead, it is experiences that shape and constrain the cognitive commitments to various spiritual practices and understandings. I am not arguing for a simple reversal of causation—that it is *only* practices that shape ideation and worldviews—but rather I aim to illustrate that participation in specific groups and exposure to their norms and spiritual sensibilities during highly affective moments shape normative and religious sentiments in important ways.

Outstanding questions remain. Do these transitory, practical, improvisational spiritualities translate into any measurable differences in behavior outside concert or festival venues? Do experiences of *communitas* and engagement in *liminoid* experiences challenge a general desire in everyday experience for comfort, security, and predictability? Do contemporary improvisational rock subcultures represent a resurrection of the revolutionary social movements of the late 1960s, or the opposite, and are they capitalist structures that participate in the domestication of dissent through the corporatization and commodification of popular music?[50] Certainly some people have been so moved by their musical experiences that they have enacted new behaviors, and participation in these subcultures have convinced some individuals to divest from the "real world" and to live in intentional communities. But my sense is that this is the exception, that most scene participants treat these experiences as another joyous occasion to "unplug" from their usual routines and commitments. The consolidation of record labels and ticketing agencies contributed to the economic stratification of concerts as VIP and Super-VIP tickets became common. The same trends ensured that performances are occasional *liminoid* experiences rather than an enduring lifestyle commitment. These are the remnants, the hot coals and ashes that continue to smolder from earlier countercultural movements, and it remains to be seen whether they spark, or indeed catch fire again.

8

The Spirit of Place: Identity and Media in Relation to Cornwall

Garry Tregidga
University of Exeter

Spirituality can be regarded as a core component of the cultural and political identity of Celtic Cornwall. At one level this is evident in the competing discourses of religious groups such as Cornish Methodists and Celtic Pagans that claim to have an indigenous association with this peripheral area situated in the far South West of Britain. Yet the territorial concerns of the Cornish regionalist movement as a whole can also be expressed in spiritual terms. The passion of local campaigners is evident in a variety of settings such as cultural festivals, sites of memory, political campaigns for greater autonomy, and the everyday defense of the Cornish language.[1] Yet there has been little research into the underlying relationship between media, place, and identity in articulating this sense of Cornish distinctiveness. After a brief discussion of the Celtic-Cornish Revival since the nineteenth century the focus moves to a consideration of notions of spirituality and identity. The chapter concludes with a preliminary appraisal of the role of media, ranging through time from the historic role of newspapers in promoting a greater interest in Cornish culture to the contemporary use of the Internet, particularly Facebook, in articulating and sustaining the territorial concerns and belief systems of activists in Cornwall and its Diaspora.

Celtic Cornwall: From the "reawakening" to the neo-revivalists

Before investigating the relationship between media and practical spirituality in the cultural construction of Cornwall it is necessary to consider the paradoxical nature of the territory's identity. Bernard Deacon remarked, "In order fully to appreciate how and why Cornwall is different from (and similar to) other parts of the British Isles we must recognise a fundamental tension structuring Cornwall's past and pervading its present. Cornwall is seen by some as a Celtic country or nation, by others as an English county, and can even be imagined as both at the same time."[2] Scholars conclude that a critical period in the advancement of the Celtic dimension of its identity occurred in the early decades of the twentieth century.[3]

The creation of Cowethas Kelto-Kernuak (Celtic-Cornish Society) in 1901 meant that a pressure group now existed that could campaign for the region's ancient language and culture. By 1904 the activities of its members had resulted in the Pan-Celtic Congress accepting Cornwall as the sixth Celtic nation. Henry Jenner, regarded by many as the founder of the movement, claimed that even at this stage the "reawakening" of interest was attracting considerable interest from across the social spectrum.[4] Subsequent developments included the formation of a locally based network of Old Cornwall Societies starting with the first branch at the town of St Ives in 1920 and the first Gorseth Kernow in 1928, which was consciously based upon Breton and Welsh cultural institutions. Indeed, the Celtic-Cornish Revival was in itself part "of a wider 'Celtic Revival' that had already by the late nineteenth century made a significant impact in Scotland, Ireland, Wales and Brittany."[5]

But what is meant by the term "Celtic Revival?" Sean Kay suggests that the phrase can be applied in framing the discussion of contemporary events.[6] Indeed, there is a need for a detailed reappraisal of Celtic Revivalism in regard to establishing a chronological framework, comparisons between territories and the ongoing role of diasporic communities throughout the world. Cornwall is a good example since there is evidence that the Revival goes beyond the conventional period of the early twentieth century. Placed in a chronological context, the Revival can be seen as a long-term process dating back to the nineteenth century if not before. For example, in 1877 the centenary commemoration of the death of Dolly Pentreath—reputed to be the last person to speak Cornish—attracted widespread interest, particularly from the local farming and fishing communities.[7] This was well before the formation of Cowethas Kelto-Kernuak and might be regarded as a pivotal event in the subsequent Revival.

Similarly, in the aftermath of the Second World War there was a renewed interest in the need for a political dimension. Mebyon Kernow (Sons of Cornwall) was formed in 1951 with the goal of domestic self-government, and it operated initially as a pressure group before entering the electoral arena of parliamentary politics in the 1970s. Since the last quarter of the twentieth century there have been indications of a new Revival centered initially on the performance of identity. The emergence of groups such as Bucca and Cam Kernewek in the 1970s meant that the indigenous music and dance of Cornwall started to penetrate mainstream culture. With the creation in 1978 of Lowender Peran, Cornwall's annual music and dance festival, a core institution now existed, and links could be maintained with musicians and dancers in the other Celtic nations.[8] Additionally, in 2002 the British government included Cornish in the list of indigenous "minority" languages in the United Kingdom within the framework of the European Charter of Minority and Regional languages. This led to the injection of financial support from central government and the creation of MAGA, a new language agency, to promote Cornish in schools and communities.

An opportunity for further cultural advancement came in April 2014 when the British government recognized the Cornish people themselves as a distinct group in line with the Council of Europe's Framework Convention for the Protection of National Minorities. It is interesting that some activists continue to apply the word "Revival" to these recent developments, thereby pointing to the perceived scale of its significance for the cultural life of Cornwall and perhaps highlighting yet another revival following on from earlier "reawakenings" in relation to language and politics in the early and middle decades of the century respectively that were outlined earlier.[9]

Moreover, this neo-Revival appears to be more sustainable and broadly based in the way in which it has been able to both link cultural and political agendas and at the same time penetrate mainstream culture. A classic example was Keskerdh Kernow (Cornwall Marches On) in 1997, which was an ambitious program of events that marked the 500th anniversary of the Cornish Rebellion against the Tudor regime in 1497. The centerpiece of this Public History commemoration was a re-enactment by activists of the 365-mile march of the rebel army from West Cornwall to the site of their eventual defeat at Blackheath near London. It received unusually good coverage in both national and regional media since the march symbolically linked the center (i.e., London) to the Cornish periphery. Moreover, it took place in the context of the closure of Cornwall's last tin mine in 1997 and it was an opportunity to demonstrate against the perceived neglect of modern Cornwall by central government. Although the Liberal Democrats, the heirs of the old Liberal party, have been the main beneficiaries of regionalist discontent in recent years following their success in replacing the Conservatives as the main party in Cornwall in 1997, the politics of "Cornishness" is also evident in the persistence of Mebyon Kernow.

Despite its peripheral location at the edge of the United Kingdom, Cornwall is also the ancestral homeland for many people throughout the world. It has been suggested that Cornwall in the nineteenth century was "an emigration region comparable with any in Europe."[10] Economic problems, notably the collapse of the region's mining-based economy, led to roughly a third of its population moving to overseas destinations such as Australia, New Zealand, and the United States in the last quarter of the nineteenth century. Even at the time it was recognized that this had resulted in "a greater Cornwall outside than inside" as Cornish associations started to form in order to maintain links with the homeland and to preserve cultural traditions.[11] Although many of these societies started to disappear with the passage of time, Payton points out that the last quarter of the twentieth century saw a renewal of interest.[12] This resurgence was presumably based on a growing interest in family history research by individuals who wanted to rediscover personal connections with their ancestors, but as contacts developed, it contributed to the neo-Revival taking place in Cornwall. Keskerdh Kernow, for example, involved an international gathering of members of the Angove family who believed that they were related to one of the leaders of the 1497 rebellion.[13] As a result this study will draw on examples relating to identity and media in both Cornwall and its global community.

"It was good for the Cornish": The spirituality of spatial identity

The subtitle above comes from an improvised verse titled "It was good for the Cornish and it's good enough for me" that is frequently added to the popular gospel song "Give me that old time religion." Significantly, this verse is not just sung in the sacred setting of a church or chapel but in community singing sessions in a wide variety of public venues especially village pubs. It is therefore symbolic of the view that Cornish identity is closely associated with some form of spiritual belief.

A useful starting point is the Celtic Revival, discussed earlier, since expressions of Cornish identity in the nineteenth and twentieth centuries were often articulated through the language of Christianity and denominational conflict. One such example was Canon Gilbert Doble, the noted scholar of the early Celtic saints, who declared in 1924 that standards of morality had declined in Methodist Cornwall and that the only hope was to copy the "discipline" of their Celtic cousins in Brittany and Ireland.[14] Such sentiments echoed the views of earlier activists such as Jenner and Louis Duncombe-Jewell who consciously saw the Revival as a "project" to "rebuild a pre-industrial Celto-Catholic culture in Cornwall."[15]

But the Methodists, with nearly two-thirds of church worshippers in 1851, also linked Cornish identity to religious nonconformity. Nonconformists before the First World War advocated the regional disestablishment of the Church of England on the grounds that Cornwall was similar to Wales in having a separate Celtic past.[16] Edmund Hambly, a Quaker and the founder of the Cornish youth group Tyr ha Tavas (Land and Language), lamented in 1933 that John Wesley, the founder of Methodism, had not lived a century earlier since the "religious zeal that he aroused might have arrested the decay of the language" if it had been used in religious services as in nonconformist Wales.[17]

Cornish spirituality can also be interpreted from a Pagan perspective. The Cornish Culture Association notes: "Despite its reputation as a land of the Saints, paganism and witchcraft are just under the surface in Cornwall."[18] The role of "new" media will be discussed in greater detail later, but it is worth noting at this stage how the Internet is enabling Pagan and non-Christian groups to (re)claim "a continuity of Goddess tradition in remote Cornwall from ancient times up to the present day."[19] With echoes of neo-Revivalism, local witches declare that: "In Cornwall, over the past few years, there have been very exciting developments with regards to the revival of our traditional calendar of festivals and customs, and it would seem that there is a real surge in interest in traditional community events."[20] A classic example is the Montol Festival, a relatively new event in Penzance that celebrates the traditional midwinter solstice on December 21. Although aimed at a wider audience, there is a perception that Cornish Pagans play a prominent role in Montol and that it actively "incorporates many traditions and customs from Cornish heritage, some of which are suitably sinister and mysterious."[21]

From an academic perspective there are examples of scholarly articles on certain aspects of paganism in Cornwall, notably in relation to spiritual tourism and the esoteric nature of the Gorseth.[22] But it is perhaps surprising that other topics—notably ongoing relations with Christian denominations and the role of Pagans in the Cornish neo-Revival—have not been the subject of detailed investigation. One might add that given the perception of a distinctive religious history, particularly in relation to the early Celtic Saints in the Dark Ages and the rise of Methodism in the eighteenth century, Cornwall would serve as an appropriate case study for contemporary beliefs in general.

But a sense of spirituality in regards to "Cornishness" goes beyond religious beliefs. Ethnographic researchers have noted, "the deep meanings people have around their Cornish identity, and how that involves the land, the ancestors, the religious faiths/traditions, the politics, the food and more." Monica Emerich on a research trip to Cornwall in 2002 found that the region's industrial landscape "holds a deep spiritual meaning as the source of nurture and identity."[23] For local residents tin mines and clay tips could be considered just as "Celtic" as the more conventional symbols of "holy wells, standing stones and Arthurian connections."[24] This is in line with other scholarship such as that from Fernand Braudel who wrote in 1990 of the way in which French "landscapes and panoramas are not simply realities of the present but also, in large part, survivals from the past. Long-lost horizons are redrawn and recreated for us through what we see; the earth is, like our own skin, fated to carry the scars of ancient wounds."[25] Similarly, Christopher Tilley observed, "when a story becomes sedimented into the landscape, the story and the place dialectically help to construct and reproduce each other."[26]

In a Cornish context, however, it might be said that "place" takes on particular importance in relation to "practical spirituality." Deacon concluded in the late twentieth century, for example, that territory was the main cultural pivot around which the ethnic culture of Cornwall could be mobilized and that territory is a highly mediated phenomenon that develops meaningfulness through increased mediation as a spiritualized marker of Cornishness. Deacon based his findings on research by Daniel Conversi's cultural values model (also called the Pivots Model). Conversi argued that there were five possible "pivots" (race, language, family, religion, and territory) that symbolized the "social and identificational system" of an ethnic group.[27] The dominant pivot could vary over time, so in a Cornish context it meant that the language was no longer dominant following its historic decline in the Early Modern period. Similarly, while kinship links might be important in Cornwall, the impact of in-migration since the 1960s has transformed society at the local level, and the same applies to an exclusive appeal on the grounds of race. The pivot of religion, according to Deacon, had also been dominant in the past, but by the 1990s the process of secularization was even undermining the membership base in nonconformist strongholds like Cornwall. This left "territory" as the dominant pivot by the late twentieth century with an underlying concern over "threats to the integrity of Cornwall."[28]

There is perhaps another way of understanding how the concept of territory operates in a Cornish context. Although Deacon emphasizes the point that Conversi's model is based on one particular pivot being "stressed as symbolic of the group," it could be argued that consideration also needs to be given to the relationship between the pivots. Thus, if "territory" is combined with "religion," then it is likely to have an even greater emotive power. Kayleigh Milden, investigating the relationship between nationalism and religion in contemporary Cornwall, found evidence in the early years of this century that both atheists and agnostics would use symbols of the area's religious past to support their case for greater autonomy in the present.[29] Spiritual language could therefore reinforce Cornwall's politics of "cultural defense" even if organized religion was in decline. Moreover, the land ("tyr" in Cornish) provided a natural stimulus for spiritual values. Elliot Binns writing in 1955 concluded "the Cornish love their land and all that concerns it, with a love as tenacious and enduring as the grim cliffs of their coastal landscape."[30]

A classic example of the spiritual overtones of territory can be seen in the words of "Hail to the Homeland," which is often regarded as the second Cornish "national anthem" after "Trelawny":

Hail to the Homeland,
Great bastion of the free,
Hear now thy children
Proclaim their love for thee.
Ageless thy splendour,
Undimmed the Celtic flame.
Proudly our souls reflect
The glory of thy name.

Sense now the beauty,
The peace of Bodmin Moor,
Ride with the breaker
Towards the Sennen shore.
Let firm hands fondle
The boulders of Trencrom,
Sing with all fervour, then
The great Trelawny song.

Hail to the Homeland,
Of Thee we are a part.
Great pulse of freedom
In every Cornish heart,
Prompt us and guide us,
Endow us with thy power,

Lace us with liberty
To face this changing hour.

The words by Pearce Gilbert clearly evoke a sacred image with pseudoreligious phrases that are more reminiscent of a hymn than a patriotic song. Kenneth Pelmear, a prominent religious composer in Cornwall, enhanced the sacred feel of "Hail to the Homeland" by setting the words to a moving hymn-like melody, and it naturally complemented the male voice choir repertoire that tended to be performed in Methodist chapels.[31] The anthem was written in 1959, which was significant since it meant that it could grow in popularity at a time when Cornish Methodism was still a strong religious and social force. But it is effectively a hymn to the spirit of place symbolized by references to specific landmarks marking the territorial boundaries of the region, notably Bodmin Moor in the east and then down to Sennen and the prehistoric site of Trencrom in the far southwest.

With the land of Cornwall, rather than God or Jesus Christ, presented as the guide and protector of "thy children," this meant that "Hail to the Homeland" could also appeal unconsciously to a variety of audiences by the late twentieth century. For example, members of the Cornish Diaspora are also likely to construct a spiritual narrative when talking about their ancestral homeland. A typical example can be seen in the following extract from a Facebook conversation between two apparent strangers brought together by a shared interest in Cornish ancestry and culture. The context for their discussion was a simple photograph of Carburrow Tor, a scenic site overlooking Bodmin Moor, uploaded on a personal Facebook site. This iconic landscape was to act as a cultural trigger since it led "John," an Australian citizen who had recently joined a Cornish society in Australia and had been engaged in genealogical research, to state, "I truly hope to visit Cornwall one day." "Jim," a frequent visitor from the United States who has been active in promoting global connections between Cornwall and Cornish societies overseas, then responded by encouraging the Australian to return to the land of his ancestors:

> I'm sure that you will receive a lot of advice about where to go, what to see, etc., and that it will be good advice. But be sure to take some time to 'just be there'. Some of my best experiences in Cornwall have been from simply, quietly realizing the fact of actually being in Cornwall. Not to go all mystical, but I really believe that there is something about the place that you can feel if you try that is different from anywhere else in the world. I and others have said that when taking the train from England to Cornwall, we can feel something happen as we

cross the Tamar heading west, and that it stops when we cross heading east. I always say that each time I go, I leave a bit of my soul behind and that when back at home, if I sit quietly, I can hear it calling me. Cornwall is a very special place. What you experience, and how you express it, will be your own, of course, but I'm sure that you will be moved and will know that you have been to someplace unique and, in a sense, magical.[32]

This narrative is a good example of Tilley's point about story and place reinforcing each other. Although "Jim" expresses a desire to avoid giving a spiritual testimony on his Cornish experiences since he states that he does not want "to go all mystical," the reality is that the constant use of words such as "soul," "calling," and "magical" have that effect. By highlighting the River Tamar as the boundary between England and Cornwall (the boundary was historically established in 936 AD), he fuses this spiritual narrative with notions of the territory's political identity. The concept of Cornwall as a spiritual territory can therefore reinforce campaigns for greater autonomy and the protection of its language and traditions. This was evident at the time of Keskerdh Kernow in 1997 when the personal reflections of the modern-day marchers highlighted an essentially spiritual association with the historic sites of their ancestors, starting with impromptu ceremonies at places like Helman Tor during the march through Cornwall and ending at an unmarked mound at Blackheath near London that was reputed to be the mass grave of the Cornish rebels.[33]

Projecting Cornwall: The role of media in the past and present

These examples of an underlying sense of spirituality in relation to "Cornishness" raise questions over the role of media in articulating and shaping this strong sense of territorial identity.

In recent decades media technologies in other parts of the "Celtic World" have been strengthened considerably. The launch in 1982 of S4C, the first television channel targeted at a Welsh-speaking audience, established a model that was followed by TG4 in the Irish Republic in 1996 and BBC Alba, a pioneering digital television channel for Gaelic speakers in Scotland in 2008.[34] These initiatives reinforced an existing media infrastructure provided by broadcasting services organized on a territorial basis such as BBC Scotland, STV, and BBC Wales. And, although newspaper circulation shows signs of decline, partly as a result of younger audiences turning to the Internet, the existence of papers such as the

Daily Record in Scotland and *Western Mail* in Wales are important in enabling a small nation's cultural and political identity to be expressed and debated in the public sphere.[35]

Cornwall, in juxtaposition, lacks a strong media infrastructure to project its identity. In the first place there is no regional television channel and only limited coverage given to the area by BBC Spotlight—a regional news program stretching from the Isles of Scilly to Somerset—and ITV Westcountry, which covers an even larger area and is now unable to offer any local program opt outs from the national schedule.[36] Newspaper provision on a Cornwall-wide basis is also effectively nonexistent; the regional *Western Morning News* based in Plymouth and local newspapers such as the *Cornishman* and *Cornish Guardian* focus on smaller areas and only publish once a week. Only local radio, notably BBC Radio Cornwall and Pirate FM, targets a specific Cornish audience.

The invisibility of Cornwall presumably explains why there has been relatively little academic work on the local nexus among media, place, and identity. Admittedly, there are occasional references on such topics as the limited coverage of Cornish culture by mainstream media or the symbolic importance of media programs in relation to the contemporary usage of its indigenous language.[37] There has also been some preliminary research on the spiritual meanings and values of such media as popular film, books, and oral history.[38] Nonetheless, there remains a clear need to explore the wider subject of media in Cornwall in far greater detail.

The rest of this chapter focuses on two brief case studies. In a chronological perspective, consideration will be given to the role of newspapers in promoting a spiritual dimension to the Celtic Revival in Cornwall. Contemporary forms of media will then be discussed to show how individuals and groups have attempted in recent years to harness the power of the Internet to present a Cornish perspective.

Newspapers in the nineteenth century served as the principal media for promoting causes and beliefs on an everyday basis. Cornwall at that time was no exception since the existence of competing papers such as the *Royal Cornwall Gazette* and *West Briton* provided an appropriate framework for debate in the public sphere. However, with the exception of Amy Hale's brief survey of the response of the local press to Cornwall's acceptance as a Celtic nation by the Pan-Celtic Congress in 1904 there has been no specific investigation into either the role of newspapers in disseminating the ideas of the Revival or its potential as a rich primary source for studying the phenomenon in general.[39] A good example is the *Royal Cornwall Gazette* since by analyzing letters to the paper, reports on specific events and regular editorial columns, it's possible to build up a wider picture of how the Revival developed before the creation of Cowethas Kelto-Kernuak. At a time when the emerging movement lacked an agency to promote its activities, Cornish newspapers provided an essential mechanism for generating interest and reaching out to a wider audience. For example, when a regular correspondent to the *Royal Cornwall Gazette* had a feature on Cornish cultural traditions published in 1880, it provided an opportunity for a noted local antiquarian to write a letter on the subject from a Cornish language perspective.[40]

It can be argued, however, that the Cornish experience does not compare with that of Wales. In the latter case radical politicians in the Liberal party were able to proactively link the "power of the chapels [and] the local press" to effectively create a Liberal-Nationalist agenda at the grassroots.[41] Despite the rivalry between the Conservative *Royal Cornwall Gazette* and its pro-Liberal competitors like the *West Briton*, research appears to indicate that debates were mainly along national lines.[42] But by the early 1900s there are indications that Cornish identity was becoming a political issue. A local comparison with Wales can be made with the *Cornish Guardian*, which was founded in 1901 and emerged in the years leading up to the First World War as the leading pro-Liberal newspaper in mid- and east Cornwall.

Alfred Browning Lyne, the editor of the newspaper, personified the political and religious instincts of the area since he was chairman of his constituency Liberal association and a prominent Methodist preacher. Significantly, he was able to make connections between his personal beliefs and Celtic Revivalism. The newspaper contained numerous references to Liberal MPs being the anti-metropolitan champions of Cornwall, the "Celtic temper" of Cornish Methodism and prewar calls for devolution from London. Even before the First World War the paper was receiving publicity material from activists in the Cornish movement and promoting news about the Celtic Revival in Brittany.[43]

Newspapers such as the *Cornish Guardian* therefore played a prominent if unconscious role in creating a spiritual language of identity. Callum Brown remarks that Christian values in Britain were traditionally expressed through the medium of everyday conversation and publication.[44] The religious beliefs of individuals like Lyne meant that secular events and ideas would naturally be presented with Christian overtones. It is worth speculating on the importance of this factor for the inner spirituality of "Cornishness" in contemporary society.

Since the Celtic Revival was championed by individuals with strong religious views—arguably regardless of their individual Anglican, Catholic, or Methodist affiliations—it is perhaps not surprising that Cornwall has been constructed down to the present day as a spiritual place. A classic example appears in an article on a parliamentary by-election in Cornwall published in the *Cornish Guardian*. It was claimed that the scenes at the "declaration of the poll beggared description. They were Cornish of the Cornish, the enthusiasm of nonconformist farmers, of earnest young preachers, of dark-eyed women and fiery Celtic youth had something religious about it." Subsequent references in the article to "fervour" and "ancient faith in Liberalism" further reinforced the underlying impression of Cornwall and its people as sacred.[45] Such statements seem curious especially since the contest was not ostensibly about a religious issue on this occasion. The campaign instead revolved around the failure of the British government to support Cornwall's mining industry and moral indignation over its postwar interventionist policy in the Middle East instead of addressing domestic problems at home. But this also provides yet another clue to understanding the cultural dynamics of place: In a provincial community where the language of moral protest was closely connected to that of religion, it was only to be expected that the defense of Cornish interests would be presented in similar terms. The "fiery Celtic" image of Cornwall generated through the press draws on its past and arguably provides a sense of continuity through narrative construction that endures down to its post-Christian present.

Moreover, the influence of the local press on Cornish identity formation was not restricted to Cornwall itself. In the late nineteenth-century newspapers provided the traditional means for reporting on Cornish migrants overseas with regular features on the cultural and economic activities of individuals, families, and societies. For example, the *Royal Cornwall Gazette* reported in the early 1890s on the progress of the South Australian Cornish Association including the formation of a Cornish music society and plans for a library that would include regular issues of newspapers posted from Cornwall.[46] In some cases migrants associated with the communications media maintained a press network. In 1890, Moses Roberts, the editor of the *Kimberley Daily Independent* and described as a "thorough Cornishman," organized an annual Cornish dinner in South Africa. Newspaper reports indicate that the event was consciously modeled on the Celtic "clannishness" of the Irish, Scottish, and Welsh communities of South Wales who "cling to the memory of their fatherland, and take every opportunity of keeping home associations in remembrance."

Roberts used his press connections to promote the event and ensured that newspapers back home in Cornwall were kept informed.[47] Kinship networks meant that links between Cornwall and its diaspora communities remained strong well into the twentieth century, and this raises the need for detailed historical research on how newspapers maintained this connection at a public level.

Moving forward in time there is evidence that modern forms of communication have reinforced those global connections. This is one area where academic research on Cornwall has been evident, with David Crowther and Chris Carter writing on the subject in the early years of the Internet revolution. Following an online survey in 2001 they concluded that the Internet was already helping to define and maintain a sense of Cornish identity. This was particularly the case for activists living overseas who felt that it was a vital medium in which to participate in a range of activities including the "politics of Cornish rural life, regional cookery tips and local history."[48] New forms of identity were also possible. A fluid definition of Celtic identity was now possible, in contrast to the tensions that sometimes existed between groups settling in overseas destinations in the past, so that "Cornishness" was more likely to be viewed "as part of a larger Celtic cultural identity."[49] They also highlighted the comments of Philip Payton in 1999 who was predicting a "deterritorialized virtual community" with the future of Cornish ethnicity being championed overseas by a "newly re-emergent Cornish diaspora." He concluded that the "homeland" was in no position to promote "Cornishness" in the future since it was "confronted continually by threats to its own territorial integrity and identity." In contrast, "Cornish enthusiasts across the globe are in almost constant contact through email communication" and this factor would "bridge the gap between the global and the local."[50]

This research was obviously conducted before the emergence later in the decade of social media sites. Facebook, for example, has been able to provide a platform for a variety of diaspora groups including the California Cornish Cousins, Cornish in New England, and the Cornish Downunder.[51] From a political perspective Mebyon Kernow appears to be utilizing the potential benefits of using social media for campaigning purposes with 1,473 supporters currently on its Facebook site. In contrast, the Liberal Democrats, Labour, and UKIP have failed so far to establish a comparable Cornwall-wide site, while the Cornwall Green Party and Cornwall Conservatives have just 585 and 142 supporters respectively.[52] Social media has also been a catalyst for the recent Kernow King phenomenon. Edward Rowe from mid-Cornwall (otherwise known as Kernow King) was able to win a television competition organized by tourism chiefs in California. He then launched a series of comedy films on YouTube along with a traveling stand-up show, and Facebook has been a powerful publicity tool with 40,847 supporters.[53] Rowe's platform has been essential in enabling him to link his comedy career with a genuine interest in promoting Cornish culture to a wider audience both in Cornwall and further afield. It is a model that has been pursued by the Cornish Oafs, two young performers that have combined comedy with social media to promote the Cornish language, while Radyo an Gernewegva, an online radio channel in Cornish, has been established following a successful Crowdfunder campaign publicized through Facebook.[54] New media therefore offers an alternative route for cultural activists when confronted by what they perceive as a centralized communications system controlled from outside the region.

There are implications for "Cornishness." In the first instance, social media provides an additional medium for the individual to express a sense of affinity with Cornwall. It is significant that "Jim's Story," discussed earlier, was articulated via Facebook, enabling a conversation between two strangers to reach a far wider audience, and to share, and perhaps, build spiritualized meanings about Cornwall and their Cornish identity. A positive interpretation of new technology is that "it is at the level of the individual that changes effected by the Internet take place." This means that an ability to combine with other individuals and small groups as in the Cornish case can potentially lead to "a revolutionary redistribution of power."[55]

The Facebook site of the California Cornish Cousins illustrates how the global projection of Cornish identity is operating in the media age. Alongside reports and photographs of the group's activities are online news features gathered from media channels and organizations based in Cornwall. The result is an interactive communications channel with individuals having access to news and films relating to such topics as culture, history, and contemporary politics.[56] Although there are echoes with the way in which newspapers in the nineteenth century operated in exchanging information, social media enable the California Cornish Cousins to have an instant knowledge and connection to events back "home" but at the same time have the opportunity to create and discover their own Cornish world, both internal and external.

Moreover, Facebook enables Cornish activists to engage more effectively with both government agencies and mainstream media. This can be seen in the recent emergence of an online pressure group titled *It's Our Cornwall*. Their key aim is to challenge what they perceive as central government's unsustainable housing program for Cornwall that is being implemented through its National Planning Policy Framework. But there are also difficulties in using social media. *It's Our Cornwall* has struggled to build up support in contrast with the sudden rise of the so-called Nostalgic sites focused on preserving old photographs and reminiscences relating to specific towns and villages in Cornwall. In some cases success has been dramatic with Nostalgic Camborne building a base of over 6,000 members in just four months.[57] Scholars have pointed to a "turn to the past" in recent decades, and the Internet plays a prominent role in creating what has been termed as the "Heritage Society."[58] An escapist desire to preserve "great stories and photos" of an area's past is perhaps more likely to be sustained since it reflects the strength of Facebook in acting as a social platform to share photos and videos.[59] It can be argued that certainly in a Cornish context it is more difficult to generate widespread support for a political cause on a permanent basis. The one exception perhaps has been Say No to the Pasty Tax with nearly 5,000 members, but significantly this was a short-lived, though successful, campaign to oppose central government's attempt in 2012 to impose 20 percent VAT on a traditional food that is a famous symbol of Cornwall.[60] An effective way of using Facebook as an effective medium for advancing Cornish interests on a less sporadic and reactive basis still needs to be established.

Conclusion

By exploring Cornish media, migration, identity, and activism through time, it is possible to highlight the importance of a spiritual and religious narrative in relation to the region's cultural construction. The close association between spatial identity and spiritualized language and images in the past means that even today it is natural to perceive Cornwall as a land of deep meaning, as a place with a landscape that is inherently sacred, and as a representation of an axis mundi, if you will, for the self, centering one's place in the world and in time.

Newspapers at the turn of the twentieth century provided an important medium for articulating such values in the public sphere. However, despite evidence of a further strengthening of Cornish identity in recent years, there is less opportunity to articulate "Cornishness" through Britain's relatively centralized communications network. There is a need for detailed research to investigate this paradox. Certainly a key part of such research will take into serious consideration the manner in which people—from activists to migrants to tourists—have embraced social media to fill that void, if indeed it truly is one. By using Facebook, a sense of identity for Cornwall's global community is maintained and articulated on an everyday basis.

This chapter has argued that Cornwall as a place is experienced as a practical spirituality—practical in that it forges identity for individuals and groups that in turn drives purpose(s) and generates deeply held values—and that this practice is and has been renewed, shaped, and birthed via media. Future research might look at the manner in which this spiritualized meaning projected onto the actual site of Cornwall is inextricably linked to political sensibilities and acts, and where that occurs and for whom. Interestingly, the very lack of centralized media in Cornwall might be enabling and shaping the rise of these sentiments, concretizing ideals of Cornishness as spiritualized activism.

9

Spiritual Narratives and The Icarus Project: Disidentification and Rhetoric of Liberation

Liz Barr
University of Wisconsin-Madison[1]

> *I don't think I could dissect my spiritual life from my "mental health" even if I tried. I am whole. I can't be cut apart. I see things on a regular basis that others don't see on a regular basis since I was 14. This is not a symptom. And it's not even super weird. It's just part of how I exist in the world, how I sense things, and how I connect to the divine.*[2]

The Icarus Project is a radical mental health collective founded in 2002 by a small group of young activists who were experiencing extreme states of consciousness and were frustrated by the options available to them for healing.[3] The Icarus Project has published several books and zines, but the roots of their project are thriving online discussion forums. Here, members post to threads on a large number of topics including spirituality and its relationship to madness. The above epigraph was posted in a public discussion forum about spirituality and mental health on Icarus' webpage. As the poster writes, spirituality and mental health—which are often understood as separate—are actually intimately connected, interrelated, and overlapping.

Spirituality is key to The Icarus Project's self-definition and activism, and members engage with all forms of spiritual experiences as they forge uncharted paths through "madness and brilliance." Icarus proposes a framework of peer support and community building to reframe "illness" as "gift." Espousing a rhetoric of "cultivation and care" for these gifts, The Icarus Project encourages its members to forge new paths through the world and to abandon the oppressive dogma of traditional biomedical understandings of mental health. Spiritual experiences are essential to The Icarus Project's activist practices, the members' creation of community, and their self-definition as individuals who experience extreme states of consciousness. As part of its spiritual activist project, The Icarus Project puts forth an alternative framework of "mental health" and "mental illness." This alternative framework looks at madness as a door to spiritual experience and approaches traditional religious practice through a process of what Jose Esteban Muñoz calls "disidentification."[4]

Muñoz theorized disidentification as a queer practice, as "the survival strategies the minority subject practices in order to negotiate a phobic majoritarian public sphere that continuously elides or punishes the existence of subjects who do not conform to the phantasm of normative citizenship."[5] Muñoz continues that disidentification allows subaltern subjects to find ways to exist in an oppressive world—by "neither opt[ing] to assimilate within [dominant ideology] nor strictly oppos[ing] it; rather, disidentification is a strategy that works *on and against* dominant ideology."[6] While disidentification is not theorized specifically in relation to spirituality or religion, it is still quite relevant to The Icarus Project's engagement with religion. Icarus members disidentify with religion in that its members choose not to engage with religion on strictly straightforward terms. Instead, they work on and against religion to create spiritual narratives that allow them to survive in an inhospitable world that fears and punishes madness. It is through these spiritual narratives that members are not only able to survive, but also to forge a new path to psychic and spiritual liberation.

The Icarus Project engages in discursive and material activism with two primary aims. First, it works to reframe mental illness as a nonpathological, beautiful (but sometimes dangerous) aspect of one's psyche that ought to be understood as a gift rather than a curse. Second, it uses the mediatized space of the Internet and online discussion boards to create a sense of community, a place for safe(r) space, and peer-support networks for individuals experiencing what members term "extreme states of consciousness." Both forms of activism rely on the process of disidentification, working on and against dominant discourses. Through these disidentifications, The Icarus Project undertakes a worldmaking project that offers its participants linguistic and lived liberation, acceptance, and ways to cope in a mad world.

A major facet of The Icarus Project's rhetoric is that Icaristas,[7] despite their psychiatric symptoms, are not pathological. Rather, they are beautifully flawed and possess dangerous gifts that must be cultivated and cared for. Their survival as mad individuals, then, entails the ability to forge new paths of existence in a world that medicalizes and pathologizes extreme states of consciousness. In this chapter, I explore the ways that Icarus' online discussion forums take up spiritual narratives as part of its larger political project. I demonstrate the different ways that spirituality is invoked—shamanism and seeing/hearing angels and spirits—through disidentification with traditional religious practices. In other words, Icaristas take discursive fragments from multiple religions and consciously choose to use them in new ways. They tweak and rework religion in order to redefine it as an alternative, spiritual framework that accounts for radical politics, community building, and self-care. Further, I am interested in how the third space of the Internet enables and constrains these disidentificatory worldmaking projects. My analysis concludes that online spiritual narratives of disidentification facilitate a community-building project that allows The Icarus Project to use the Internet creatively and productively to offer its members discursive and embodied freedom from dominant mental health discourses.

Online discussion forums as community-building projects

Although The Icarus Project's website is fairly traditional in layout and color scheme, its aesthetics make it unique and strikingly beautiful. The incorporation of drawings (in the corners of pages and as icons) personalizes the webpage and makes it appear more than a simple drag-and-drop template. The Project's home page features a delicate drawing of an Icarus figure flying out of the frame in the upper right corner. Below the Icarus, icons link to the discussion forums, a donation page, a link for the mailing list, and a link to get involved. These icons feature imagery that is central to The Icarus Project's discourse: a winged Icarus riding a bike, a pair of clasped hands, and the phrase, "You are not alone." The center and focal point of the page is an area helping visitors navigate the page: hyperlinks to forums, groups, contacts, and so forth. The top banner of the page includes these same links to the different parts of the webpage. Finally, in the upper left corner of the page, The Icarus Project provides space for members to log in and for new members to sign up.

Clicking the "forums" icon takes the viewer to The Icarus Project's online discussion boards. Topics are listed vertically and organized into individual threads. Members are able to post on any thread, and the public can view most of them, although some are restricted for Icarus members only. Each topic has a brief description informing viewers of the scope of the thread, and the right column indicates who made the last update and when it was made. Topics include "Introductions," "Experiencing 'Madness' and 'Extreme States,'" and "Making

Maps, Swimming Upstream and Building Islands of Community." Across all the discussion boards, there are currently 288,671 posts on 30,642 topics.[8] In this chapter, I examine the "Spirituality" thread with 4,487 posts on 560 topics.[9] This forum asks:

> What place does spiritual practice have in our lives and in our emotions? How do our visions of the divine and feelings of interconnectedness relate to living with madness? What is our place within a framework greater than human civilization and how does this affect our daily struggles?

I also look at the forum "Alternate Dimensions or Psychotic Delusions?" with 4,546 posts on 599 topics,[10] which is:

> A place to talk about everything from mysticism to lucid dreaming to psychosis to telepathy to conspiracy theories. How do we make sense of the things we see and feel even though we know most 'normal' people don't acknowledge them? How do we harness our mutant powers? Is there really 'power' in what they call 'madness' or are we just a bunch of loons?"

These two forums are rich sites for rhetorical analysis. In them, members of The Icarus Project work through what spirituality means, what spiritual experiences look like, how they relate to madness, and how these experiences shape their lives. It is fascinating to take up questions of how "our visions of the divine and feelings of interconnectedness relate to living with madness" and how "we make sense of the things we see and feel even though we know most 'normal' people don't acknowledge them." The Icarus Project uses these forums for consciousness raising and community building, two key components of their activist practices.

Disidentification, worldmaking, and spirituality

Disidentification grows out of queer theory and is closely related to the practice of queer worldmaking. Several scholars have taken up disidentification as a way to understand how subordinated groups and subjects are able to navigate hegemonic discourse.[11] As a theoretical tool, it is useful to understand the myriad ways that subjects engage with dominant discourse, working and reworking it as a way to survive. Like disidentifications, worldmaking is a "constructive and deconstructive process" that resists majoritarian discourses.[12] Through dismantling and rebuilding, worldmaking allows us to focus on futurity and offers hopeful possibilities for navigating an oppressive world. Both disidentification and worldmaking help us understand how discursive queer resistances shape the material conditions for queer lives. This is to say, changing language doesn't only change what we say. It is widely accepted that discourse shapes practice, and disidentifications and worldmaking use a queer theoretical lens to understand resistances in this arena. Through a focus on queer subjects and heteronormativity, the theories of disidentification and worldmaking attempt to shift power dynamics by centering or reterritorializing the margins. Donna Haraway argues that subordinated subject positions are better able to see structures of power, bringing us closer to an understanding of how these power structures are upheld and maintained.[13] This feminist and queer framework places power in the subaltern as a worthwhile subject of study and frames subordination as a valuable subjectivity for resistance.

The ideas of forging new paths, of survival, and working on and against appear throughout The Icarus Project's discourse. Its printed material features tropes of navigation and mapmaking where Icaristas are encouraged to disengage with dominant ideology and "draw their own lines" on the maps they were given by dominant culture. One way that Icaristas are forced to draw their own lines is through decisions regarding psychotropic medication. Icarus's ambivalent stance toward medicating madness reflects this sort of navigation; Icaristas are encouraged to embrace the embodied experiences of madness, whether or not they are medicated. This process can be seen as a disidentification because Icaristas neither "assimilate . . . nor strictly oppose" the medicalization and stigmatization of mental illness. Icaristas acknowledge the constraints within which they live and find ways to rework and refashion spirituality (and other topoi) in order to survive those constraints. The disidentificatory spiritual practices that many Icaristas take up are not only essential to their identification, but also to their survival in an inhospitable world as well.

The Icarus Project's spirituality comes about through members' lived engagement with institutional religions. Institutional or organized religion can be understood to mean "the sacred rituals, practices, symbols, prayers, and faith of the people," while lived religion or "people's religion" can be "defined as the totality of their ultimate values, their most deeply held ethical convictions, their efforts to order their reality, their cosmology."[14] While religion might be more formalized and institutionalized, its practices are often taken up and internalized by individuals, creating a lived, everyday religion. This lived religion ends up being extraordinarily valuable to those who practice it, as it frames people's deepest beliefs, their ways of understanding reality.

Scholars sometimes use the term "folk religion" to refer to these practices, which Don Yoder defines as "the totality of all those views and practices of religion that exist among the people apart from and alongside the strictly theological and liturgical forms of the official religion."[15] Expanding on Yoder's work, Leonard Primiano argues for the use of the term vernacular religion, explaining that "The need to do justice to the experiential component of people's religious lives can only be satisfied by a term which specifically addresses the 'personal' and 'private.'"[16]

Robert Glenn Howard continues this tradition of exploring everyday religion in *Digital Jesus*, using his framework of the dialectical vernacular to understand online vernacular Christian fundamentalism.[17] Howard adds to Yoder and Primiano's definitions by focusing on how authority is deployed in this everyday/vernacular/folk religious discourse; attention to "authority accounts for both vernacular and institutional power by emphasizing the dialectical definition central to the ancient meaning of the vernacular."[18] Howard's work is particularly valuable for this project since, like him, I am interested in the ways that vernacular religion happens online. Describing an online church, Howard writes, "Not a lifeless structure lifted and turned by the chance of circumstance, this vernacular web [the online church] is emergent from the aggregate authority of an untold number of individual human choices to engage in ritual deliberation about the End Times."[19] Although the radical activists of The Icarus Project and the Christian fundamentalists who Howard studies are wildly different in terms of their politics, their online presences bear resemblance to one another, if only in that they allow believers to gather and develop community, and by so doing, to inspire activism. Lived, folk, and vernacular religion, while nuanced and slightly varied, all share an attention to the details of everyday lives, of the ways that individuals take up—and disengage with—religion.

This relationship between religious belief and action is certainly not a new phenomenon. Writing about art and religion, Gordon Graham notes, "virtually every religion makes a connection between venerating the sacred and being inspired to act, and holds that this is the place where a large part of the importance of religion lies."[20] This is to say that almost all religions see a relationship between worship, reverence, and action. Graham explains, "storytelling has a much deeper significance, connected in some important way with finding/giving/transmitting meaning to human existence."[21]

While Graham is particularly interested in art and artistic practices, his analysis is relevant to this project on The Icarus Project as well. First, aesthetics are key to The Icarus Project's establishment of ethos. Members draw on do-it-yourself and punk aesthetics to claim authority as a radical alternative to institutional psychiatry. This sort of radical opposition is important to The Icarus Project's self-definition. Second, Graham's work on religious literature can be used to illuminate the spiritual narratives presented on The Icarus Project's website. Like the discourse of the traditional literature Graham studies, The Icarus Project's discourse gives and transmits meaning to its readers, which is key to building a mad community.

Defining spirituality

In what follows, I use spirituality to refer to lived, everyday practices of connection to a divine, immaterial (although sometimes material), or psychic presence. Spirituality thus defined encompasses actions such as chanting, meditation, prayer, yoga, and ritual, reflecting what Paul Heelas terms an expressive, experiential, New Age "spirituality of life."[22] Although it is likely that not all Icarus members would consider themselves New Age spiritualists, there are certainly elements of the spirituality Heelas describes in their discourse, particularly the idea "that experiential contact with inner-life spirituality enables it to 'flow' through other aspects of one's being to integrate, 'harmonize' or 'balance' oneself."[23] This type of spirituality can be separated from religious practice in that it is framed as a personal experience while religion may be mediated through more formal organizations (the church, formalized ritual, and texts). Of course, people regularly access spirituality through religious means, and there is obviously overlap between the two terms. Because The Icarus Project is made up of thousands of members across the world, Icaristas put forth numerous and varying definitions of spirituality; however, the definition I provide above encompasses almost all of the definitions I have found in the discussion forums.

Despite the diversity of Icaristas' discourse, their definitions of spirituality generally share several common features, including an attention to the interrelationship between spirituality and mad identity, madness as access point to spirituality, and the incommensurability of traditional religions with Icaristas' lived experiences. To return to the epigraph of this chapter, (which was posted in the thread "Spirituality and mental health not talking to each other") that Icarista defines spirituality in terms of an integration of "spiritual life" and "mental health." The poster suggests that while some might classify the experience of seeing unseen things as a pathological symptom, for them, these experiences are "just part of how i exist in the world."

The full passage reads:

> I don't think I could dissect my spiritual life from my "mental health" even if I tried. I am whole. I can't be cut apart. I see things on a regular basis that others don't see on a regular basis since I was 14. This is not a symptom. And it's not even super weird. It's just part of how i exist in the world, how I sense things, and how I connect to the divine . . . Spirituality it is not some aspect of my personality. Making meaning, connecting to the divine/God and and serving others in compassion is my life. Relationships, basketball, drawing, work conflicts, all are spiritual experiences for me. Because what often falls into religious categories cannot be sorted out from the rest of life. I am integrated.

This description of "relationships, basketball, drawing, work conflicts" as "spiritual experiences" differs from traditional understandings of religion and spirituality. The poster continues this definitional work, writing two posts later that spirituality includes "angels, voices, hands catching them, ghosts, out of body, near death, visions, prophetic dreams, warning signs of evil, ecstatic union with the divine." Unlike traditional religious rituals or practices, these experiences are all private, personal, and internal. The individual and the divine are the only participants in the experience. However, part of this Icarista's work is to share and make public experiences in the hopes of creating community. In this way, spirituality can be understood for this poster as divine connection that is essential to self- and community-definition.

This passage's reframing of spirituality as encompassing basketball, drawing, and work is part of the process of disidentification that many Icaristas use to build their spiritual narratives. Integrating these seemingly secular practices into the spiritual arena is a way to expand spiritual discourse to account for the poster's actual experiences; rather than use an institutional definition of what counts as spiritual, they[24] draw a new line on the map. The online arena is crucial to this poster's disidentificatory work. The collaborative, interactive, and communal nature of the discussion forum allows Icaristas to think through what spirituality means, to work out spiritual identity in conversation with other Icaristas. The thread received many responses and this online deliberation and debate allows for a community to coalesce around these reinterpreted spiritual practices.

Many Icaristas share stories of turning to wider definitions of spirituality after being rejected or displaced by organized religions. Members often post that they feel as though traditional religion fails to account for their extreme states of consciousness. They recount frustration that religious institutions view their experiences with madness as separate and unrelated issues. When members of The Icarus Project disidentify with traditional organized religions through a lens of madness, it allows them to create community and safe space. Again, disidentification "is a mode of *recycling* or re-forming an object that has already been invested with powerful energy."[25] Often, members will post about how they tweak, alter, and personalize aspects of organized religions to better reflect their own spiritual experiences. Members might take pieces from several religions in order to create a patchwork or mosaic spirituality. For example, posting about chakras and Kundalini awakenings, an Icarista explains:

> So that's satori or samadhi or whatever the hell, i've lost track, *that is why i have my own terms now*, it is eggsactly like being 158% endarkened. personally, i humble student in all matters re: darkness, i am at 58%, so if i were to put it in kundalinistical, i'd say that's more like a little lower than the heart chakra? yeah, i'm about belly level, i think, but now i can't be sure if there's a chakra associated with the belly, i do know there's one right about the ass/prostate level.

This Icarista engages with the Eastern philosophy of chakra energy centers and Kundalini yoga, but only pieces of each. Further, while these practices are traditionally associated with enlightenment, the poster refers to endarkenment, writing that they are "58% endarkened." This subversion of tradition is an excellent example of the disidentificatory practices The Icarus Project undertakes. This disidentification is significant to The Icarus Project's activist project because it validates members' experiences that might not match perfectly with institutional religion. By providing the space for members to share experiences like this, The Icarus Project allows community to develop organically. Because spirituality is often a personal and intimate experience, Icaristas bare their souls to one another in these threads, drawing them closer and building community. And again, the mediatized space of the Internet allows this poster to work through their understanding of spirituality and religious disidentification collaboratively, in communion with other Icaristas. Spiritual identity formation becomes a community activist project that is facilitated by the public-yet-private space of relatively anonymous online discussion forums.

Shamanic awakenings

Shamans are often seen as mediators between this world and other worlds, as healers who are able to bring messages and enlightenment from other psychic and spiritual plains. For many Icaristas, this description resonates with their experiences of "psychosis" and "delusion," and often Icaristas write about shamanistic states they have experienced and share articles written about shamanism, spiritual awakenings, and "mental illness."[26] One poster writes, "I specifically set out to explore my brain and shamanism . . . ultimately my friends ended up bringing me to the hospital after I had completely exhausted their collective ability to care for me. I repeatedly tried to tell the hospital staff that I was having a shamanic initiatory crisis and that all I really needed was to sleep. I was labeled as delusional for talking in this way, and the staff would threaten to remove my friends if they tried to talk to me about my experiences/beliefs." This Icarista specifically links "delusions" to a "shamanic initiatory crisis," and believes that the extreme state of consciousness was in fact the experience of passing through a portal into other realms of consciousness. This approach to shamanism can also be seen in numerous other posts that link "psychotic breaks" to shamanistic trances.

While many Icaristas see their extreme states of consciousness as emblematic of shamanistic experiences, others see the two as distinct, although perhaps related, and many report feeling troubled by Western individuals taking up shamanism as an identity term. Distinguishing between his experiences and his understanding of shamanism, an Icarista posts:

> From what I've met of true shamans, true people of healing who do in fact commune through other realms, it's only obtained through a medium of endless work and set backs. from how I understand it, the shaman is born into this world broken, and the shaman learns to heal themselves, and from that knowledge they learn to heal others if in fact that is there calling.
>
> From ancient times the shaman history is revealing that the people who did act on these types of principles were often times gatekeepers of knowledge for the community, they acted on behalf of there peers and the well being of those around them. They were the ones who would created systems for understanding the migration patterns so the warriors knew when to hunt. They would learn the plants and the different uses, even if it meant dieing, if only to create that prosperity for their people, above all they concur all fear.
>
> If anything, the link between shamanism and mental illness should be realized first by the pain, and second by overcoming, *otherwise they remain separate.* (Emphasis added.)

As the above passage shows, this poster separates madness from shamanistic work. The Icarista explains that the shamans must engage in "endless work and set backs," thereby distinguishing shamanism from his (and other Icaristas') experiences.

Because individual Icaristas variously pick up, tweak, and problematize shamanic identities, I view their interactions with shamanism as a disidentification. Pieces of this tradition are useful to individual experiences (understanding their extreme states of consciousness as part of something meaningful, perhaps) but parts of the tradition are problematic (the appropriation of indigenous tradition). The above post provides an example of this disidentification, as the poster concedes that there is a link between shamanism and mental illness in that both share experiences of pain and overcoming. Shamanism is useful for them, but on different terms that it might be useful for others. This is a disidentification because it moves on and against shamanism as a religious practice; shamanism is recognized as commensurate with "mental illness," yet the poster refuses to fully appropriate or reject it. Rather, the poster looks for a productive third space that creates new political identity and possibility.

Whether Icaristas see shamanism as a full or partial explanation of madness, they often write about transformative experiences of pain, despair, and mania, viewing the cycles of emotions as something that enhances spiritual connectedness. The transformations afforded by shamanism allow Icaristas to continue "drawing new lines on the map" and forging new ways of being mad in the world. The trope of map-making is essential to The Icarus Project's activist mission, as members seek to create a new framework for understanding "mental illness." Reframing psychotic breaks and delusions as shamanistic experiences allows them to redefine madness *and* to disidentify with shamanism. In other words, The Icarus Project's discursive or linguistic activism can be seen in members' disidentification with shamanism. Spirituality is key to their worldmaking project, and shamanism is a common theme that emerges in the discussion boards.

Visionary moments

Another common theme for the discussion boards is seeing or hearing visions, angels, and spirits. Like shamanistic experiences, these visionary moments take a variety of forms and are triggered by all sorts of everyday experiences, or from nowhere at all. Often, Icaristas write that their visions give them spiritual guidance and direction, as seen in the following post: "I started having visions on my bike ride home, which culminated in the voices I hear on-and-off dictating a ritual that I carried out which involved drawing five sigils[27] on myself and masturbating while doing some really intense processing of rape trauma. . .At the end of the ritual the voices instructed me to take a shower and symbolically wipe off the sigils, which I did." Here, this Icarista recounts the ways that they were instructed and led by the voices they heard to engage in a purification and healing ritual. For them, these voices are not an extraordinary phenomenon, rather, the voices are just something they hear "on-and-off." They are not frightened by these voices and visions; rather, they feel perfectly comfortable following the voices' direction.

Many other Icaristas share stories of hearing voices and visions, and of following their directions. These stories are almost always presented as un-extraordinary, noteworthy only for the insights they reveal or the healing they provide. The visionary moments that Icaristas describe from their extreme states of consciousness work to challenge the idea of voices as delusions. When re-understood as part of a spiritual gift, visionary moments are simply an everyday part of the experience of mad folks. The discussion forums create an important space for Icaristas to share their experiences with one another without judgment. The forums' communal nature normalizes Icaristas' visionary moments as members are able to see that, like Icarus' home page promises, they are not alone. Sharing and reading each other's experiences of visionary moments or other extreme states of consciousness helps to create community and safe space for mad individuals.

This crucial re-definitional work demonstrates how The Icarus Project's mission is enacted. As this analysis suggests, Icaristas' visionary moments are disidentifications. Disidentification involves a process of enclaving, of seeking strength from within a minoritarian community to use as an impetus for social activism. Icaristas work on and against the idea of delusions as pathology to reframe those as common, nonextraordinary experiences that are simply a part of the fabric of members' lives. This disidentificatory practice reveals the ways that spirituality can be deployed in the service of social activism and worldmaking.

Discursive and material activism

The disidentifications discussed above are key to the ways that The Icarus Project develops its online and offline discourse of community building and safe space. Part of The Icarus Project's practical activism includes using the third space of the Internet to create community and peer support for mad folks. The discursive work discussed above is key to reframing extreme states of consciousness and creating this online community. Community building emerges across the discussion boards, as members engage in dialogue, banter, and sometimes disagreements. Ultimately though, the online nature of the discussion forums really enables community building. For example, one Icarista asked: "Does anyone know what can help one get out of a paranoia psychotic state? My friend has been fucked up on his meds for over a year. He is now in a psychotic state. I call it a different spiritual plane. He is super paranoid. Thinks the devil has a hold on him. Thinks his parents are 'gone' . . . Does anyone know of anything spiritual or related to ground someone out of psychosis?" This poster's first instinct—as someone embodying The Icarus Project's discourse—is not to seek to have her friend committed. Rather, she reaches out to the supportive community of The Icarus Project and seeks a spiritual solution to the issue. Here, we can see The Icarus Project's discourse of dangerous gifts; *the problem* is that a friend's gift is spiraling out of control, and he sounds as if he is lost on a spiritual plane. For this Icarista, *the solution* is obviously spiritual in nature, not pharmaceutical or institutional. By reaching out to the forums, the poster is actively taking advantage of the community of support that The Icarus Project cultivates. In their printed materials, The Icarus Project outlines specific, concrete steps that mad folks can take to set up peer support systems, and the above post reveals an instance when those action plans can be put into place.

These two forms of activism (discursive and material) can be seen as disidentifications for two reasons. First, Icaristas take up discursive bits from multiple frameworks and rework them to create a unique discursive mosaic of their own. Second, this work is part of a resistant and re-definitional practice that counters majoritarian discourse. As Muñoz tells us, "Disidentification is a point of departure, a process, a building. Although it is a mode of reading and performing, it is ultimately a form of building. This building takes place in the future and in the present, which is to say that disidentificatory performance offers a utopian blueprint for a possible future while, at the same time, staging a new political formation in the present."[28] The Icarus Project's activism, as exemplified through the posts on the discussion boards, are also a process of building—building community, building safe space for exploration of spirituality, and building a new world that understands spirituality and "mental illness" as intimately and intricately connected.

Conclusion

Over the course of more than a decade, Icarus has enabled thousands of individuals, scattered across the globe, to create meaningful relationships with one another and find ways to reinterpret their experiences outside of dominant biomedical frameworks. For Icaristas, this reinterpretation often happens through an uptake of spiritual discourses and a disidentified appropriation of spirituality and religion. My analysis shows how the theory of disidentification can be used to understand these vernacular or lived religious and spiritual practices. This is significant to my case study because The Icarus Project provides an excellent example of what spiritual disidentification may look like in practice. Icarus shows us how individuals take up (and set aside) discursive fragments from institutional religions to create a patchwork or mosaic of lived, everyday spiritual experience.

The mediatized space of the Internet has allowed The Icarus Project to create a vibrant community of mad folks trying to make sense of their lives and experiences in a world that tells them they are flawed, pathological, and broken. Their practical spiritual practices—embodied in the online arena—show us how new media can be essential to identity formation and community building. On Icarus' discussion boards, Icaristas are able to break apart and refashion spiritual and religious discourses in a safe space that is simultaneously anonymous and communal. The online discussion boards create space for radical reunderstandings of madness and spirituality, and the linkages between the two. The Internet is crucial to The Icarus Project's worldmaking efforts as it brings a scattered community of individuals together in a safe space where pathologized spiritual experiences—hearing voices, seeing visions—are reframed as key to identity formation.

This chapter investigates the fruitful terrain of madness in the hopes of providing new ways of talking about mental illness and spirituality that might better reflect individuals' self-understanding and ways of being in the world. I hope to have revealed that ways that spiritual disidentifications can enable discursive and material activism—how disidentification with spirituality is an embodiment of practical spirituality. By working on and against dominant discourse, The Icarus Project seeks to bring about social liberation. Through an analysis of alternative frameworks of mental health, discourses of shamanism, seeing and hearing angels and voices, and activist practices, I hope I have broadened conversations about spirituality, social change, and vernacular identity. This broadened framework can allow us to more fully account for the realities of our everyday lives, and perhaps bring us closer to the liberated world that The Icarus Project envisions.

10

Strategic Confession: Pragmatic Religion and Spirituality in the PostSecret Community

Rachael Liberman
University of Denver

Stewart M. Hoover
University of Colorado

In a contemporary moment where cultural practices increasingly engage with the social affordances of digital media, accounts of identity, and "identity projects"[1] have resulted in a noteworthy connection to interactivity, agency, and prosumption. Digital media—the Internet, in particular—have become a space for negotiating the self, and the decision to engage or abstain from online activity has become not only lifestyle choice, but a moral one as well. Questions surrounding "authentic" community building and "meaningful" interpersonal activity have entered our public consciousness and, despite warnings of alienation from scholars such as MIT's Sherry Turkle,[2] many individuals have found that digital media offer a mode of identity construction that can be rewarding and productive. It is against this analytical backdrop—one that has been developed by scholars such as Manuel Castells,[3] Henry Jenkins,[4] and Clay Shirky[5]—that we can begin to acknowledge the digital sphere as intersecting with identity projects at a variety of registers. One such register is spiritual practice, but not just as an extension of offline, organized spiritual activity. Rather, as we have found in our case of the *PostSecret* project, individuals harness this project, as well as its digital features, to question personal religious and spiritual beliefs while simultaneously contributing to a therapeutic practice that might be considered "spiritual" in and of itself.

At its core, *PostSecret* is a community art project that invites the public to anonymously share secrets in a fundamentally creative way. Creator Frank

Warren's vision for *PostSecret* grew out of an earlier project, The Reluctant Oracle, which centered on the anonymous distribution of Warren's own postcard confessions.[6] In 2004, Warren stopped the strategic circulation of his own postcards and began inviting Washington, DC residents to send him *their* secrets by handing out generic postcards with the following instructions as well as an address for submissions:

> You are invited to anonymously contribute a secret to a group art project. Your secret can be a regret, fear, betrayal, desire, confession or childhood humiliation. Reveal *anything*—as long as it is true and you have never shared it with anyone before. Steps: Take a postcard, or two. Tell your secret anonymously. Stamp and mail the postcard. Tips: Be brief—the fewer words used the better. Be legible—use big, clear and bold lettering. Be creative—let this postcard be your canvas (postsecret.com).

Owing to the influx of responses he received, Warren was able to collect enough material to create what is now the "largest advertisement-free Blog in the world," according to the site (which was created through WordPress), and as of October 2014, has received 690,411,892 visitors, has received 336,000 "likes" on Facebook, and linked to 38,400 Tweets on Twitter (postsecret.com). The website is updated by Warren each Sunday, under the heading "Sunday Secrets" with twenty to thirty new postcards. Each installation is left up for only a week and are only selectively archived on the *PostSecret* site. Owing to this ephemerality, statistical evidence of such things as topic areas is impossible to collect. However, our longitudinal textual analysis of the site revealed common themes such as (in no particular order): body-image issues, family problems, relationship issues, suicide, sexuality, religion, and as this paper explores, spirituality. The following offers a sample of postcard texts from the October 18, 2014 edition of Sunday Secrets:

> "I love Christian rock, but I'm an atheist!"
> "I'm so afraid that you only told me you loved me because I am a U.S. citizen."
> "I'm afraid to tell my parents I'm depressed. But I need help."
> "I feel if they knew what I wished for they'd hate me, but I keep wishing . . . "
> "I bought my wife stockings. She won't wear them so I do!"
> "It makes me smile when tourists fall on the subway."

Owing to its immense online success, the *PostSecret* project has grown into a media empire, which includes six books published by William Morrow publishers, a lecture tour—*PostSecret* Live!—hosted by Warren himself, an international traveling art exhibit, an upcoming album that features spoken secrets from the *PostSecret* Live!, a UK and Ireland tour, and offline community-focused picnics and other meet-ups. The website itself has undergone changes to adapt to the growing following of *PostSecret*; there is now a "*PostSecret* Community" page that includes *PostSecret* Chat and the less popular "Video Secrets." Alongside the commercial popularity of *PostSecret*, Warren has also established a firm connection between this project and suicide prevention; according to the official *PostSecret* press kit, he works as a volunteer and advocate for HopeLine, a suicide prevention organization and in 2008 helped raise over $500,000 for the National Suicide Prevention Hotline 1(800)SUICIDE. Although Warren publicly considers the sharing of secrets as therapeutic and healing, the self-realization and self-reflection associated with confronting such secrets has consequences, as he discusses at his *PostSecret* Live! events. This ideology of "healing through secrets" has not only built cultural capital for *PostSecret*, it has also increased its economic capital through emotionally driven consumption within popular culture.

Although Warren does not explicitly connect the project of *PostSecret* to religious or spiritual practice, he has consistently drawn connections between confession, therapy, and "our spiritual selves." In an interview with *Relevant* magazine, he framed *PostSecret* as "the things we really can't say in church": "I just think that we have so many more hopes and fears and thoughts about our spiritual selves that we're unable to express, and we don't feel comfortable talking about them."[7] In the epilogue to one of the *PostSecret* books, *Confessions on Life, Death and God*, he discusses a "spiritual secret" that may or may not have influenced his decision to create The Reluctant Oracle: "When I was in high school, I attended a Pentecostal church five days a week. After every service, I approached the altar, raised my hands, and prayed fervently to speak in tongues like the other church members. Two years passed without success. I felt lost, a failure in God's eyes. I left the church and never talked about this experience. It became a spiritual secret."[8] Comments such as these, combined with the publication of an entire volume of secrets rooted in religion and spirituality, the popularity of spiritual secrets in the blog's Sunday Secret editions, and the featured "Secrets of Spirituality" thread in *PostSecret* Chat all account for a presence of spirituality in the *PostSecret* project. However, what is this presence and how does the digital sphere facilitate such a presence? Can we call participation in the *PostSecret* community "spiritual practice?" What counts as spiritual practice in the digital sphere? Would such spiritual practices be ancillary to other forms of "the spiritual," supplemental to them, or a replacement for them? To answer questions such as these, it is necessary to come to terms with the affordances of *PostSecret* for the category of spirituality, and it is the purpose of this chapter to explore these affordances and their implications beyond.

Questions of religion and spirituality have roiled discourse about social and digital media and vice versa. As with in other domains of life, there has been a consistent tendency to claim both too much and too little for the affordances of these practices. And, it is a focus on practice, consistent with current trends in the fields of media studies and religious studies, that we bring to the argument here. We do not seek to define the "essential" nature of religion or of digital space or of religion *in* digital space (we would note that there is an important and growing literature in this area, cf. Campbell, 2013, for a review).[9] Instead, we want to explore how, in practice, the meaning of "the spiritual" is engaged, nuanced, and deployed in social spaces through the affordances of digital media. This is not unrelated to the larger question of what spirituality is. In fact, part of the constitution of the social meaning of spirituality must in some sense always rest in its deployment in social discourse and social relations. And, as the digital sphere is today an important context for the exploration of the meaning of spirituality (both for the demographic we might call "digital natives" and others) it can be seen to provide both the language and the language-of-practice through which the meaning of spirituality is evolving today.

PostSecret has proven to be an exceedingly rich example of online explorations of "the spiritual." But, its status as a central statement must be seen in its own terms, not in relation to some substantive definition of "spirituality." The whole question of what constitutes spirituality today is, of course, very much up in the air. A broad discourse about spirituality describes it as in some ways being the normative category of "the religious," with a growing segment of the American public now describing itself as "spiritual but not religious."[10] While complex, the discourse of "spiritual but not religious" can be said to have several characteristics. First, it is a claim about the status of religious traditions and more importantly, religious institutions. People today distrust institutional religion, and some observers argue that the choice of "spirituality" as a category is a convenient shorthand identity marker that can separate an interest in things spiritual or religious from the embodiment of institutional religion.[11] Second, it must be said that even the category of "spirituality" must reside in traditions and histories. An account of this in the *New York*

Times quotes religion scholar Courtney Bender, who notes that contemporary practitioners of what they think of as "spirituality" explore a wide range of ways of "doing spirituality":

> [while the idea that] spirituality "is not sui generis," but rather learned in communities that persist over time, actually runs contrary to spiritual people's conceptions of themselves, she said. "There is something in the theology of spiritual groups that actually refocuses their practitioners from thinking about how they fit into a long continuous spirituality."[12]

These two sides of contemporary "spirituality" that, on the one hand, can be a kind of marker or label distancing effervescent and meaningful practice from the perceived inadequacies of institutional religion, and, on the other hand, can generate exploratory practices that are seen to stand outside of history—to be meaningful and generative on their own—are important themes in the discourses surrounding digital spiritualities. Both meanings can be seen in the various practices and claims that surround it. It is important to note as well that these two somewhat disparate projects of spiritual identity compete for coherence in some of the narratives that we can see emerging and surrounding the ways that a phenomenon like *PostSecret* is seen and valued.

PostSecret has, as we've noted, verged on, and invoked, ideas of "the spiritual" from its earliest days. This is acknowledged by Frank Warren himself on the *PostSecret* website's pages that reproduce selective archives of notable cards. Introducing one of the earliest collections, Warren notes: "These postcards in the second set were posted in late 2005. Even this early in the project, I was receiving a number of spiritual secrets." (He pointed to two cards. One depicts the tortures of hell accompanied by two blocks of text on either side: "I tell people I'm an aethiest" and "But I believe I'm going to hell." The second card depicts a newspaper clipping of two women holding little dogs accompanied by a block of text that reads "While others pray at church, I bow my head and think about the TV programs I plan on watching.")

We can see here the conditional definition of "spirituality" as something that is simply "not religious" or is in fact "irreligious." We have argued elsewhere[13] that *PostSecret* has a deeper and more important implication for spirituality than simply standing for something that is "not religious." Its primary significance is deeper than that. Many of the cards that address issues of religion and spirituality are, in fact, articulations of ideas about contemporary spiritual and religious identity that link broad communities of shared meaning. But those shared meanings are broader and deeper than implied by Warren's suggestion here that the "spiritual" is simply "not religious."

PostSecret can be seen in the context of broader online discourses about the meanings of religion and spirituality. It is a participant in these discourses but also an exploration of the capacities and affordances of digital space. More focused and determined discourses of spirituality exist, discourses that attempt to connect spirituality with digital space in fundamental ways. Even a cursory review of online reflections on the question will reveal at least three perspectives on "the spiritual." The first can be represented by a recent blog interview with media/personal growth guru Deepak Chopra. Mashable.com engaged Chopra in a discussion of social media and spirituality. "Chopra wants users to realize that social media not only has the power to better personal health, but also the potential to spark a global shift toward a more mindful future," the account began. In answer to the question, "What excites you about social media and the impact it can have on spirituality?" Chopra opined:

> I think that it's the evolution in a way of human consciousness. What are social networks? They are the extensions of our mind . . . when this info is put on a social network, it influences the minds, and therefore, the neural networks of everyone participating. So unbeknownst to us, society is moving in the direction of a planetary mind through the social networks.[14]

Social media, then, are coterminous with consciousness, and their relationship to spirituality is a kind of connectedness that blends together into collective mindfulness. The spirituality is a distinctly Asian spirituality, but more importantly to our point here, it can be said to be integrally linked to the nature of social media, with the latter seen as universal, encompassing, and on some level beneath consciousness. The social media are like neural networks, and through their extension into and out of the biological forms that are the basis of consciousness, a global spiritual harmony can be achieved.

Contrast this view of digital spirituality with one that is equally sympathetic to online explorations, but from a distinctly religious perspective. Writing for the millennial/entrepreneurial blog *Life Without Pants*, Methodist youth minister Gavin Richardson looks for the consonance of digital practice with traditional modes of religious and spiritual expression and exploration. Richardson contrasts digital practice with what he sees as traditional Christianity's focus on Biblical inspiration, with the sacred text being the sole source of inspiration.

Instead, he claims, religion has always been enlivened by individual expressions and stories and the centuries-long focus on Christianity on the printed work is in fact an aberration.

> What people forget in all this, is the insinuation that dwelling on God's word is *about you and your individual experiences*. In fact, if you wanted to get back to learning from the early days of your faith, language isn't the biggest change. You need to go to the town square or the temple (whatever you have) and trade stories about God, your ancestry, prophets, and make sacrifices. Maybe then you'd get lucky that the one sacred book maybe Psalms or Exodus would be brought out for all to hear a reading. You see, technologically, the greatest item to change the way we've lived out our faith is not PowerPoint or video, guitars or keytars, Twitter or voting, but that modern 1400's invention of the printing press.[15]

Social media, then, are something that has long been sought by Christian reformers across the ages: a return to the primitive, or first state, of Christianity.

> Social media/web 2.0 and the continued interweavings & collision of people on the Internet could turn a reversal to . . . living out one's faith expression as was done before the technological advance of the printing press.[16]

Both Chopra and Richardson thus provide different versions of a sort of utopian vision for social media in relation to spirituality. Notably, neither presents a singular definition of spirituality, preferring instead to mashup spirituality with something else: a discipline of mindfulness in Chopra's case, a vision of the primitive, authentic version of Christianity in Richardson's case. Both of them, though, take a slightly different approach than that implied by Warren and by other voices around *PostSecret*. To them "spirituality online" is more than just a way of differentiating a practice from "religion," it is a generative center or force in spirituality in and of itself. The distinction is both definitional and practical. Warren and *PostSecret* in a sense objectify the category of spirituality in a certain way as it is expressed online, while Richardson and Chopra want to see it as something that is suffused in the technical and practical linkage of the digital, the social and human consciousness.

A more explicit distinction from *PostSecret* is evident in an essay that appeared on the website of the (conservative evangelical) Christian Broadcasting Network under the title "Postcard Confessions."[17] Noting the breadth and success of Warren and *PostSecret*, the author, Hannah Goodwyn, seeks to differentiate this sort of online confession from the real thing. Confession is a good thing, she notes, and is even prescribed in the Bible, but the kind of confession done on *PostSecret* falls short of that ideal.

> Confessing our secrets to each other isn't a bad thing to do. In fact, the Bible encourages it . . . Ultimately, the forgiveness doesn't come from sharing your secrets with a stranger or even fellow believer. God is the One with the power to take your shameful secret and replace it with forgiveness.[18]

Noting that the problem with *PostSecret* is both in this misplaced object (the "secrets" are given to "the World," not to God) and the content of the secrets (Goodwyn finds some of them even "shocking"), Goodwyn identifies a flavor of what she calls "humanism" in Warren and *PostSecret*. Goodwyn objects to the very things that Chopra and Richardson celebrate about digital space, its openness and diversity. Such a "humanistic ideology is fragile because it has no foundation outside of mankind's understanding of life," she concludes.[19] In a way, Goodwyn confirms what Chopra and Richardson (and perhaps Warren, too) suspect: that the very nature of digital space is to be open, broad and linked to human autonomy and agency. To her, such an unruly space will necessarily be in conflict with a "God centered" universe of meaning and action. The contrasts are slightly different in each. Richardson, like Goodwyn, has a fundamental commitment to Christianity and the Christian message. But they disagree on the nature of authority and media (textual) authority. For Goodwyn, authority is in the book, for Richardson, it is in the collective, realized through the modern context of social interaction around meaning and spirituality, the digital realm. The contrast with Chopra would be even more challenging, it would seem, as he suggests that the very nature of digital space is to draw a completely different form of religious or spiritual meaning or expression out of practice. The Christian focus on individual salvation is not the point, individuals' ability to connect together to realize a kind of common consciousness is the point.

We wish to argue that *PostSecret* is a very different project than any of these. When it addresses itself to religion and spirituality, it does so with a vitality and energy that goes way beyond merely challenging received versions of religious faith (though it does do this). Frank Warren's approach to "the spiritual" is to treat most or all of the Secrets that in any way reference religion or spirituality as fundamentally the same sort of thing. They are all about "religion," which is true, but the most compelling, fresh, and thought-provoking among them are more than just "about religion," they are direct, heartfelt, and in some cases searing challenges *to* religion.

Expressions of spirituality and religion in *PostSecret* chat

Although the steady stream of religious- and spirituality-inflected postcards work to substantiate the claim that *PostSecret* does, in fact, facilitate a unique space for this type of identity work and practice, the "Secrets of Spirituality" discussion thread within *PostSecret* Chat reveals a digital community of individuals *seeking* extended conversations. It is worth noting that *PostSecret* Chat does not offer a thread dedicated exclusively to religion; rather, religious discussions are typically found within this thread. The moderator for this thread identifies himself as "Casey," a band teacher who was raised in the Methodist church, and he introduces the discussion board in the following way:

> Spirituality is something that almost everyone seems to have an opinion about, and most people have a story to tell in regards to how it has affected their lives—some stories are positive, some are negative, but all of them contain a lesson for us. Hopefully by coming here and sharing our secrets, our stories, our opinions, and our beliefs—our even lack of them—we can learn something important about how to understand one another.[20]

For Casey, as well as the thousands of others that have either "viewed" or "posted" to various threads on this board, the practice of learning from one another through discourse and debate offers a way to strengthen their spiritual and religious selves. One of the most popular "topics" is "Dear God," with 1,022 posts and 20,950 views to date. User "Matt," who created the topic, offers an extremely inclusive invitation for posts: "Post whatever prayer is on your mind right now. If you don't believe in God just way what would be your prayer if you did."[21] The majority of posts follow these instructions, but many of them offer comments to other prayers in the form of support and suggestion; in fact, some users even offer a prayer in response to another user's post.

Other topics have considerable range from one another, yet all reveal the ways in which this space offers a forum for democratized discussion and discourse; users seem to capitalize on the affordance of digital media for multiple voices and viewpoints. Most users are interested in crowdsourcing their religious and spiritual questions while seeking support and community. For example, user SancturaryGoneWrong posted "Pagans! Gather!!!" and wrote: "Samhain is coming up, what's everyone got on their agenda?"[22] On the other hand, user Kradilicious (who also offered their Skype handle and personal phone number at the end of their post) posted "Encounters with the spirit world and other explainable things" and had the following post: I have an encounter with spirits all the time. They are always around us. I tend to really be in tune with my spirituality which allows me to encounter them more than others. They typically leave me alone, though, if I do the same for them. What about you?"[23] In addition to these interactive posts, many others could be categorized as practices in questioning and challenging received notions of religion and spirituality. Such posts do not elicit hundreds of responses, but they allow the user the opportunity to reach out to the *PostSecret* community nevertheless. Example topics include: Strange; Youth Camp; I'm jealous of polygamists; Grappling; I wished I believed; That awkward moment when everyone prays; and Less like a journal entry, more like a miracle.

Such digital practices of the *PostSecret* community point toward interests that move beyond what might be categorized as "reverse discourse"[24] or other forms of direct opposition to traditional religious or spiritual authority. Rather, as the topics in the *PostSecret* Chat community illustrate, users are navigating between what Raymond Williams might call "residual" or offline religious practices and new "emergent" practices. [25] In this way, users contribute to *productive* spiritual and religious discourses that create new meanings and values for not only themselves, but for a global network. Owing to the success of *PostSecret*'s aesthetic logics, not only have online communities (via *PostSecret* Chat) and related, offline communities (via *PostSecret* Live! events and gatherings) emerged, other digital trajectories have been created that model themselves after the "online confession" framework.

In fact, within the last decade, there were several attempts made by religiously affiliated individuals and organizations to create their own version of *PostSecret*, including "Permission to Speak Freely," a blog from Anne Jackson, manager of a Christian bookstore and recovering pornography addict, that was created to accompany her book by the same name; "PostSacred," a Mormon-based iteration (now removed); and Patheos' "Soul Secret," which began with the option to create a digital postcard, but is now simply a blog where users can enter text-based confessions.[26] One website that continues to thrive in the digital confession marketplace is *Whisper* which, according to the website, boasts: "Whisper is the best place to express yourself online."[27] The website, and its accompanying app, serves more as a curation of users' secrets rather than a fluid display of individual submissions with opportunities for interaction and connection; for example, the current home page offers links to stories such as: People Used these Wacky Excuses for Calling in Sick and Siblings Share the Most Hilarious Things They Did to Each Other Growing Up. Here, the moderators of the website sift through submissions—which consist of digital images and text—and frame them within catchy titles and headlines. If you scroll down the page, you are able to click on individual "Popular" or "Related" Whispers and can post a reply, but they remain categorized into eight categories. Interestingly, of the eight categories on the masthead, "Faith" has been included, signaling the popularity of this form of discourse. Example stories include: Children of Religious Leaders Share Their Most Private Thoughts and 12 Good Deeds That Will Warm Your Heart.

When compared to *PostSecret*, the *Whisper* website and application appears to share a similar framework: the anonymous posting of secrets; the ability to interact through commenting on user submissions; instant, digital access; and the encouragement to share secrets based on various topics. However, there are also fundamental differences between the two that highlight the received authenticity of *PostSecret*—albeit within the limits of digital media production. Aside from the fact that *PostSecret* begins with the submission of nondigital postcards, includes a separate Chat community (i.e., not just a "reply" section connected to individual submissions) with hundreds of topics, offers the opportunity to meet Frank Warren and other "fans" at the *PostSecret* Live! events, and includes published collections of postcards that anyone can purchase, the online showcasing of the *PostSecret* postcards—through the weekly "Sunday Secrets"—is not curated or categorized by the logics of the website. While the postcard submissions from that week have been narrowed down for the website, they are not framed by masthead categories or catchy subheadings; rather, they exemplify a sampling of postcards that were constructed without the intention of "fitting" a particular category. *PostSecret*, then, offers a less programmed or constrained experience for their community as compared to the *Whisper* website, and therefore operates as a "third space" of spiritual practice that maintains a fluid relationship between various modes of personal, collective, digital, and offline experiences.

As a spiritually significant affordance of digital media, *PostSecret* offers a "third space" for various discourse to "crash" into one another via direct submission as well as voyeurism. The aesthetic logics of this project offer opportunities for production at various levels: constructing a postcard, constructing a pseudonym for the chat rooms, and so on. Such various constructions contribute to *PostSecret* in meaningful ways, but are ultimately determined by the logics of digital media. For example, decisions are made as to which offline contributions are able to enter the construction of the site, and thus, the construction of the space. At the same time, however, *PostSecret* invites competing discourses to operate, together, within a digital space and due to this logic, these discourses merge together and become a new form of spiritual knowledge and practice (i.e., sharing secrets as therapy).

In this way, *PostSecret* is an example of what Hoover and Echchaibi call a "third space."[28] This formulation suggests that phenomena such as *PostSecret* derive a large measure of their force and meaning from the affordances of digital practice where participants can reflexively engage in negotiations and strategies from a position "in-between" more formal and structural dimensions. "Third Spaces" can exist—and endure—in a kind of suspension between institutional and individual practice, between agency and structure, between received doctrine and individual autonomy, among other "poles." What is important is to see how *PostSecret* functions as if it were a real place where new forms of meaning practice, new communities, new networks, new gestures, and new recursive discourses can find a basis. It is not enough to see *PostSecret* only as a re-formulation of received categories such as "confession." It is also not merely about "therapy," or about "resistance," though these are important themes and affordances. It operates according to its own logics to perform important personal and cultural work and in that process can have a dynamic relationship to evolving senses and meanings of spirituality.

Conclusion

We can think of *PostSecret* as having at least two meanings in relation to questions of "the religious" or "the spiritual." First, it represents an invocation of spirituality (or in a lesser way, religion) in that many of the cards do, in fact, represent explorations of spiritualities or spiritual themes. Secondly, it represents a marker or commentary on the meaning and prospects of "spirituality" and religion today, how they are defined, what their prospects are, and how their place in the culture is being redefined by contemporary meaning practice. Each of these valences of spirituality in *PostSecret* stands in contrast (though in different ways) to the received notions of how spirituality and digital space ought to relate to one another. Against the idea that "the digital" provides unique affordances of spirituality (a view we might attribute to Deepak Chopra's ideas introduced earlier) the actuality of spirituality in *PostSecret* seems not to be very much about that.

In fact, the thing that defines what *PostSecret* and the "*PostSecret* Community" call "spirituality" stands in a dialectic relationship to such a hermetic "digitally spiritual." The representations of spirituality in *PostSecret* are self-conscious, reflexive, discursive, and rhetorical. They are not, in the main, attempts to invoke or introduce spirituality into the aesthetic forms of the cards. They exist alongside such practice, using the "Third Space" of *PostSecret* as a context for negotiating and reimagining the meaning of religion and spirituality. This also places them in some conflict with the view we attributed to a Methodist Pastor earlier. Rather than being a place where people can digitally explore their own ideas of spirituality in some ideal or normative form, *PostSecret*'s explorations seem more prone, as we have said, to distance themselves from actual practices of spirituality and move instead to discourses *about* religion and spirituality.

These considerations are not helped by the linguistic or rhetorical challenge that what much of the *PostSecret* Community (including, notably, Frank Warren himself) means by "spirituality" is less an ideal or idealized form of "the spiritual" and more a statement about the nature and status of contemporary *religion*. Thus the approach in *PostSecret* is consistent with much contemporary discourse, which considers "the spiritual" to be a singular, ideal, and normative form that contrasts with the socially and culturally suspect category of "religion."[29] There is a normativity here, in that Warren—and many voices in the community—consider it to be an almost-sacred task to wrest the idealized spiritual away from religion and to allow it to be expressed-and expressible, in autonomous, individual practices of expression online.

The sheer weight of this practice, the critical mass of discourse that is represented by *PostSecret*'s exploration of spirituality, is significant to the overall discourse. It provides powerful and salient moments where the expression of ideas about the Manichean choice between the "old" *religion* and the "new" *spiritual* become important moments of community, and solidarity between individuals who share these ideas. These can be seen in the Sunday Secrets, as well as in the discussion boards, the Community, in Warren's live events, and in the various *PostSecret* books and other publications. *PostSecret* is not all about spirituality, but when it is about spirituality, it speaks with a powerful voice drawing in the aesthetic and social-practice affordances of its forms, contexts, and content.

This momentum is obviously potentially quite threatening to the meaning of religion and to religious authority. It is missed by authorities such as our Methodist Pastor (above) who see within digital practice opportunities for autonomous searching and self-expression but who miss the deeper cultural meaning of the social critique implicit in the practice. It is also missed by observers such as Deepak Chopra, who see the digital only in the narrowest terms (though we doubt Chopra would be particularly concerned about deeper implications for formal religion anyway). Ironically, it is also missed by critiques such as the one we presented earlier from conservative Christianity.[30]

Goodwyn, as we saw, was primarily concerned with the potential for online practice to presume to occupy the same spaces in faith and piety as those claimed by traditional religion. Consistent with some Catholic critiques of *PostSecret* and the other "confession" sites, Goodwyn laments the potential for such prosumption to lure the unwary into a Godless, irreligious space almost unawares. This misses two essential things about *PostSecret*. First, that it represents a voluble and self-conscious exploration of a "third space" where powerful explorations of meaning (around loss, lifecourse, relationships, etc.) can be articulated in ways that stand outside (and in some ways surpass) the affordances of traditional religion. Second, it misses that these explorations are both self-consciously and inferentially about contesting the place of religion and religious authority themselves. It is not a simple matter of people going to a superficial source for things that ought more appropriately and effectively be done in the context of the "received religious," it is about a practice whose affordances directly contest and undermine the prospects and aspirations of religion.

Is *PostSecret* an example of "digital spirituality?" If we mean to ask by that question whether it can stand in for, or replace or fuse or bind with ideals of spiritual practice per se, then perhaps the answer is "no." But, if we take *PostSecret* as a digital "third space" on its own terms, then the answer can be found in the ways that it inhabits a dynamic place in contemporary discourse, offering its "community" opportunities to contest and remake the meaning of religion and spirituality today. This is not to say that this is only a project of cultural politics around religion. The act of contesting and of re-positioning that *PostSecret* makes possible is by all accounts a deeply meaningful project, one that has important implications for meaning, identity, community, and solidarity in contemporary lives.

11

A Constructed Category: Baby Boomers Navigating Aging through Spirituality and the Media

Anne Maija Huffman
Sofia University

Defining generations and cultural complex

The American Psychological Association (APA) defines the field of psychology thusly: "Psychology is the study of the mind and behavior."[1] Part of how we understand ourselves is by how we understand our behavior and actions, and how those are reflected back to us—often through popular culture and media. Both media and psychology have made major contributions to our understanding of western culture throughout the 20th century[2] and will no doubt continue to impact our interpretation of ourselves as the 21st century continues. Importantly, how we define our cultures will be determined by the constructs and categories we associate with and assign to ourselves and others. Age and generation are such constructs, and the central focus of the research supporting the recommendations in this chapter.

Markus and Kitayama noted that "the study of culture and self has renewed and extended psychology's understanding of the self, identity, or agency and casts it as central to the analysis and interpretation of behavior."[3] Further, people and their sociocultural worlds are entwined and give rise to an understanding of "self" as an individual in America.[4] One sense of self that people use as a reference relates to age and age categories. As Leerom Medovoi noted, "age categories might be thought of as the crystallized or reified forms of the practices that represent an individual's temporality, understood more precisely as one's position within that duration that imaginatively corresponds to the life span."[5] As a construct, aging is a broadly represented category that includes identifiable brackets, among them childhood, adolescence, middle age, and old age. These brackets intersect with gender, sexuality, race, socioeconomic status, education, and religious and/or spiritual beliefs. Identification with a dominant group or culture within the society makes it possible for people to be valued as significant members of a meaningful world and contributes to an individual's self-esteem. In this context, culture "is a set of meanings created by society, manifested in values, beliefs, and norms to regulate the requirements of the societal institutions and the group behaviors necessary to fulfill these requirements."[6] These shared beliefs can also become part of a cultural complex.

Overall, humans live their lives in context.[7] For many this context includes the dominant culture they belong to as well as the ethnic, religious and/or spiritual, gender and/or sexual, political, regional, and national identities that make up an individual's personality. Here these pieces of a person can be organized individually into his or her psyche or collectively into a group complex. Cultural complex is a theoretical term that extends Carl Jung's original conception of a complex and Joseph Henderson's[8] cultural unconscious into group phenomena. A cultural complex is defined by Abramovitch as "akin to personal complexes in that they are based upon repetitive, historical experiences that have taken root in the unconscious."[9] Kimbles originally envisioned cultural complex as a way to understand deeply rooted religious, social, racial, and/or ethnic conflicts in the world today.[10] Cultural complexes provide a conceptualization of "the twilight zone between the archetypal and the personal"[11] and may provide a theoretical basis for understanding the structure of the cultural unconscious.[12] Gold and Douvan noted that "people are carriers of beliefs that are derived directly or indirectly from their cultural environment, but in their minds these ideas are motives, resources, and so on."[13] This can be a useful way to frame cultural complexes and how people interact with them: The individual does not recognize the activated complex, but does act upon the impulses generated by it, and names the impulse as an individual motive or resource which also keeps them safe and within the normative whole of the in-group.

Further, cultural complexes are "repetitive, historical group experiences which have not only taken root in the collective psyche of groups but in the individual/collective psyches of the individual members of the group as well."[14] Singer noted that cultural complexes are "lived out in group life and are internalized in the psyche of individuals."[15] Whole groups can often behave as if they are in the grip of a specific cultural complex. This type of cultural complex activates in the group's behavior, emotion, and life as a self-care preservation system. Here the goal of the defensive self-care preservation system is the protection of the collective spirit rather than the individual spirits that make up the whole. The unquestioned assumptions and underlying beliefs in a cultural complex are held to be true by most members of the group[16] and continue to be reinforced through such media as social networking. This chapter looks at how Baby Boomers act, think, and feel around the topics of aging and spirituality.

Between 1946 and 1964 the United States experienced a population boom: approximately 77.3 million babies were born, creating the Baby Boom generation.[17] The Baby Boomers epitomize the birth cohort concept in sociology. The demographic, social, political, and economic significance of this cohort marks them as a generation with the ability to influence all those around them. Strauss and Howe suggest:

> Whatever age bracket the Boomers have occupied has been the cultural and spiritual focal point for American society as a whole. Through their childhood, America was child-obsessed; in their youth, youth-obsessed . . . Always, the Boom has been not just a new generation, but what Brackman has termed "a new notion of generation with new notions of its imperatives." . . . Boomers have always seen their mission not as constructing a society, but of justifying, purifying, even sanctifying it.[18]

The concept of generation is not a new one. For Mannheim the status of a generation was determined by the confluence of a particular cohort with a historical period, in a particular social context. This convergence created a "community of location," which formed the necessary (but insufficient) conditions for realizing a "generation unit."[19] Mannheim noted that a further element was needed to constitute generation as an actuality. This was participation in a "common destiny," which then and only then created a distinct "generational style."[20] These three elements: a shared temporal location (i.e., birth cohort), shared historical location (exposure to a common era), and shared sociocultural location (i.e., a generational consciousness or "generational entelechy"[21]) comprise the modern elements of what is considered a generation.

Eyerman and Turner further update and define a generation as: "a cohort of persons passing through time who come to share a common habitus, hexis [state or disposition] and culture, a function of which is to provide them with a collective memory that serves to integrate the cohort over a finite period of time."[22]

Baby Boomers can be viewed as such a generational unit, formed by a community of location, namely membership in a cohort born in the late 1940s who reached young adulthood during the 1960s and whose next common destiny will be retirement during the 2010s.[23] As Gillon stated "While past generations have shared common experiences, they developed only a loose sense of generational identity. Largely because of their size and the emergence of mass media, Boomers are the first generation to have a defined sense of themselves as a single entity."[24]

Almost from the time they were conceived, "Boomers were dissected, analyzed, and pitched to by modern marketers, who reinforced a sense of generational distinctiveness."[25] This generation became known among other monikers, as "War Babies, Spock Babies, Sputnik Generation, and Pepsi Generation,"[26] thus giving them a sense of themselves as an entity unto their own, especially as depicted and reflected back to them by the media.

Youth culture, initially considered a subculture within sociology,[27] was rendered prominent with the births of the Baby Boomers and "it subsequently became massive and commercialized. Being young became especially popular in the 1960s. Not only adolescents, but adults also, were inspired by this idea."[28] This subculture is highly visible as more and more advertising turns toward preserving youth as we age here in America. With the first of the Baby Boomer cohort having turned 65 in 2011, American society is going to contain a proportionally larger population of long-lived elderly men and women[29] whose realities of aging become increasingly apparent as will the shadow of infirmity and death looming over this cohort.

It is a paradox that an aging American society is seemingly obsessed with youth[30] and clearly reflected in media. All these elements contribute to a cultural complex that helped shape (and still shapes) the Baby Boomers. As Roszak noted, in a nation and world attempting to put the horror of World War II behind them, with all its death and destruction, a desire for renewal and vitality swept across the land. People, "wanting to start over again were swept up in the cult of youth."[31] America at that time became the ideal society, one based solely on the young and their needs, a prospect that was not very difficult with such a large demographic dominating the culture. In America the future belonged to the young, "an ageless class, permanently endowed with vitality, daring, and optimism, a deathless Pepsi generation that would always be there."[32]

Spiritual seekers

As befitting a rebellious youth culture, many of the Baby Boomers turned away from organized religion in the 1960s and 1970s and turned their attention to those things they deemed "spiritual."[33] Unlike their parents, Baby Boomers moved across religious boundaries, often trying out various different religions or the then-seemingly-exotic Eastern traditions and religions. Boomers often ended up in nondenominational settings that combined elements from many different traditions, but were generally based on a mix of spirituality and self-help traditions.[34] Baby Boomers came to understand spirituality (and religion) to be an inward reflection about knowing oneself, essentially independent of any involvement with a church, synagogue, or any other religious organization.[35] One church marketing consultant stated, "Baby boomers think of churches like they think of supermarkets . . . They want options, choices, and convenience. Imagine if Safeway was only open one hour a week, had only one product, and didn't explain it in English."[36] Thus, for Baby Boomers seeking spiritual and religious sustenance, "Spiritual quests are at the core of their personal narratives and . . . these quests bear directly upon not only their inner feelings, but their religious identities, their family life, and moral and ethical issues."[37] This stance on spirituality has implications for Baby Boomers' understanding of how they will age. This spiritual seeking may well be part of a cultural complex in that the eternal spiritual quest will help ward off anxiety associated with aging, death, and dying, by giving the Baby Boomers a sense of their symbolic immortality within the experience of transcendence.[38]

The Boomers quest for self has been a central theme through the rising adulthood and continued aging of the cohort. An individual's capacity to cope with age-related threats and adversities is a central facet of adaptive competence in later life.[39] Thus the self plays an active role in the selection of age identities such as age group or generation. Through this process the self-identity determines whether group stereotypes are applied to oneself and serve as self-defining. For example, older adults may refuse to accept negative age stereotypes and distance themselves from those that they perceive to be negatively "old."

In contrast, older adults' identification with their generation may be based on socially shared experiences that provide a sense of belongingness and continuity[40] such as the advent of rock and roll music or the sexual revolution. Thus, generational identity may buffer individuals' psychological well-being through the beneficial effects of collective identity.[41] Weiss and Lang found empirical evidence that "older adults were found to differentiate between people their [own] age and people in their generation, clearly favoring their generation identity."[42] Here the benefits of a collective identity over an individual identity provide better psychological well-being. In other words, meaningful cognitive representations were found in the generational identity, such as shared identities and a common fate, whereas the same age group was the repository for the more threatening aspects of old age and its attendant specters of death and dying. For the Baby Boomers this may look like investment into a generational identity of eternal youthfulness. In this instance others might grow old (in a negative sense), but the individual invested in a collective identity will not.

As a generation, "The baby boomers are likely to reject many of the traditional associations of old age. In making personal fulfillment after 50 their priority, the research shows that many will use their purchasing power, connections and self-awareness increasingly to dominate the images and rituals of popular culture."[43]

The desire among the Baby Boomers to hold onto their youth, perpetuating that cultural perception, can be seen through media advertisements that tout pills, creams, and procedures that will help one maintain one's youthful appearance and ward off physical decline. Vitamins, exercise, and healthful eating, all components of the Boomers childhood, may also be used in defense of dying and to continue to age well and live an active lifestyle.[44]

At each stage in the life cycle the Baby Boomers have shaped American culture[45] and will continue to do so for quite some time. Arndt et al. found that cultural complexes may help groups transcend death either literally through religious or spiritual beliefs such as "heaven, or reincarnation, or symbolically through identification through entities beyond oneself."[46] The author of this chapter conducted a qualitative study inquiring into the ways culture, attitudes, and beliefs offer Baby Boomers a protected way of viewing aging and death and how media can support Baby Boomers in exploring the physical, psychological, and spiritual aspects of their own senescence.[47]

Illustrations from the study

The original research question posed was: Have the Baby Boomers unconsciously invested in a cultural complex of youthfulness to help buffer their anxiety about aging and death? Using thematic analysis[48] informed by virtual ethnography[49] the study surveyed 39 Baby Boomers via an online survey hosting service.

This method captured individual experiences as well as potential collective experience, particularly among the large Boomer population that is leaving a unique imprint on American life[50] and whose personal narratives construct shared narratives through the use of mass media. As Gillon noted, "starting in the 1950s Americans across the country watched the same shows, laughed at the same jokes, and watched the same news stories unfold."[51] Television connected the nation and set a standard of knowledge that in turn created a shared group experience with its own identity. "A group identity is made and maintained, then . . . through highly regulated storytelling practices."[52] Modern storytelling often takes place online. Furthermore technologically mediated communication is now commonly incorporated into most aspects of daily life, and the distinctions between online and offline worlds are therefore becoming blurred as these realms become increasingly merged into society.

Currently in North America 77.4 percent of the population are Internet users (Internet World Stats 2010).[53] Furthermore, according to Pew Internet Research[54] as of March 2012, 80 percent of Baby Boomers use the Internet, comprise 34 percent of the Internet population, and are 32 percent of the traffic on a typical day with 69 percent of them averaging once-a-day usage. Indeed, Boomers are comparable to the Millennials (18–32-year-olds) in their Internet usage and online activity.[55] As Capurro and Pingel stated, "being human is more and more a matter of being online" particularly as we as a society move more deeply into a digital age.[56] Therefore virtual ethnography forms an important component because "'virtual reality' is not a reality separate from other aspects of human action and experience, but rather a part of it."[57]

Participants who were born in the United States of America, excluding its Territories, between the years 1950 and 1960, with a minimum age of 50 and a maximum age of 62 were recruited. However, there were two age outliers, both aged 65, who were not screened out of the survey, most likely due to a screening preset failure of the survey design. Participants were located across the United States with access to a computer. Participants could be of any race, ethnicity, sex, gender, sexual orientation, relationship status, religious or spiritual preference, and from any socioeconomic status. The average age was 56.5 years, and the mode was 55 years of age (5 participants). Overall the age spread of the participants was fairly evenly distributed across the middle Boomer lifespan, with most of the participants falling into the "pre-senior (aged 55–64)"[58] category for those born 1950–1960. Not surprisingly, the study was comprised of 28 women (71%) and 11 men (28%), which reflects the trend of 96 Boomer men per 100 Boomer women.[59] This is also reflected in the online presence of Boomer men and women, as Underhill[60] has noted that Facebook's fastest growing demographic is women over 55, while Wortham pointed out that "more than 60 percent of baby boomers are avid consumers of social media like blogs, forums, podcasts, and online video."[61] They were able to speak, read, and write English proficiently to give consent and were able to clearly articulate subjective experiences in writing. The purpose of this study was not to discover a universal truth applicable to all Baby Boomers. Rather it is to learn what an aging generation is experiencing and to capture an experience that may relate to a cultural complex and affect subsequent generations as they themselves age.

The most eclectic category for the participants was the religious/spiritual affiliations. As befitting a generation that has viewed itself as part of "a country of believers not belongers,"[62] 1 participant was agnostic, 1 participant was an atheist, and 12 (31%) had no religious or spiritual affiliation. Six participants (15%) had an earth-based Pagan and or Wiccan affiliation, 4 (10%) were Christian, and 3 (8%) were Catholic. Of the remaining participants 2 were Interspiritual/Interfaith, 2 were Christian with Buddhist practices, 1 was Buddhist, 1 was Sufi, 1 was a practitioner of the Science of Mind, and 1 was United Church of Christ (UCC). This reflects a wide array of seekers who have a fluid idea of who their spiritual self is and their likely discontent with scripted categories of belief.

The purpose of this research was to explore the premise that Baby Boomers may have consciously and unconsciously invested in a cultural complex of youthfulness to help buffer their anxiety about aging and death. Interestingly, the participants (all identified with pseudonyms) responded with similar thoughts about the world and their place in it, thus, unknowingly corroborating their socially constructed conception of reality and collectively, as individuals, coming together as American Baby Boomers. As Festinger noted, our particular beliefs are fortified when others believe similarly and thus substantiate our conceptions of reality. These beliefs then are often reified in the world around us, through the movies and television we watch, the music and advertisements we listen to, and the books and websites that we consume.

Three major themes emerged from this study:

1. World Change Agents
2. Individuality
3. Scarcity.

For those participants to whom the Baby Boomer identity was important, the major themes were that they felt part of something larger than themselves, they had many opportunities, and also were part of a movement that changed the world (world change agents). Several participants expressed this eloquently: "Being a Baby Boomer means I grew up with the belief that I could do/be anything. Endless possibilities. Free love. No limits" (Devi). Other perspectives included:

> I think we changed society in some drastic ways. I identify with civil rights and protesting as part of my activist years, drugs were also a part of my generation and ridding ourselves of puritan views of sex . . . we opened eyes in several areas and still fight to have all people respected and allowed to show up in the world as themselves. (Spirit)

Interestingly, all participants saw themselves as bracketed by war, specifically World War II and the Vietnam war, with a few mentions of the Korean War as part of defining who they were as Baby Boomers. Lynda noted: "Baby Boomers are a generation that came after WWII and enjoyed some happy growing-up years before the Vietnam War and racial unrest challenged our generation to deal with things in the world that we did not like." Inger also spoke to this theme, stating that "I am a part of the post WWII blip I am defined by war—WWII, nuclear, Vietnam." Beverly pointed to the impact of Boomers in her response: "Being born after WWII. The largest segment of the population. Baby boomers have affected all facets of life as they passed through each decade." Here Beverly's statement seems to illustrate the experience implicitly affecting the majority society, of pointing to the unconscious idea of having in-group status, when she speaks of having "affected all facets of life" as a world change agent.

Finally, one participant noted the advantages of being part of a large cohort that is aging and their impact as a world change agent:

> I think the impact of [being the largest group of aging adults in the country] may be that more services, goods, and advertising will cater to this generation. I knew that something radical had changed the day I heard the Rolling Stones being played in the grocery store. Wow, I'm the target demographic! Wow, my generation has the buying power! (Krista)

Four themes emerged from inquiring into how Boomer identity impacted the aging process: Baby Boomers will reinvent aging and change how Americans age and grow older in this society (world change agents); there are too many Boomers and not enough resources (scarcity); Baby Boomers are more active as they age; and Baby Boomers really did not think they would age. One participant, Devi, captured several of these themes in her response:

> I am in graduate school at age 58 and that is partly because of the idea that as a Baby Boomer I can do what I want at any age. It's a belief that if I keep my mind active it will be healthy and not age as quickly. Of course there is more to it than that but there is that element. I go to Pilates to keep a healthy body. There is a culture of youth with the Baby Boomers. We grew up believing we would never grow old. "Don't trust anyone over 30" was a saying when I was a teenager. Death was kept hidden.

Several other participants concurred:

> Growing old is becoming the next thing my generation is redefining. It means that we are expected to do it uniquely. It also means that the social safety net is thinning and there may not be enough services for my large generation to actually make it into old age. It means that we are likely to have company in the "old folk's home" because, this too, we are doing together. (Glinda)

In this case it would seem that for these participants the identity of Baby Boomer does indeed buffer against fear of aging since there seemed to be a strong belief in the ability of their generation to change how America ages.

Surprisingly, within the framework of asking about maintaining physical appearance, the dominant themes were: a healthy diet and exercise to age well; a contentedness with one's aging appearance, but dislike of the physical aspects of aging; and a mismatch between the physical/outer appearance and the internal experience of self. There was also a hint of nostalgia for some aspects of younger selves.

Liss articulates the three themes well:

> My changing body has been a challenge for me as I have aged! My hair began to turn gray when I was in my 30s. I chose to have it dyed for about 10 years and then discontinued that practice. My hair is "salt and pepper" now and one of my significant features! (I receive many compliments!). Although I was very trim and athletic into my 30s, I began to notice some real shifts in my body when I entered into perimenopause and full-blown menopause. Weight gain had never been an issue and suddenly was . . . I value a strong, healthy, physically fit body because I feel better and because I am a woman who has previously enjoyed hiking, backpacking, horseback riding, and cross-country skiing. I can feel the stiffness and decreased range of motion that is settling into my body when I am not active. I am tall (5'9") and attractive. I have historically garnered positive

> attention and compliments. This has mattered to me. I would like to be seen as an attractive, fit, healthy, vital older woman!

Preston speaks to his experience as a man.

> I'm blessed to look younger than my age. I've been graying for about 15 years and don't much like it, but have come to accept it—it's not so bad. My hair started thinning about 5 years ago and I am taking Propecia to combat that. I exercise regularly, hard. I pay attention to my diet and attempt to maintain a reasonable weight. I play in the mountains. I'm on a search and rescue team where the average age is somewhere about 34, and it's a good motivator to stay fit. No plastic surgery, though I've thought about getting the lower portion of my eyes done. I'm sad that my jawline is starting to sag. That really bugs me when I see it.

Conversely, GG owns his appearance and echoes the overarching theme of individuality. "My hair is grey, I am overweight, and my chin is growing a sibling. I am what I am and I don't give a damn what anyone else thinks." Delia captures the mismatch of the inner self and her outside appearance: "I am a little shocked by the fact that I have wrinkles, etc. because I don't feel as old inside as I am beginning to look on the outside . . . I don't feel like I have had time to really live yet!"

Within the responses, many of the participants reported that they colored their hair. For some it was camouflage for grey, for others it was a "creative outlet" (Betty Boop) or a "decoration" (Devi). Several participants also had minimal plastic surgery and other cosmetic procedures done, more to feel better or correct a defect rather than a pursuit of youth, the overall feeling expressed was that aging was okay with them, at least in response to this question. Ultimately Wild Turkey sums it up succinctly, "wrinkles don't hurt." Paradoxically the participants all rejected plastic surgery as a means for maintaining youth, which may speak more to how Madison Avenue thinks of them rather than how the Boomers think of themselves. The participants focused more on what they as individuals could control, such as exercise and accepting oneself. It may be that there is more interest in selling the Baby Boomers the idea of youthfulness via advertising about plastic surgery and fat-melting pills, than there is investment in these things on the part of the Baby Boomers themselves, at least as reported by these participants. It may also be a case of the world change agents coming into play, with some authority telling the Baby Boomers what to believe or think about aging, and this group's rejection of that notion.

In concluding notes, participant Oakson noted:

> I have been analyzed since I enrolled in public school. The Baby Boom has been under constant scrutiny from every branch of medical and social research. We were the first to have fool proof contraception and the free love that it ushered in. We were also the first to face HIV and AIDS. And I think quite significant, the Civil Rights movement lead by Dr. King was comprised of the prior generation, for the most part, but it was burned into Boomer consciousness by the evening news (in living black and white). So, I think the various liberation movements that followed were to a great degree inspired by what the boomers saw and learned. And we did it without Twitter or Facebook.

Maude captured the themes of individuality and world changers well.

> There are lots of us. We came of age during the Viet Nam War, peace protests, drugs, free sex, Woodstock, rock and roll, acid rock. We broke convention and seeded the way for a new world. We were post WWII affluent/middle class. We had Helen Caldicott, 11 minutes to midnight and the specter of Nuclear War. We were raised on pharmaceuticals, a pill for everything, canned vegetables, TV dinners, Laugh-In, Ed Sullivan, The Beatles, Bob Dylan, Joni Mitchell, Simon and Garfunkel, Jimi Hendrix, The Cream. Demonstrations, radical politics, Kent State.

However, she also speaks to the theme of world change agents indicating the under-belly, or negative impact of Baby Boomers:

> A sense of entitlement that does more harm than good. A sense that the world is a mess so we can live like there's no tomorrow. My generation has single-handedly destroyed the environment, caused the decay of morality, escalated greed to a religion, created a debt society, destroyed the food chain and contributed to alarming rates of obesity and diabetes. On the whole, I can't say I'm proud of Baby Boomers.

Finally, Preston notes that, "we as a society really, really don't have our act together when it comes to caring for the aging, and it scares the bejeezus out of me." Overall the participants seemed to be in sync with their responses, reflecting their participation and consumption of the culture reflected back to them by each other and media.

Wider ramifications of boomer youth obsession

Gold and Douvan noted "people are carriers of beliefs that are derived directly or indirectly from their cultural environment, but in their minds these ideas are motives, resources, and so on."[63] The individual does not recognize the activated complex, but does act upon the impulses generated by it, and names the impulse as an individual motive or resource, which also keeps them safe and within the normative whole of the in-group.

A cultural complex of eternal youthfulness of the American Baby Boomer can be posited from the study data. More specifically, youthfulness for the Baby Boomers can be operationalized as a state of mind, the idea of what the Boomers are becoming. Smith and Clurman sum it up well, stating that "youthfulness is the spirit of possibility and plasticity"[64] thus allowing for the flexible neotenic (or younger) mindset that allows the Baby Boomers to constantly redefine the self to stay mentally "with it" even as they age chronologically. Youthfulness can also be further operationalized to include the idea of agelessness, in which the participants remain active and aware, pushing past the traditional limits of old age, and staying relevant in order to impact the world, a worldview consistent with the themes in this study. This also allows for the paradoxical adoption of the idea of being eternally youthful even while aging, a powerful yet fluid characteristic for all the Baby Boomers.

Yet, everyone wants to feel they belong in the world they live in. Belongingness is a very basic human need. Kohut noted that people seek to confirm a subjective sense of belongingness, or being a part of a larger human family, in order to avoid feelings of loneliness and alienation. For humans, a sense of connectedness begins to emerge during adolescence and extends throughout the adult life.[65] This sense of connectedness allows people to maintain feelings of being "human among humans"[66] and to identify with those who may be perceived as different from themselves. Further this sense of belongingness can provide psychological buffering to the self-esteem structure of the individual, particularly if the individual identifies with belonging to the in-group or dominant culture. For these participants, it seemed almost as if there was this need to be a part of the society at large, of "being an American, coupled with the search for individuality, [which] has been historically part of the fabric of American culture."[67] Singer noted, "the cultural complex can possess the psyche and soma of an individual or a group, causing them to think and feel in ways that might be quite different from what they think they should feel or think."[68] Thus an archetype that the Baby Boomers' cultural complex may be clustering around is that of the rugged individual, again demonstrating the theory that unconscious cultural traits are manifesting in the individuals' stances.[69] Media that the Baby Boomers have consumed, from *The Graduate* (1967) through *The Big Chill* (1983) and *The Big Lebowski* (1998) to *The Bucket List* (2007) reflect the Boomers' quest for an authentic inner life[70] and individual spiritual self has been magnified and mirrored back to them and has informed the culture at large around them, reifying the archetype.

There is a commonly held view in personality and social psychology that people strive to distinguish themselves from others and that they have a basic motive to achieve distinctiveness. In some cultures, people want to be distinguished as individuals, whereas in others, people want to be part of larger entities and may even seek to avoid distinctiveness from other members of those entities.[71] Weiss and Lang have demonstrated that as people grow older they develop a sense of a dual-age identity, referring to their age group and generation.[72] Further research has revealed that age-group identity was more frequently associated with loss and decline, whereas generation identity was more frequently associated with positive characteristics and increased levels of agency.[73] Interestingly for the Baby Boomers, as much as they wish to be regarded as individuals, when asked, such as in the research reported herein, they *do* identify with their generational character.[74] Bollas noted that for individuals, becoming aware of the passage of time facilitates "a keen sense of their own generation. They can define it clearly, differentiate it from older and younger generations, and in some respects analyze why their generation is the way it is."[75] Here again is where media influences how we see ourselves, especially as we age. Are we doing well, as reflected in pharmaceutical commercials about older adults and sexuality, which portray active and attractive older adults who ride motorcycles into rosy sunsets? Or are we doing poorly, as depicted in films such as Yasujirō Ozu's (1953) masterpiece, *Tokyo Story* (often cited as one of the greatest films of all time), about an aging couple who come to the title metropolis to visit their far-too-busy-to-care kids. As film blogger Bill Gibron noted:

> That's why the movies rarely venture into the realm of age and aging. We don't want to see Grandpa and Grandma suffering or suggesting that their Autumn years are anything but a breeze. No, we like our elderly characters cocky, over sexed, and dealing with beneficent aliens. They should be cracking jokes instead of breaking hips, cursing like sailors instead of settling in for the inevitability of . . . well, you understand.[76]

Physical health is one factor in contributing to functional health. A study by Lachman and Agrigoroaei[77] found that physical fitness contributed to the maintenance of functional health and contributed to maintaining a healthy life as one aged. Given that, in the study reported herein, overall the participants reported good health, they well may be on their way to increasing their functional health as they age. Indeed, many of the participants reported healthy behaviors such as eating well and exercising regularly. In America there is a tendency to believe that health equals youth, while illness equals aging.[78] As The Who so famously sang, "I hope I die before I get old"[79] when talking about the Baby Boom generation, and now this generation are beyond thirty years and are alive and aging, rejecting the notion of old. Unsurprisingly, this generation has embraced the idea of health in ways not available to previous generations. This generation was on average freer from malnourishment, better clothed, and given greater hours for leisure and play.[80] This generation was also relatively free from infant and childhood disease and mortality with the advent of vaccines and vitamins.[81] Further, for the Baby Boomers at large, health can be seen as a moral issue connected to the rights of older people and the fairness of policies and regulations that might affect their opportunities to control their own destinies and self-invent, as individuals, their futures.[82]

The commitment to fitness and health by this generation can also be seen to have a buffering effect on death and aging anxiety by giving them the illusion of total control over their own well-being. A majority of the participants reported good health and behavior that supported their good health, such as the changes they had made in their lifestyles to take care of themselves. The good health of the participants allowed them to diminish concerns about ill-health as they age, preserving that youthful outlook and investing in another cultural worldview about youthfulness.

It would also seem that the projected pandering to the Baby Boomers and advertising moguls' ideas of youth might be overstated. Advertising for wrinkle creams, plastic surgery, Botox injections, and other anti-aging remedies are prevalent on television, radio, and online communication, yet this set of participants rejected these ideas as solutions to ensure youthful good looks. Consistent with their worldview of themselves as individuals and change agents, they, on the whole, rejected the idea of plastic surgery as a means to a youthful end. This group of self-selected participants would rather age naturally, without unnatural intervention, and view themselves as part of a demographic who will change how Americans age. It may also be that this set of participants is taking the idea of aging yet living youthfully forward as a new ideal for how older adults can do this successfully in a country that continues to deny the reality of death. Nonconformity has always been a trademark for a majority of this generation, and the advertisers may have seriously underestimated this among the participants and Baby Boomers at large. Pew Internet Research noted the proliferations of blogs for and by Baby Boomers that cover a range of topics from aging abundantly, ongoing sexual health and well-being, technology, social advocacy, and changing stigmatized models of aging.[83] Baby Boomers are blogging and taking charge of their own nonconformist narrative.

Another concept that could be part of the greater cultural complex is the idea of collective narcissism, "which describes an in-group identification tied to an emotional investment in an unrealistic belief about the unparalleled greatness of an in-group."[84] While the Boomers have often been categorized as self-centered and narcissistic, sometimes unfairly, the self-focus of these highly individual adults may in turn have led to an unconscious enjoinment in a collective narcissism that in turn could also be feeding the fires of the defenses that buffer them against the fear of aging and death. Thus the "culture of competitive individualism,"[85] which may have led to a "narcissistic preoccupation with the self"[86] may allow the Baby Boomers to proclaim self above others and elevate such ideas to a place of spiritual life, again tying to the sense of transcendence that the Baby Boomers have been seeking since their youth.[87] This type of worldview belief, of one as a spiritual seeker, also allows for the symbolic immortality that in turn helps buffer fear of death and dying. As Roof noted:

> Nowhere is this greater emphasis upon the seeker more apparent than in the large chain bookstore: the old "religion" section is gone and in its place is a growing set of more specific rubrics catering to popular topics such as angels, Sufism, journey, recovery, meditation, magic, inspiration, Judaica, astrology, gurus, Bible, prophecy, Evangelicalism, Mary, Buddhism, Catholicism, esoterica, and the like. Words like soul, sacred, and spiritual resonate to a curious public. [88]

Therefore, for the Boomers, this emotional investment in the in-group identification can be seen to be in harmony with the self, and further reinforces their belief in themselves as an ageless generation who has the ability to be flexible and adaptable.

> So do we baby boomers embrace our positive legacy, declare victory and fade away? My research says no. We are the generation that made L'Oreal and Just for Men necessary. We identified ourselves as "youth" and aren't letting go. So boomers will find new careers and hobbies and volunteer. They are a big part of what I call secular spiritualism, a growing rejection of materialism. People are embracing the notion that the American dream is measured in spiritual, not material, fulfillment. [89]

The Baby Boomers are a generation that was born into relative peace and prosperity to parents who had suffered through the Depression and World War

II who desired to give their children everything they possibly could. They were a cosseted generation who nevertheless had the shadow of the nuclear bomb and their immanent death hanging over their heads.[90] Is it any wonder then that this generation seems to have sought safety and buffering in an identity of perpetual youth to continue to protect them from the perceived threat of dying? The story of the first thirty years of the Baby Boomers is a story of an unprecedented baby culture turning into a youthful celebration, with all the self-absorption inherent in young people at that age.[91] However the inconsistencies that the Baby Boomers seem to embody are explicable when one recognizes that their mindset is not fixed, closed, or finished.[92] Their ability to change the world, innovate, and think outside the boxes, is laudable. This generation reshaped many social norms, including family life, religion and spirituality, and sex. This ability to adopt and adapt as they move along demonstrates the flexibility and plasticity of their thinking, even as it might seem inconsistent, allowing them to avoid the trap of a rigid mindset. This also gives credence to the idea of Baby Boomers as free agents. Free agents "are players who negotiate their contracts as individuals rather than as part of a team. Today there are more free agents off the playing fields than on them"[93] negotiating their way through life much like the Baby Boomers. This negotiation and self-reinvention demands a youthful sensibility, and for the participants in this study, there seemed the possibility of holding onto the worldviews of world change agents, individuality, and even scarcity, as a way of understanding the world and their place in it.

Without doubt this group will change how we think about aging and dying, and they will do things differently than previous generations, but perhaps that is their generational mission, to question the status quo and help us all rethink what we know, thus allowing for new and fresh perspectives to come into play, especially with the new technology available to us. It may be their purpose is to lead America into a new era of awareness about aging, death, and dying, where everyone may choose the right path for him or herself, and that, in the end, it may not be so dreadful. This ties back into Roof's reflection that for the Boomers, spirituality (and religion) are an inward reflection about knowing oneself, and that this generation's collective ideas and thoughts about aging are part of that spiritual path and about expanding the conversation.

12

Food, Sex, and Spirituality

Graham Harvey
The Open University

In widespread popular usage "spirituality" is often used to speak of more personal, more individual, and more immediate experiences than is "religion." In such uses "religion" is deemed to be institutional and hierarchical. In some perspectives, at its best religion is said to facilitate and encourage spirituality. At its worst, religion is vilified for constraining and policing individual or personal experiences of transcendence so as to protect the institutions of religion against enthusiasm, syncretism, and other messy realities. However, religion and spirituality are often thought to share a common focus on transcendent, otherworldly, or sacred realities rather than on the bodily concerns and relationships of the material world. This view is increasingly challenged by the rising tide of scholarly interest in vernacular, material, lived, and everyday religion, and by broader multidisciplinary attention to interactions or relationality. This is the context in which I seek, here, to test my argument for a thoroughly relational definition of "religion" by considering what "spirituality" is in real life.[1]

While many people do emphasize transcendence, subjectivity, and individuality when they speak about their religion or spirituality, frequently they also insist that religion and/or spirituality are intimately fused with every aspect of their lives. Scholars of religion are now increasingly interested in the material, bodily, and relational nature of religion in the real world in which food and sex are also generative activities. A definitional accentuation of "practice" or "doing religion" raises important questions about the practicality of religion and spirituality. A significant implication of this is that "religion and media" debates are not about secondary matters of the representation of transcendent experiences but are vital to improving understanding of the relational interactions that define religion and spirituality.

My discussion begins by welcoming recent understandings of religion that focus on lived religion. It casts the "relational turn" into sharper relief by a relatively brief tracing of the historical development of the modern privatized and belief-centered notion of religion that continues to misshape scholarly and popular understandings. A second section establishes that the focus of this chapter is not so much about food and sex themselves as it is about the practicality of spirituality as it is lived and enacted in the real world. Before discussing examples of practices that could be religion or spirituality or both, I invite you to consider chimpanzee religion and spirituality. This is an "elsewhere" in which we might see things differently so that we can be more bold in our analysis and theorizing about spirituality.

Whether or not this experiment succeeds, the term "spirituality" is widely employed in relation to varied phenomena. Thus, three sections of this chapter are devoted to considering phenomena that can be labeled "animism," "shamanism," and "indigenous spiritualities." I summarize the diversity of ways in which the terms are understood and presented both by "insiders" and by "observers." If Lewis Carroll's *Through the Looking Glass* character, Humpty Dumpty, had made these words "work hard" (as he says, he uses a word to mean "just what I choose it to mean—neither more nor less") he would also have "paid them extra."[2] While "animism" and "indigenous" are rewarded by playing central roles in dynamic debates about important matters, "shamanism" is largely exploited and abused. The chief point of these case studies is, however, to contribute to the "extra pay" being awarded to the word "spirituality" in this volume. Along with colleagues, it concerns me that popular claims about spirituality, and common assumptions about its relation to religion, are inadequately tested and contested. In particular, underlying many definitions of "spirituality" is a particular ontology that uncritically over-privileges immediate experience and other aspects of putative interiority. The three case studies are therefore followed by a section considering what makes "spirituality" either useful or misleading when applied to such phenomena. A final discussion outlines ways of differentiating religion from spirituality when we conceive of both as interactions in the everyday "food and sex" world.

Lived religion and licensed impracticality

In *Food, Sex and Strangers*, I built on incitements to emphasize vernacular religion,[3] lived religion,[4] and materiality.[5] I ought also to have included "everyday religion" among the terms that enable and enrich new approaches.[6] These writings and other colleagues have insisted that religion is something people do, though not all have adopted the verbal form "religioning" as a way of saying this.[7] Taking seriously the understanding that religion is (or may be) infused throughout people's lives (rather than being "just for festivals"), I sought to encourage greater efforts to see, understand, theorize, and discuss religion as a real-world engagement. If religion is an aspect of the pervasive relationality of life, it may be best observed in social interactions. To that end, I examined selected ways in which people do religion and, in the process, re-examined some of the critical issues that have engaged scholars of religion since the late nineteenth century. My enquiry is structured by questions about Maori *tapu* (taboo), Anishinaabe "totemic" relations, Yoruba "animist materialism," Jewish *kashrut* (purity systems), and Pagan ritualism. All of these exemplify the centrality of doing, acting, or practicing. They make the standard association of Christianity with "believing" rather than "doing" seem eccentric. When freed from the dominance of believing as a touchstone, religions may be seen as ways of living in relationship with others. (Importantly, such relationships often include differentiation from or opposition to others.) If Christianity is all about believing, then, I assert, "either Christianity is the only religion, or it is not a religion at all."[8] The evident flaw that generates this rhetorical flourish is that Christians, like other people, claim that they do not do Christianity only by believing irrational, unscientific, or nonempirical things, or by having private ideas or attitudes. Rather, many Christians assert that Christianity is an everyday matter. Toward the end of *Food, Sex and Strangers*, therefore, I offer a chapter titled "Christians do religion like other people." Building on research about the lived realities of Christianity strengthens my argument that religion is definitively about acts of relationship.[9]

In seeking to emphasize the relationality of religion(ing), my work resonates with the "relational turn" occurring in and between many disciplines. Here, the key fact that requires and rewards scholarly attention is interactivity—between humans, between human and other-than-human persons and species, and between those we commonly call "persons" and those we might call "things," "media," or even "places." In *Food, Sex and Strangers* I discuss the real-world relations within which religion is produced, takes place, and has some sort of this-worldly, practical role, outcome, or benefit.

The context of this discussion is a contrast between lived religion and what I will call "licensed impracticality." The alternative to theorizing religion as interactions between people in the real world is to limit it to the realm of private beliefs that have no contact or concern with everyday, secular or political domains, commitments, or activities. A key moment for the now dominant definition of religion (as "believing about transcendence") is the series of early modern European conflicts over the establishment of nation-states. These violent upheavals (often misidentified as "Wars of Religion") required the privatization and interiorization of religion.[10] Re-constituting Christians primarily as "believers" was a significant part of re-forming them to be citizens of modern states rather than as members of transnational communities or networks.[11] As modernity spread, so these processes reconfigured other religions, cultures, and communities. Religion was forcibly redefined as personal beliefs that *must not* have any contact or concern with matters deemed appropriate to the public duties and rights of citizens of nation-states.

When religious people acquiesced to this process, they became "believers" of licensed forms of impracticality, kin to entertainments and hobbies of an "improving" kind. This riffs with John Bowker's evocative term for religion, "licensed insanities," but plays to the modernist/Calvinist and capitalist denigration of unproductive leisure.[12] It was precisely the practicality or constructive power of religion that was a threat to the ideologues of early modernity, and it can still be a threat to the rule of contemporary nation-states. While private or personal ideas can be licensed, tolerated, or ignored (and even protected under United Nations rights charters), acted-upon affiliations with other constituencies cannot. When religions link people into communities that transcend or transgress national, ethnic, gender, class, and other boundaries they are often treated as having become dangerous. In such conditions, religions do sometimes invite commitments to activities that conflict with the totalitarian (if subtly mediated) demands of citizenship. However, evidence that "we have never been modern," as Bruno Latour has asserted, may be found in diverse overt or subtle acts of resistance to these processes of privatization, individualization, and interiorization.[13]

The media regularly broadcasts indications that religion remains central to many people's everyday lives, communal relations, identity construction, (inter) networked interactions, and other forms of belonging, becoming, and behaving. These include public acts of violence. Were this not so, researchers interested in religion would have little to do beyond quibbling about what causes such failures of rationality. The fact that religion remains potent in the twenty-first century gives us something to do. In that context, the fact that religion has some relation to "spirituality" requires more attention.

Food and sex

In truth, this chapter is not about food or sex themselves nor even about their role within religions or spiritualities. Rather "food and sex" is a merism that refers to everyday and ordinary lifeways and relations. These, I argue (here and elsewhere) have been paid inadequate attention in discussions of religion and spirituality.

It would be possible to treat food and sex in a different way. They are, after all, among the acts that form people into "us" over against "others" or "strangers." Rules, rituals, and discourses about food and sex are among the most common markers of religious identities and boundaries. They are not mere expressions of religion—they *are* religion in action. Religion is not a reification of society but an instance of people's socializing together. Therefore, rather than awarding priority to beliefs or believing while treating food and sex (or clothing, jewelry, institutions, symbols, or rituals) principally as media through which beliefs are declared, modulated, or disseminated, we are enabled to theorize more interestingly. The inherent relationality of foodways and sexuality (e.g., as creators or maintainers of families and friendships) makes them significant among the media by which religion is recognized as a communal, interactive practice. Equally, however, precisely because food and sex can be matters of private, personal, and individual choice, they may stand as emblems of (putatively) individualized spirituality. A discussion of people's choices of sexual and socializing partners and practices could tell us far more about the doing of spirituality in everyday life than the tired metaphor of the "spiritual supermarket" that often suggests that "spiritual shopping" is peculiarly random, impractical, and without regard to other social acts or relations.

Food and sex may be both religion and spirituality in their stereotypical forms while also requiring us to get beyond those stereotypes. They stand for the many acts that are inescapably both individual and communal, private and public, personal and shared, experienced and performed. They are transgressive of neat binaries. However, my intention is largely to leave food and sex in peripheral vision while focusing attention on the question of how spirituality and embodied, located, performed, and material engagements relate together. Therefore, the chapter is not primarily concerned to present data about food or sex in relation to specific religions or spiritualities (though the case studies do not entirely ignore them). The chapter's chief focus is on the commonalities and contrasts between religion and spirituality that relational acts reveal. In particular, what requires further thought is the mapping of community onto religion and individuality onto spirituality. What is at stake is understanding the links or barriers between spirituality—allegedly "inner experience" and/or personal encounters with transcendence—and people's practical, material, and relational concerns. Understanding that spirituality is something that people do in the world of birth, growth, death, decay, and recycling, I am provoked to think that it must necessarily have everyday purposes and outcomes. Going "elsewhere" in the following section may strengthen our intention to think new thoughts.

Chimpanzees and ants

If we seek evidence of religion and/or spirituality elsewhere than among humans, we may find it among the closest of our other-than-human relations, chimpanzees. We co-evolved for millennia and still have much in common, including DNA, tool use, propensities toward intimacy and violence, and inquiring minds. Thus, asking whether or not chimpanzees do anything recognizable as religion makes sense.[14] In discussing the evolution of early humans, Steven Mithen could have integrated religious rites and taboos into his compelling book-length argument that language and music originated in what he calls a "holistic manipulative multi-modal, musical and mimetic" communication system, at least partly shared by prehuman primates.[15] Perhaps religion evolved alongside language and music to express respect between species, especially, perhaps, those deemed edible. This is, of course, speculative. Primatologists have, however, observed evidence that we might recognize as religion among contemporary chimpanzees. Volker Sommer demonstrates that some chimpanzees eat ants but not termites (although they could eat both) while others eat termites but avoid eating ants. He concludes that chimpanzee dietary rules are similar to activities readily recognized among humans as religiously founded taboos, that is, an "arbitrary/non-practical aspect of certain behaviours that assist to create some sort of random in-group/out-group identity (sometimes with violence)."[16]

Whether this is the same as saying that chimpanzees are spiritual or possess spiritualities among their cultural repertoires is now at stake. James Harrod advances an argument that chimpanzees behave in ways that match his "non-anthropocentric, trans-species definition of religion."[17] That is, chimpanzees engage in complex and deliberate behaviors that demonstrate prototypical characteristics of religion such as "reverence, careful observation, wonder, awe, and empathic intimacy."[18] For instance, Harrod presents data about actions indicative of awe, wonder, or fascination while watching sunsets or encountering waterfalls or fires. These and some negative forms of awe lead Harrod—citing Nancy Howell's work—to think that chimpanzees possess "connectedness, interdependence, and sociality" and "symbolic capacity."[19] His definition of religion emphasizes matters that are commonly labeled "spirituality." If Sommer and Harrod are correct, chimpanzees structure their communities by taboo protocols and also experience and communicate awe, fascination, reverence, and interdependency.

I am not proposing that "spirituality" should be employed as a critical term for specific experiences, feelings, or attitudes (like awe). To the contrary, part of what needs testing is the word's frequent association with such "inwardness." The following three sections consider what "spirituality" can mean when used in relation to communities, networks, or practices associated with "animism," "shamanism," and "indigenous spirituality." Then I will ask whether "spirituality" is helpful in analyzing these and other phenomena.

Animism

In recent decades, "animism" has taken on a new meaning. While the echoes of Edward Tylor's usage (defining religion as the "belief in spirits") continue to be heard in some cognitive studies of religion, it is more commonly treated as a label for one type of religion among many.[20] For example, it can be alleged that animists believe in ancestors or ghosts, whereas theists believe in deities. Sometimes West African populations are said to be divided between Christianity, Islam, and animism. However, a third use of the term interests me more.

In 1999, Nurit Bird-David signaled a "re-visiting" of the "animism" following fieldwork among the Nayaka of India and reflection on ethnography and philosophy. Like others involved in this "re-visitation," she cites the research of Irving Hallowell among the Anishinaabe of southern central Canada.[21] In contrast with Tylor's animism, much of this new approach understands animism to be rooted in the recognition "that the world is full of persons, only some of whom are human, and that life is always lived in relationship with others."[22] Here, the important questions are not about life but about living, for example, "what constitutes good ways to live alongside other-than-human persons?" and "how should we show respect to those who we wish to eat?" There are multiple versions of this understanding. It is, for example, the underlying ethos and inspirational provocation of a "Bear Feast" that takes place at midwinter in southern England.

The primary purpose of this festive gathering is to say "thank you," "please," and "sorry" to those other-than-human persons who have been or will be (if they are willing) food. The expression of gratitude and sorrow, and the seeking of permission from food-persons, is ritualized as an encounter with a bear. This is inspired by those arctic and subarctic cultures in which bears are respected as close relations of humans, powerful persons, responsive to the polite etiquette of hunters and their kin-groups, and as good food. The "Bear Feast" brings together around sixty people each year at midwinter at a relatively secluded venue. Over a long weekend, the group (many of whom participate every year) share communal sleeping, cooking, and eating arrangements. Around fires, they share stories, music, life-experiences, and food. The centerpiece of the Feast is a day-long ritual-complex, which begins before dawn with the hunting of a bear who is made present both by an antique Siberian bearskin and by a ritualist dressed (both playfully and powerfully) as a bear. A feast is prepared throughout much of the day, utilizing ingredients brought to the site by all the participants. This features venison from locally culled deer, but since between a fifth and a quarter of the participants each year are vegetarian or vegan, these and other diets are also catered for. The resulting evening feast is, unsurprisingly, a highlight of the event and the focus of speeches and songs addressed to the bear and other food-persons. These liturgical elements are adapted from such texts as the *Kalevala* (a Finnish and Karelian epic compiled from folk sources by Elias Lönnrot in 1835 and ethnographies of other bear traditions).[23] The idea that the consumed bear returns to another realm to be reborn is dramatized in the ascent of the bearskin through the smoke-hole of the impressive wood-timbered and turf-roofed building used for the feast. The community then process outside to see the bear in its stellar form in the northern sky.

Similar bear-ritual focused groups and events exist elsewhere. Facebook pages, websites, and word-of-mouth recommendations are crucial to their dissemination and development. Some of these movements and events continue indigenous cultural practices, especially in the arctic and subarctic. Others are newly minted to meet the needs of people for whom this seems a natural step on from efforts to evolve an "ecologically responsible spirituality." They find that practical matters such as foodways ground their religion or spirituality in everyday life. For those who espouse the kind of animism that seeks to respect all other-than-human persons, eating is an immensely intimate act. While participants in the Bear Feast and similar movements do not all identify with one religious organization or institution, many do self-identify as Pagans. As the label "animist" gains currency among Pagans and others, addresses to food-persons are likely to become increasingly popular. Indeed, they may become even more popular because they create a feedback loop in which "saying grace" to food-persons (rather than to transcendent creators) roots ritual or etiquette in everyday and ecological life. The crucial question (for this chapter) as to whether this phenomena evidences religion or spirituality will be considered after an introduction to two further case studies.

Shamanisms

Shamans first entered European and then global vocabularies in the writings of eighteenth-century travelers and missionaries returning from Siberia to metropolitan centers in Russia and Germany. The term has carried so many meanings that it would be foolish to attempt to restrict its applications. In 1705, Nicholas Witsen depicted a Siberian Evenk shaman as a "priest of the devil" in a woodcut illustration.[24] By the twentieth century shamans had been transmogrified from world-manipulating magicians concerned with the everyday needs of localized kinship-groups into the embodiment of elevated spirituality. The "shamanism" constructed around them is often said not to be a new religion but the original spirituality. The path from magician to spiritual leader is way-marked by the work of Mircea Eliade,[25] Carlos Castaneda,[26] and Michael Harner.[27] It also benefitted from significant cultural shifts, including Christianity's loss of pre-eminence in defining proper religion, the elevation of individualist interiority as modernity's primary ontology, and the way in which concerns about environmentalism, gender, and health had made the denigration of nature and bodies less easy to articulate. These and other factors enabled the emergence of what we might call spiritual-shamanism or shamanism-as-spirituality, although this is more often called (often with a sneer suggestive of outright dismissal) "neo-shamanism."

Eliade's construction of indigenous shamanism privileged what he called "techniques of ecstasy" that enabled shamans to "journey to the upper world." These techniques included rhythmic sounds and/or movements, sensory stimulation or deprivation, guided visualization, and psycho-dramas involving costumes or masks that disrupt ordinary expectations and experiences. Castaneda's teachings (allegedly those of a Jacqui medicine man) on accessing "non-ordinary reality" were attractive to some in the long-1960s but their embeddedness in psychedelia limited their acceptance beyond the counterculture. Harner has more successfully popularized some of Eliade's "techniques" as ways of achieving "altered states of consciousness" (ASC) or "shamanic states of consciousness" (SSC). In particular, rhythmic music and visualization have become typical within this new universal kind of shamanism. Under the guidance of workshop facilitators, people may, while listening to particular drum rhythms, visualize descending into an underworld in which they meet a "power animal" or "helper," usually understood as archetypal aspects of themselves. The animals most commonly reported in the "talking circles" that follow such meditative encounters are those of North American prairies. In more advanced workshops participants ascend into an upper world to seek knowledge and power to aid them in therapeutic efforts for themselves or their clients. The resonances of Harner's "core shamanism" with Jungian and other individualized, psychologized self-therapies form bridges into the kind of human-potential or self-development practices and communities that are often labeled "new age." Shamanism websites and events often also sell CDs of drumming recordings, smudging fans, and other accoutrements of the practice. They typically emphasize the "self-knowledge" and "self-empowerment" that define the claimed foci and outcomes of such shamanism.

Carlos Fausto asserts that "the most noticeable fact about this myriad of neoshamanic sites and rites is not its profusion but rather the absence of blood and tobacco."[28] While Siberia is the *locus classicus* of shamanism, Amazonian cultures have inspired much of the new style. The contrast between Harner's more anthropological book about the Amazonian Jivaro/Shuar and Conibo[29] and his manual for core shamans[30] is suggestive. The first narrates powerful experiences following from the ingestion of *ayahuasca* (a potent brew of plant extracts that induces vomiting and visions). The later book is clear that consciousness can be altered largely by visualization. Even the continuing growth in popularity of "*ayahuasca* shamanism tourism" demonstrates the salience of Fausto's contrast. In such contexts *ayahuasca* is a technique for gaining self-knowledge rather than a purifying purgative. Similarly, neo-shamans might use tobacco smoke to cleanse individual auras but not to disguise the smell of blood, because they do not combat cannibalistic sorcerers. Ayahuasca, tobacco, and blood are, then, helpful media to convey differences between the ritual repertoires and rhetorics of these shamanisms.

Indigenous spiritualities

Like "animism" and "shamanism," "indigenous" is used in many ways, few of them straightforward or uncontested. Its synonymity with "native" is, for example, made more difficult when referring to extensive diasporas.[31] While the United Nations makes use of the term "indigenous peoples" (e.g., in its Permanent Forum on Indigenous Issues, UNPFII), the roughly synonymous "aboriginal" or "First Nations" are preferred elsewhere. All these terms can imply the precedence of dwelling and belonging, and contest assertions of colonial conquest or ownership. Against this, the rhetoric of invasive nation-states inverts the celebration of prior relation with lands, insisting on replacement and ownership by either individuals or state governments. Here, indigeneity, aboriginality, and natality are, at best, reasons for consideration of special or minority protection or rights that must be subject to colonial settler rule. Unsurprisingly, such positions are contested in global, national, local, and online forums, including in activist movements such as "Idle No More."

Growing interdisciplinary interests in indigeneity is advanced in *Constructing the Indigenous*.[32] In my contribution I argue that both "indigenous" and "religion" are correctly deployed strategically rather than as bland descriptions.[33] It encourages a concerted effort to rethink what phenomena, approaches, and theorization may be possible if "religion" and "indigenous" are considered in relation to emerging debates. Much the same is true of "spirituality." Something changes when we collocate "indigenous" not with "religion" but with "spirituality." Although many invasion-era texts denied that particular indigenous peoples displayed any evidence of "religion" (and linked this to primitivity or animality), it has now become common to fantasize indigeneity as the epitome of spirituality. Internet searches for "Native American Spirituality," for example, are likely to return valorizations of wisdom, profundity, elevated consciousness, harmony with nature, and cosmic interconnectedness.

There is nothing neutral about these clichés. It is an aspect of "imperialist nostalgia,"[34] that is, a "romanticization that assumes a pose of innocent yearning thus concealing its complicity with often brutal domination."[35] "Appropriation" is frequently used for the activities of other-than-indigenous people who consider it appropriate to imitate indigenous "spiritual" practices or cultural technologies such as sweat lodges, smudging, and "dreaming" rites.[36] If "appropriation" seems neutral, perhaps its use in fiscal and military contexts may aid understanding of the colonial power dynamics involved. The beneficiaries of such processes are rarely, if ever, those being imitated but the "takers."[37] This is integral to the problematic collocation "indigenous spirituality." To be blunt, indigenous people are not "spiritual" in the way that "spiritual" people wish them to be, and what is appropriated is not "indigenous."

Shorter tackles this apparent enigma by demonstrating that "spirituality" is the wrong word to associate with Native American peoples' traditional lifeways.[38] He demonstrates that the pervasive theme of indigenous knowledge systems is relational, locational, and interactive engagement. "Spirituality" misdirects attention toward supernatural, disembodied, dislocated, and quietist tropes. It is too strongly flavored by dualist separations of body from mind and/or "spirit" and by over-emphasis on individualist interiority. In contrast, Native American lived realities require a redirection of attention toward practical matters embraided with actual and desired relationships within the larger-than-human community in the everyday world. In Shorter's words:

> In the very long history of this continent's inhabitation, native people were relating socially, across species and life forms, in material ways, and for practical reasons, much longer than they have not been doing so.[39]

He proposes that "spiritual" should be replaced by "related" as it encapsulates the this-worldly, embodied and emplaced ontological necessities, ethical imperatives, and communal interactivities that are the *leitmotifs* of the majority of Native American traditional cultures.

Unsurprisingly, therefore, I cannot supply an example of what truly indigenous "indigenous spirituality" might look like. The practice of those who wish to be "as spiritual as indigenous people" may be exemplified by forms of "vision quest" in which, by meditative visualization, people encounter power animals at the heart of their true or higher selves. They may imagine that Lakota style feather- and bead-accoutrements link them to "the sacred earth" or other emblems of cosmic harmony and ecological sagacity. One fashionable sonic marker of such a spirituality is Lakota flute music, though the sounds of Andean pan-pipes, Aboriginal didgeridoos, and "Celtic" bodhrans may compete for popularity. Importantly, it is rare for practitioners to devote themselves to one cultural source. Most fuse their "indigenous spirituality" with elements of yoga, Reiki, tantra, Sufism, and more. For some academic and skeptical observers this very eclecticism makes such practices suspect. There is, however, no justification for separating the lived practices of religion or spirituality from the broader culture of practitioners, which in this case is largely eclectic and globalized. Over-emphasis on the boundedness of cultural traditions does not advance our understanding of religious or spiritual phenomena. The question that remains is what scholarly value there is in categorizing activities and ideas as "religion" or "spirituality."

What makes these things spiritual?

The phenomena I have introduced can be identified as religious or spiritual or both. Different schemas and reasons may be deployed in people's preferred terminology. Here, I set out some elements of animism, shamanism, and indigenous spiritualities that may be allocated to either the "religion" or "spirituality" category.

My "animism" case study is of an emerging network of people who celebrate a shared effort to re-constitute themselves as co-dwellers within the larger-than-human world. Most identify as Pagans of various kinds, others as Christians, Buddhists, Humanists, and "unaffiliated." Some "Bear Feast" participants may think that the intensity of the event is "spiritual." At the height of their immersion in the central ritual, they may have senses of being within a community that transcends both humanity and their "ordinary experience." While the "Bear Feast" has easily identifiable organizers and an emergent liturgical tradition, these act as facilitators rather than as imposed constraints. These and other factors may fit the pattern generally accepted as "spirituality" rather than "religion."

The feast also includes matters that might be "religion." It is thoroughly ritualized, not only when addressing "food persons" but also even when tending fires and donning costumes that are not only about keeping warm in winter. It is framed by a taboo in which the word "bear" is avoided and participants address "honey paw," "golden one," or "bee wolf." Ritual and taboo are marginalized in dominant rhetoric about spirituality, even if they are recognizable once attention is paid. The most stereotypical contrast between religion and spirituality, however, is a profoundly ontological one. The Bear Feast is not a self-empowerment event, and altered states of consciousness are rarely spoken about. What places the Feast firmly within the boundaries of the "new" animism is its focus on relationships between persons (human and other-than human; participants and those who they eat). The interiorized "self" of post-Reformation modernity is deconstructed as participants devote themselves to the "in between" relational personhood of animism. In gratefully addressing food-persons, Bear Feast animists transcend a history that would make religion impractical and irrelevant to everyday life.

Neo-shamanism is more about spirits than stomachs, more about individuals than relations, more about "non-ordinary reality" than the everyday world of food and sex. This is not to say that individuals are not, in reality, members of communities. As Martin wisely says, "[T]he problem with the ideology of individualism is not that it dissolves community but that it obscures how 'individuals' are constituted by their communities."[40] Neo-shamanism is not an individual practice but that of networks or assemblages. What makes this a "spirituality" rather than a "religion" is not that such people are individualized or individuated but that they commit themselves to the construction of an ontology that privileges imagined forms of individuality and interiority. "Traditional" Amazonian and Siberian shamans can be equally disjointed from their communities, especially when they are feared. However, their work constructs both themselves and their communities as relational beings. These shamans and neo-shamans engage in rituals, even if the latter sometimes denigrate "mere ritual." Both are embedded in cultural and social complexes of production, distribution, and consumption. The distinction between the religion of shamans and the spirituality of neo-shamans may not, then, be what it is thought to be by many participants and observers, that is, a conflict between community and individuality. Mere affiliation to a movement or ideology does not re-organize reality or ontology. However, the *attempt* to drive shamanism deeply into private and personal realms is what usefully links neo-shamanism with "spirituality."

Unsurprisingly, the label "indigenous spirituality" evidences a tension between religion and spirituality. I agree with Shorter that "spirituality" is unhelpful when applied to indigenous religious traditions and practices. "Religion" is a more useful term with which to refer to locally appropriate etiquette in which human and other-than-human persons interact.

However, the kind of "indigenous spirituality" that is constructed and disseminated in many neo-shamanic or so-called new age websites does match popular usage of the term "spirituality." Despite claiming to be holistic, this indigenous spirituality is largely disconnected from the real lives of real communities (including the everyday lives of many practitioners). Exemplifying this, after one First Nation leader spoke in Britain about the struggles of his community against poverty, racism, suicide, alcoholism, and other daily realities, he was asked "how can we be as spiritual as you?" as if he might serve as a personal development guru. The question that seems required by this is what practical use spirituality has in the real, food and sex, everyday world.

Spiritual as privatizing religion

Despite Orsi's assertion that "either/or is not the appropriate register for the critical study of religion," in widespread academic use, religion and spirituality are often contrasted quite starkly.[41] Their dualistic usage replays and reinforces distinctions between individuals and communities, interiority and institutions, and experiences and rules. But, as Martin suggests, just because people claim to be individuals with a personal, interiorized spirituality, we do not need to agree that such atomization is real.[42] "Individuals" are necessarily members of communities, albeit of networks that over-determine individuality and interiority and employ media to support their epistemology. Ontologically, we are all related and relational. Something more interesting becomes visible when we place these distinctions in a wider historical and cultural context. Orsi argues that:

> The modern world was not supposed to look the way it does . . . This sort of [everyday] religion . . . was fated to be outgrown by the world's cultures, beginning with the West (specifically northern Europe) and then spreading across the globe, to be succeeded by a modern liberal faith sanctioned by (and providing sanction for) law, political theory, epistemology and science.[43]

Orsi also introduces a "fundamentalist modern religion"—not defined by literalist biblicism, but by a refusal to separate religion from politics and all other social domains—but this invites a different discussion. "Spirituality" is an apt term for the most determined forms of this "modern liberal faith," or what I have called "licensed impracticality." When people acquiesce to the conversion of religion into personal beliefs and private believing, spirituality is a way to build communities that resonate with the wider (alienated, consumerist) milieu. The epistemology required when nation-state ideologues re-created people as individual citizens is, unsurprisingly, productive of and mediated by spiritualities of inwardness (of spirit, soul, mind, consciousness, or self). In turn, since these match the practical demands and processes of globalized markets, accusing "new agers" of being the tools of capitalist consumerism is too banal. There is no more practical way to be "spiritual" and live within this modern world.

"Liberal modern religion" or "spirituality," "fundamentalist modern religion," and the still enchanted "everyday religion" all have practical outcomes in the construction or maintenance of communities, each using a range of ancient and contemporary media in appropriate ways. Each can match the needs of practitioners to engage with the modern world. However, academics studying religion have largely colluded with the liberal, nation- state project by emphasizing religious subjectivity and by neglecting materiality and relationality (except as mediations). Had the study of religions been shaped by the study of indigeneity, we might have paid more attention to food and sex, but not as "expressions" of a prior and inward spirituality. Instead, we may have better understood Te Pakaka Tawhai's statement that among his (Maori) people "the purpose of religious activity is doing violence with impunity" as people seek to feed and shelter guests within a radically interpersonal and interactive multi-species world.[44] In this "food and sex" world, religion is practical when it enables human relationality within the larger-than-human community to flourish.

Notes

Chapter 1

1 Paul H. Ray and Sherry Ruth Anderson, *The Cultural Creatives: How 50 Million People Are Changing the World* (New York: Three Rivers Press, 2000).

2 Sara MacKian, *Everyday Spirituality* (New York: Palgrave Macmillan, 2012), 69. http://www.palgraveconnect.com/pc/doifinder/10.1057/9780230365028.0001. E-book.

3 Jack Gilbert, "The Forgotten Dialect of the Heart," in *The Great Fires: Poems, 1982–1992* (New York: Alfred A. Knopf, 1994). Accessed February 8, 2015, The Poetry Center at Smith College, http://www.smith.edu/poetrycenter/poets/theforgottendialect.html.

4 Wade Clark Roof, *Spiritual Marketplace* (Princeton, NJ: Princeton University Press, 1999), 29.

5 Wade Clark Roof et al., "Forum: American Spirituality," *Religion and American Culture—a Journal of Interpretation* 9, no. 2: 136, 131–57.

6 Anthony Giddens, *Modernity and Self-Identity: Self and Society in the Late-Modern Age* (Stanford: Stanford University Press, 1991).

7 Roof et al., "Forum," 137.

8 Sarah M. Pike, *New Age and Neopagan Religions in America* (New York: Columbia University Press, 2004), 14.

9 Paul Heelas, *Spiritualities of Life: New Age Romanticism and Consumptive Capitalism* (New York: Blackwell, 2008), 53.

10 Ibid.

11 Ibid., 5.

12 Ibid., 55, 56.

13 Ibid., 55.

14 Roof, *Spiritual Marketplace*, 35.

15 Pike, *New Age*, 14; Heelas, *Spiritualities of Life*, 53.

16 See, for example, Roof, *Spiritual Marketplace*; Stewart Hoover, *Religion in the Media Age* (New York: Routledge, 2006), Paul Heelas, Linda Woodhead, Benjamin Seel, Karin Tusting, and Bronislaw Szerszynski, *The Spiritual Revolution: Why Religion Is Giving Way to Spirituality* (Oxford: Blackwell, 2005).

17 See, for example, Heelas, *Spiritualities of Life*; Pike, *New Age*; Steven Sutcliffe, *Children of the New Age: A History of Spiritual Practices* (London: Routledge, 2003).

18 Sutcliffe, *Children of the New Age*, 112.
19 See Harvey, this volume, p. 194.
20 MacKian, *Everyday Spirituality*, 3.
21 Pamela Klassen, "Practice," in *Keywords in Media, Religion and Culture*, ed. David Morgan (New York: Routledge, 2008), 137.
22 Discourses are ways in which we structure and create knowledge (Michel Foucault, "After Word: The Subject and Power," in *Michel Foucault,* ed. H. Dreyfus and P. Rabinow [Chicago: University of Chicago Press, 1982], 206–26). Thus, discourses include social practice as well as thought and symbol. Discourses constitute us in ways that implicate the body, as well as the mind, and, to use the language of our respondents, the spirit. Discourses situate us into ways of being and ways of knowing. Finally, discourses are fields of power and involve "strategies of domination as well as those of resistance" (Irene Diamond and Lee Quinby [eds.], *Feminism and Foucault: Reflections on Resistance* [Boston: Northeastern University Press, 1988]). Focusing on discourses allows us to examine the relationship between mystery and the mundane, aspirations, and action.
23 Stewart M. Hoover, *Religion in the Media Age* (London: Routledge, 2006). Elsewhere, Hoover wrote, "The most logical standpoint of understanding converging fields—media studies, religious studies, material culture, ritual studies—is via *practice*" (in Hoover and Clark [eds.], *Practicing Religion in an Age of Media,* [New York: Columbia University Press, 2002], 2.
24 MacKian, *Everyday Spirituality*, 2.
25 Hoover and Clark, *Practicing Religion*, 2002.
26 Nick Couldry, "Mediatization and the Future of Field Theory," *Community Formations: Working Paper* 3 (2013): 3.
27 Hoover, *Religion in the Media Age*.
28 Anthony Elliott and John Urry, *Mobile Lives* (New York: Routledge, 2010).
29 Mary Chayko, *Portable Communities* (Albany: University of New York Press, 2008).
30 Zygmunt Bauman, *Liquid Love: On the Frailty of Human Bonds* (Hoboken, NJ: John Wiley & Sons, 2013), 70.
31 S. Brent Plate, *A History of Religion in 51/2 Objects: Bringing the Spiritual to Its Senses* (Boston: Beacon Press, 2014).
32 See Hoover, *Religion in the Media Age*, 2006; Nick Couldry, *Media, Society, World: Social Theory and Digital Media Practice* (Cambridge: Polity Press, 2012); Rachel Wagner, *Godwired: Religion, Ritual and Virtual Reality* (New York: Routledge, 2012); Heidi Campbell, *When Religion Meets New Media.* (New York: Routledge, 2010); Lorne L. Dawson and Douglas E. Cowan (eds.), *Religion Online: Finding Faith on the Internet* (New York: Routledge, 2013).

33 Peter Horsfield, "Media," in *Key Words in Religion*, ed. David Morgan (New York: Routledge, 2008), 111–22.
34 The culturalist view is often linked to William Carey's seminal work, *Communication as Culture* (New York: Routledge, 1992), where he differentiates between the dominant "transmission" view of media and the "ritual" view of communication. This focus on ritual provided the spark to considerations of media as culture.
35 Horsfield, "Media," 113.
36 Ibid., 111.
37 Williams Raymond, "Culture Is Ordinary," in *Resources of Hope: Culture, Democracy, Socialism*, ed. Raymond Williams and Robin Gables (London: Verso, 1989), 7.
38 Horsfield, "Media," 113.
39 See Hoover, *Religion in the Media Age*; Lynn Schofield Clark, *The Parent App: Understanding Families in the Digital Age* (Oxford: Oxford University Press, 2013); Nick Couldry, "Mediatization."
40 Horsfield, "Media," 118.
41 Ibid., 116.
42 Ibid., 120.
43 See, for example, David Morgan, *The Embodied Eye* (Berkeley: University of California Press, 2012) and Paul Teusner, "Imaging Religious Identity: Intertextual Play Among Postmodern Christian Bloggers." *Online-Heidelberg Journal of Religions on the Internet* 4, no. 1 (2010).
44 Horsfield, "Media," 119.
45 Hoover, *Religion in the Media Age*, 68.
46 Klassen, "Practice," 139–40.
47 Elliott and Urry, *Mobile Lives*, 5.
48 Horsfield, "Media," 117.
49 Monica M. Emerich, *The Gospel of Sustainability: Media, Market, and LOHAS* (Champaign, IL: University of Illinois Press, 2011).
50 See Francis G. Couvares, "Hollywood, Main Street, and the Church: Trying to Censor the Movies before the Production Code," *American Quarterly* 44, no. 4 (1992): 584–616; Leonard J. Leff and Jerrold Simmons, *Dame in the Kimono: Hollywood, Censorship and the Production Code* (Lexington: The University of Kentucky, 2010); Terry Lindvall, *Sanctuary Cinema: Origins of the Christian Film Industry* (New York: New York University Press, 2007).
51 Nick Couldry, "Media Ethics: Towards a Framework for Media Producers and Media Consumers," in *Media Ethics Beyond Borders*, ed. Stephen J. A. Ward and Herman Wasserman (New York: Routledge, 2010), 59–73.
52 Meg Leta Ambrose, and Jef Ausloos, "The Right to Be Forgotten across the Pond." *Journal of Information Policy* 3 (2013): 1–23.

53 Couldry, "Media Ethics."
54 See, for example, Jeremy R. Carrette and Richard King, *Selling Spirituality: The Silent Takeover of Religion* (New York: Psychology Press, 2005).
55 Lynn Schofield Clark (ed.), *Religion, Media and the Marketplace* (New Brunswick, NJ: Rutgers University Press, 2007); Mara Einstein, *Brands of Faith* (New York: Routledge, 2008).
56 See Mark Andrejevic, *Reality TV: The Work of Being Watched* (Lanham: Rowman & Littlefield Publishers, 2004); and Dallas Smythe, "On the Audience Commodity," *Media and Cultural Studies: Keyworks* (1981): 230–56.
57 Elliott and Urry, *Mobile Lives*, 5.
58 See, for example, Clark, *The Parent App*; Hoover, *Religion in the Media Age*; Heidi Campbell, *Exploring Religious Community Online: We Are One in the Network* (New York: Peter Lang, 2005).
59 See also Hoover, *Religion in the Media Age.*
60 Elliott and Urry, *Mobile Lives*, 5.
61 See, for example, Chapters 2, 5, 8, and 9.
62 Robert W. McChesney, "Global Media, Neoliberalism, and Imperialism," *Monthly Review* 52, no. 10 (March 2001), http://monthlyreview.org/2001/03/01/global-media-neoliberalism-and-imperialism/.
63 Horsfield, "Media."; Hoover, *Religion in the Media Age.*
64 Elliott and Urry, *Mobile Lives*; Chayko, *Portable Communities*; Jennie Germann Molz, *Travel Connections: Tourism, Technology and Togetherness in a Mobile World* (New York: Routledge, 2012).
65 Lynn Schofield Clark invites such an approach in her work on family dynamics in the digital age. She notes, "The field of media studies reminds us to think of communication technologies not as things we merely use but as innovations that evolve in specific contexts in relation to perceived needs and which continue to evolve in relation to both those needs and to practices that specific technologies discourage or make possible" Clark, *The Parent App*, xi.
66 Jonathan Sterne, "Bourdieu, Technique and Technology," *Cultural Studies* 17, nos. 3–4 (2003): 373, 377.
67 Couldry, in fact, has taken up this effort in his engagement with the concept mediatization, which he argues, "needs to be conceived as a meta-process that *emerges from* the continuous, cumulative circulation and embedding of media contents *across* everyday social action" Couldry, "Mediatization," 3.
68 Jolyon Mitchell, "Narrative," in *Key Words in Media, Religion and Culture*, ed. David Morgan (New York: Routledge, 2008).
69 Hoover, S. and Echchaibi, N. (2012). The "Third Spaces" of Digital Religion, discussion paper, Boulder, CO: Center for Media, Religion, and Culture, University of Colorodo Boulder. Available online: http://cmrc.colorado.edu/wp- content/uploads/2012/03/Third-Spaces-Essay-Draft-Final.pdf

70 Henry Jenkins, *Convergence Culture* (New York: New York University Press, 2006).

71 Curtis Coats, *From Mediascape to Meaning and Back Again: An Interactionist Analysis of Spiritual Tourism in Sedona, Arizona* Doctoral dissertation, ProQuest, 2008, 192.

72 For a discussion of interpretive communities, see Stanley Fish, *Is There a Text in this Class: The Authority of Interpretive Communities* (Cambridge: Harvard University Press, 1980).

73 Hoover and Echchaibi, "The 'Third Spaces.'"

74 Ibid., 14.

75 It is important to remember that media access remains a critical ethical issue in media studies (see Couldry, "Media Ethics," 2010) and a global concern taken up by the UN Millennium Goals (see Target 8.F, http://www.un.org/millenniumgoals/global.shtml). Further, it is important to note those who consciously choose to *not* adopt technology in spiritual practice. See, for example, Michele Rosenthal et al., "Navigating Media Ambivalence: Strategies of Resistance, Avoidance, and Engagement with Media Technology in Everyday Life," *Selected Papers of Internet Research* 3 (2013).

76 Richard Ek, "Media Studies, Geographical Imaginations and Relational Space," in *Geographies of Communication: The Spatial Turn in Media Studies*, ed. Jesper Falkheimer and André Jansson (Göteborg, Sweden: Nordicom, 2006), 45–66.

77 Ibid., 49.

78 Ibid., 53–4.

79 Molz, *Travel Connections*, 43.

80 Elliott and Urry, *Mobile Lives*, 5.

81 Ek wrote: "The notion that space (and time) are 'compressed', or that space is even annihilated, by hyper- or late modern technologies (like information and communication technologies), and that media and communication technologies are partly 'responsible' for increased placelessness and the loss of a sense of place is fundamentally built on an ontology that claims that space and place are 'here', media and information technologies are 'there', and that space and place (here) are shaped by the influence of media and information technologies (there). This is an ontology that does not harmonise with the relational space paradigm (Ek, "Media Studies," 54, 55).

82 Ibid.

83 S. Elizabeth Bird, *The Audience in Everyday Life: Living in a Media World* (New York: Routledge, 2003).

84 Jeremy Stolow, "Religion and/as Media." *Theory, Culture, & Society* 22, no. 4 (2005): 119–45.

85 Leonard N. Primiano, "Manifestations of the Religious Vernacular: Ambiguity, Power, and Creativity," in *Vernacular Religion in Everyday Life: Expressions of Belief*, ed. Ülo Valk and Marion Bowman (London: Equinox, 2012), 382–94.

86 Graham Harvey, "Food, Sex, and Spirituality,"

87 Gregory Stanczak and Donald Miller, "Engaged Spirituality: Spirituality and Social Transformation in Mainstream American Religious Traditions: Report Supplement," (Los Angeles: The University of Southern California Center for Religion and Civic Culture, 2002), 14. https://crcc.usc.edu/files/2015/02/EngagedSpirituality2.pdf, Accessed May 19, 2015

Chapter 2

1 The material in this chapter was collected in the framework of a larger and still ongoing research project titled "Natural Parenting in the Digital Age: At the Confluence of Mothering, Religion, Environmentalism and Technology," funded through two mobility fellowships of the Swiss National Science Foundation and hosted by the Department for the Study of Religion at the University of Toronto. Interviews were conducted in conformity with the ethical protocols for research with human subjects at the University of Toronto (protocol reference number 28397). Informed consent was secured from all interviewees and respondents' names have been omitted or changed. The interview with "Vanessa" was conducted on January 24, 2013, through audio-visual communication. Other online materials quoted in this chapter were or still are publicly available contents. I wish to thank the Swiss National Science Foundation for its support and the Department for the Study of Religion for hosting my postdoctoral research stay.

2 Pamela Klassen, "Practice," in *Key Words in Religion, Media and Culture*, ed. David Morgan (London and New York: Routledge), 136–47, esp. 143.

3 Itie C. van Hout (ed.), *Beloved Burden: Baby-Wearing around the World* (Amsterdam: Royal Tropical Institute, 2011).

4 Monica Emerich, *The Gospel of Sustainability: Media, Market, and LOHAS* (Urbana: University of Illinois Press, 2011).

5 Chris Bobel, "Resisting, but Not Too Much: Interrogating the Paradox of Natural Mothering," in *Maternal Theory. Essential Readings* (Toronto: Demeter Press, 2007), 782–91, esp. 49.

6 Judith Stadtman Tucker, "Mothering in the Digital Age: Navigating the Personal and Political in the Virtual Sphere," in *Mothering in the Third Wave*, ed. A. Kinser (Toronto: Demeter Press, 2008), 199–212; M. Friedman, *Mommyblogs and the Changing Face of Motherhood* (Toronto: University of Toronto Press, 2013).

7 Friedrich Krotz, "Media, Mediatization and Mediatized Worlds: A Discussion of the Basic Concepts," in *Mediatized Worlds: Culture and Society in a Media Age*, ed. F. Krotz and A. Hepp (New York: Palgrave Macmillan, 2014), 72–87; Nick Couldry, "When Mediatization Hits the Ground," in *Mediatized Worlds: Culture and Society*

in a Media Age, ed. F. Krotz and A. Hepp (New York: Palgrave Macmillan, 2014), 54–71.

8 Krotz , "Media, Mediatization and Mediatized Worlds," 74.

9 The highly gendered dimension of parenting and babywearing cannot be engaged with directly in the limited scope of this chapter.

10 Birgit Meyer (ed.), *Aesthetic Formations: Media, Religion, and the Senses* (New York: Palgrave Macmillan, 2009), 6–11.

11 Thorstein Veblen, *The Theory of the Leisure Class* (New York: Cosimo, 1899, 2007).

12 See Janelle S. Taylor, Linda L. Layne, and Danielle F. Wozniak (eds.), *Consuming Motherhood* (New Brunswick, NJ: Rutgers University Press, 2004).

13 See Chris Bobel, *The Paradox of Natural Mothering* (Philadelphia, PA: Temple University Press, 2002) and Bobel, "Resisting," for the most extensive studies on the topic.

14 Chikako Takeshita, "Eco-Diapers. The American Discourse of Sustainable Motherhood," in *Mothering in the Age of Neoliberalism*, ed. M. Vandenbeld Giles (Bradford: Demeter Press, 2014), 117–31, esp. 118.

15 Florence Pasche Guignard, "The In/Visibility of Mothering against the Norm in Francophone Contexts: Private and Public Discourses in the Mediation of 'Natural Parenting,'" *Canadian Journal of Communication* 40, no. 1 (2015): 105–24.

16 Bron Taylor, *Dark Green Religion: Nature Spirituality and the Planetary Future* (Berkeley: University of California Press, 2010).

17 The use of a breastpump, an electronic technological device used to extract breastmilk, is an example of a welcomed technology that enables mothers to continue (or enhance) their breastfeeding, considered by many in this milieu as the (only) "natural" way to feed babies.

18 "Wrap You in Love," accessed August 10, 2014, http://www.wrapyouinlove.com.

19 Marcel Mauss already situated babywearing as a practice of the "Exotic Other," which is clear from his referring to his contemporaries and compatriots by specifying "in us" and by marking distance with babyworn babies "unlike our children." See Marcel Maus, "Techniques of the Body," in *Incorporation. Zone 6*, ed. J. Crary and S. Kwinter (New York: Zone, 1934 edition in French, 1992), 455–77, esp. 466.

20 Ibid.

21 The author wishes to thank informants and participants for allowing the use of parts of conversations as material for this chapter.

22 "Je porte mon bébé" and the JPMBB logo are registered trademarks.

23 JPMBB is a popular French brand of wraps made since 2007. I gathered most of the material analyzed in this chapter from the official JPMBB Facebook page (https://www.facebook.com/jeportemonbebe) and from that of an open Facebook group for JPMBB users called "*Le coin des utilisateurs Je porte mon bébé (JPMBB)*" (JPMBB

Users' Corner). JPMBB administrates this group page, though without monitoring it as closely as the company's official page, and without using it predominantly for advertising new products.

24 Such examples can be seen on the Facebook page of the open group of JPMBB users.

25 Claude-Suzanne, Didierjean-Jouveau, *Porter bébé. Avantages et bienfaits* (Genève-Bernex - Saint-Julien-en-Genevois: Jouvence, 2006).

26 "Our Philosophy," *jeportemonbebe.com*, accessed January 14, 2014, http://jeportemonbebe.com/en/.

27 Elisabeth Badinter, *Le Conflit. La femme et la mère* (Paris: Flammarion, 2010).

28 Michèle Lalanne and Nathalie Lapeyre, "L'engagement Écologique Au Quotidien A-t-il Un Genre ?" *Recherches Féministes* 22, no. 1 (2009): 47. doi:10.7202/037795ar.

29 Rima Apple, *Perfect Motherhood: Science and Childrearing in America* (New Brunswick, NJ: Rutgers University Press, 2006).

30 *JPMBB users Facebook group*, posted April 11, 2014.

31 This alluding to "Africa" is such a frequent trope that an article written by a member of the Swiss Association for Babywearing (ASPB, Association Suisse de Portage des Bébés) and available through its website addresses this specific concern (see Alexandra Aubert, Le Portage à travers le monde et les époques, *Swiss Association for Babywearing* [Association Suisse de Portage des Bébés], last modified November 6, 2012. http://www.aspb.ch/association/ASPB%20-%20Le%20portage%20a%20travers%20le%20monde%20et%20les%20epoques.pdf, 2012).

32 See Mauss, "Techniques of the Body," 1934.

33 Badinter, *Le Conflit.*

34 Users of JPMBB Facebook page, accessed January 14, 2014. Author's translation.

35 Meyer, *Aesthetic Formations*, 6–11.

36 Benedict Anderson, *Imagined Communities: Reflections on the Origin and Spread of Nationalism* (London: Verso, 2006).

37 Natasha Chiam, "Babywearing: Beyond the Cute Baby Carriers." Retrieved from *The Feminist Breeder*. Accessed January 30, 2015, http://resources.thefeministbreeder.com/babies-toddlers/babywearing/babywearing-beyond-the-cute-baby-carriers/.

38 Timothy Taylor, *The Artificial Ape. How Technology Changed the Course of Human Evolution* (New York: Palgrave Macmillan, 2010), 109–19.

39 Babywearing International, accessed July 22, 2014, http://babywearinginternational.org/pages/whatisbabywearing.php.

40 Babywearing skills have been forgotten in Euro-American contexts due to the widespread use of strollers for more than a century in charge of caring for and carrying a younger sibling, and thus acquire knowledge about babywearing directly.

41 Jeportemonbebe, YouTube, accessed November 3, 2014, https://www.youtube.com/user/jeportemonbebe/featured.

Chapter 3

1 Carole L. Jurkiewicz and Robert A. Giacalone, "A Values Framework for Measuring the Impact of Workplace Spirituality on Organizational Performance," *Journal of Business Ethics* 49 (2004): 129–42.

2 Many who study religion treat what is described as spiritual as a subset of religion rather than as a distinctly separate category. Further they often argue that the distinction seems to idealize the personal, demonizing the organizational, and that it tends to focus on the purely personal benefits of spiritual practice while failing to engage the larger social implications of religious/social practice. Clarifying a theoretical distinction between what is spiritual and religious bears continued reflection. However, in this chapter we want to focus on how the popular focus on the spiritual is particularly fitted for the digital media age, and how these seemingly private spiritual practices have come to shape understandings of work and the workplace as a distinctly separate category.

3 Heidi A. Campbell, "Understanding the Relationship between Religion Online and Offline in a Networked Society," *Journal of the American Academy of Religion* 80, no. 1 (2012): 64–93. See especially 68.

4 Jessica Brack, "Maximizing Millenials in the Workplace," UNC Kenan-Flagler Business School, accessed February 16, 2015, http://www.kenan-flagler.unc.edu/executive-development/custom-programs/~/media/DF1C11C056874DDA8097271A1ED48662.ashx.

5 Diana Butler Bass, *Christianity after Religion* (New York: Harper One, 2013), 48. Bass explains a secularization theory that emerged in the early in the twentieth century. Many scholars argued that the growth of science in the West would replace or privatize people's belief in God and that because of this religion would fade away.

6 Peter C. Hill et al., "Conceptualizing Religion and Spirituality: Points of Commonality, Points of Departure," *Journal of the Theory of Social Behavior* 30, no. 1 (2000): 61. Hill explains that the demographic that refer to themselves as spiritual-but-not-religious "appear to reject traditional organized religion in favor of an individualized spirituality. . .and are likely to engage in emerging religions that may include New Age beliefs and practices."

7 Jeffrey H. Mahan, *Media, Religion and Culture: An Introduction.* (New York: Routledge, 2014), p. 25.

8 Larry Myler, "Why Are 70% of Employees Disengaged, and What Can You Do About It?" *Forbes*, September 2, 2013, accessed December 22, 2014, http://www.forbes.com/sites/larrymyler/2013/09/02/why-are-70-of-employees-disengaged-and-what-can-you-do-about-it/.

9 Sukumarakurup Krisnakumar and Christopher P. Neck, "The 'What,' 'Why,' and 'How' of Spirituality in the Workplace," *Journal of Managerial Psychology* 17, no. 3

(2002): 156. Purposeful work is so significant to some people that "the 'search for meaning' has been one of the most quoted phrases in examples of people who quit their jobs to lead a more spiritually enriching life."

10 This research was conducted according to the guidelines established by the Institutional Review Board of Iliff School of Theology and the Collaborative Institutional Training Institute (CITI) that sets standards to conduct human subjects research. This reference is from "Glenn," focus group, February 9, 2014. RuthAnn Ritter, "Buddhism in the Western Workplace: Implications for a Spiritual Employee and Organization," (Master's thesis, Iliff School of Theology, 2014),14.

11 Robert Giacalone and Carole L. Jurkiewicz, *Handbook of Workplace Spirituality and Organizational Performance* (New York: M. E. Sharpe, 2002), 3.

12 "Maggie," personal interview, Ritter, "Buddhism in the Western Workplace," 9.

13 Diana Ransom, "Finding Success by Putting Company Culture First," *Entrepreneur*, April 19, 2011, accessed November 1, 2014, www.entrepreneur.com/article/219509.

14 "Community," Tom's of Maine, accessed December 22, 2014, http://www.tomsofmaine.com/goodness-report/community#Volunteer.

15 "Impact," Clif Bar, accessed December 22, 2014, http://www.clifbar.com/hubs/impact.

16 "How a Life Coach Can Help Your Employees," Zappos, accessed December 22, 2014, http://www.zapposinsights.com/blog/item/how-a-life-coach-can-help-your-employees.

17 Pawinee Petchsawang and Dennis Duchon, "Workplace Spirituality, Meditation, and Work Performance," *Journal of Management, Spirituality and Religion* 9, no.2 (2012): 192.

18 Renata M. Black, "Deepak Chopra On The Future of Business," *Huffington Post*, July 15, 2014, accessed December 22, 2014, http://www.huffingtonpost.com/renata-m-black/deepak-chopra-on-the-futu_b_5588250.html.

19 Robert Greenleaf, *The Servant as Leader* (Westfield, IN: Greenleaf Center for Servant Leadership, 2008). Greenleaf introduced the concept of servant leadership in this essay where he theorized that servant leaders would positively influence their followers.

20 Danah Zohar and Ian Marshall, *Spiritual Capital: Wealth We Can Live by* (San Francisco: Berrett-Koehler Publishers, 2004), 10. The authors point to the two goals of modern capitalism that include the assumption "that humans are primarily economic beings" and "that human beings will always act to pursue our own rational self-interest." They maintain that this type of business is not sustainable in the modern era.

21 John Mackey and Raj Sisodia, *Conscious Capitalism: Liberating the Heroic Spirit of Business* (Boston: Harvard Business Review Press, 2014), 94.

22 Louis W. Fry et al., “Spiritual Leadership as an Integrating Paradigm for Servant Leadership,” in *Integrating Spirituality and Organizational Leadership*, ed. Sunita Singh-Sengupta and Dail Fields (London: Macmillan, 2007), 73.

23 Sen Sendjaya and James C. Sarros, “Servant Leadership: Its Origin, Development, and Application in Organizations,” *Journal of Leadership & Organizational Studies* 9, no. 2 (2002): 57.

24 James William Coleman, *The New Buddhism: The Western Transformation of an Ancient Tradition* (New York: Oxford, 2001), 218.

25 Mackey and Sisodia, *Conscious Capitalism*, 95.

26 Howard Behar, *It’s Not About the Coffee: Leadership Principles from a Life at Starbucks* (New York: Penguin, 2007), 8.

27 David E. Melchar and Susan M. Bosco, “Achieving High Organization Performance through Servant Leadership,” *Journal of Business Inquiry* 9, no. 1 (2010): 76.

28 Edward Lewine, “Tony Hsieh’s Office: Welcome to the Rain Forest,” *The New York Times*, December 28, 2013, accessed November 16, 2014, http://www.nytimes.com/2013/12/29/business/tony-hsiehs-office-welcome-to-the-rain-forest.html?_r=0.

29 “Maggie,” personal interview, Ritter, “Buddhism in the Western Workplace.” The example of public and private manifestations of Buddhism in Maggie’s workplace points to the complex boundaries that emerge when workplaces embrace spirituality. The distinction between what is considered private and religious and public and spiritual is a boundary that is negotiated differently across various workplaces.

30 GT Freeman, “Spirituality and Servant Leadership: A Conceptual Model and Research Proposal,” *Emerging Leadership Journeys* 4, no.1 (2011): 129.

31 Behar, *It’s Not about the Coffee*, 53.

32 Travis P. Searle and John E. Barbuto Jr., “Servant Leadership, Hope, and Organizational Virtuousness: A Framework for Exploring Positive Micro and Macro Behaviors and Performance Impact,” *Journal of Leadership & Organizational Studies* 18 (2011): 110.

33 Mackey and Sisodia, *Conscious Capitalism*, 35.

34 Behar, *It’s Not about the Coffee*, 1.

35 Mackey and Sisodia, *Conscious Capitalism*, 84.

36 Tony Hsieh, *Delivering Happiness: A Path to Profits, Passion, and Purpose* (New York: Business Plus, 2010), 121.

37 Ibid., 230.

38 Ibid., 145.

39 Mackey and Sisodia, *Conscious Capitalism*, 31.

40 Fred Kofman, *Conscious Business: How to Build Value through Values* (Boulder, CO: Sounds True, 2006), 284

41 Mackey and Sisodia, *Conscious Capitalism*, 225.

42 Two empirical studies are cited in GT Freeman's article, "Spirituality and Servant Leadership: A Conceptual Model and Research Proposal." He cites L. W. Fry's "Toward a Theory of Spiritual Leadership" and S. Sendjaya et al., "Development and Validation of Servant Leadership Behavior Scale

43 Art Toalston, "Truett Cathy, Faith Rooted Business Entrepreneur Dies," *Baptist Press*, September 8, 2014, accessed December 22, 2014, http://www.bpnews.net/43315/truett-cathy-faithrooted—business-entrepreneur-dies. Some servant leaders are known to bring their own faith traditions and agendas into the workplace. For example, the former CEO of furniture company Herman Miller is a servant leader who openly leads from the base of his Christian values. Dan Cathy, CEO of fast-food company, Chick-fil-A, also approaches his service to others on the basis of Christianity. His father and founder of the company, S. Truett Cathy, even made the decision to close the stores on Sundays: "Our decision to close on Sunday was our way of honoring God and directing our attention to things that mattered more than our business."

44 Mackey and Sisodia, *Conscious Capitalism*, 3.

45 Ibid., 213.

46 Ibid., 87.

47 Krista Bjorn, "Colleen Barrett: On Leadership at Southwest Airlines," *Character First the Magazine*, November 29, 2011, accessed December 22, 2014, http://cfthemagazine.com/2011-12/colleen-barrett-on-leadership-at-southwest-airlines/.

48 Searle and Barbuto, "Servant Leadership, Hope, and Organizational Virtuousness," 112.

49 Zohar and Marshall, *Spiritual Capital*, 29. The authors make the distinction between consumer and spiritual capital and suggest "companies concerned with amassing spiritual capital are constantly placing their goals and strategies in a wider context of meaning and value. They are constantly reframing their aims and recontextualizing the effects."

50 "Credo" Q's for Good Leadership, accessed November 24, 2014, http://danahzohar.com/www2/?page_id=612.

Chapter 4

1 I would like to thank the many people in Glastonbury who have so generously shared their experiences, expertise, opinions, and time with me over this long period.

2 See, for example, Marion Bowman, "Going with the Flow: Contemporary Pilgrimage in Glastonbury," in *Shrines and Pilgrimage in the Modern World:*

New Itineraries into the Sacred, ed. Peter Jan Margy (Amsterdam: Amsterdam University Press, 2008); Marion Bowman, "Understanding Glastonbury as a Site of Consumption," in *Religion, Media and Culture: A Reader*, ed. Gordon Lynch, Jolyon Mitchell, and Anna Strhan (London: Routledge, 2011); Marion Bowman, "Valuing Spirituality: Commodification, Consumption and Community in Glastonbury," in *Religion in Consumer Society: Brands, Consumers and Markets*, ed. Francois Gauthier and Tuomas Martikainen (Farnham and Burlington, VA: Ashgate, 2013).

3 See, for example, Nancy Ammerman, *Everyday Religion: Observing Modern Religious Lives* (Oxford: Oxford University Press, 2007); Meredith McGuire, *Lived Religion: Faith and Practice in Everyday Life* (New York: Oxford University Press, 2008).

4 Leonard Primiano, "Vernacular Religion and the Search for Method in Religious Folklife," *Western Folklore* 54, no. 1 (1995): 44.

5 Leonard Primiano, "Afterword. Manifestations of the Religious Vernacular: Ambiguity, Power and Creativity," in *Vernacular Religion in Everyday Life: Expressions of Belief*, ed. Marion Bowman and Ülo Valk (Sheffield and Bristol, CT: Equinox, 2012), 383.

6 Marion Bowman and Ülo Valk (eds.), *Vernacular Religion in Everyday Life: Expressions of Belief* (Sheffield and Oakville, CT: Equinox, 2012).

7 Mathew Engelke, "Material religion," in *The Cambridge Companion to Religious Studies*, ed. Robert A. Orsi (Cambridge: Cambridge University Press, 2011), 209.

8 David Morgan, "The Materiality of Cultural Construction," *Material Religion* 4, no. 2 (2008): 228.

9 Françoise Gauthier, Linda Woodhead, and Tuomas Martikainen, "Introduction: Consumerism as the Ethos of Consumer Society," in *Religion in Consumer Society: Brands, Consumers and Markets*, ed. Françoise Gauthier and Tuomas Martikainen (Farnham and Burlington, VT: Ashgate, 2013), 2.

10 Ibid., 23.

11 Ibid., 18–19.

12 Mary Douglas and Baron Isherwood, *The World of Goods* (London: Routledge, 1996).

13 Gauthier, Woodhead, and Martikainen, "Introduction," 11.

14 Ibid., 18.

15 Ibid., 12.

16 Jeremy Carrette and Richard King, *Selling Spirituality: The Silent Takeover of Religion* (London: Routledge, 2005).

17 Andrew Dawson, "Consuming the Self: New Spirituality as 'Mystified Consumption,'" *Social Compass* 58, no. 3 (2011): 310.

18 Ibid., 311.

19 Ingvild Saelid Gilhus, "'All Over the Place': The Contribution of New Age to a Spatial Model of Religion," in *New Age Spirituality: Rethinking Religion*, ed. Steven J. Sutcliffe and Ingvild Saelid Gilhus (Durham, NC: Acumen, 2013), 47.

20 See, for example, Irving Hexham, "The 'Freaks' of Glastonbury: Conversion and Consolidation in an English Country Town," *Update* 7, no. 1 (1983); Bruce Garrard, *Free State: Glastonbury's Alternative Community, 1970 to 2000 and Beyond* (Glastonbury: Unique Publications, 2014); Marion Bowman, "Drawn to Glastonbury," in *Pilgrimage in Popular Culture*, ed. Ian Reader and Tony Walter (Basingstoke and London: Macmillan, 1993); Marion Bowman, "Christianity, Plurality and Vernacular Religion in Early Twentieth Century Glastonbury: A Sign of Things to Come," in *Studies in Church History 51* (Woodbridge: Boydell, 2015); Brendan McNamara, "The 'Celtic' Dimension of Pre-First World War Religious Discourse in Britain: Wellesley Tudor Pole and the Glastonbury Phenomenon," *Journal of the Irish Society for the Academic Study of Religions* 1, no.1 (2014); Ruth Prince and David Riches, *The New Age in Glastonbury: The Construction of Religious Movements* (New York and Oxford: Berghahn Books, 2000); Tim Hopkinson-Ball, *The Rediscovery of Glastonbury: Frederick Bligh Bond, Architect of the New Age* (London: Sutton Publishing, 2007); Adrian J. Ivakhiv, *Claiming Sacred Ground: Pilgrims and Politics at Glastonbury and Sedona* (Bloomington: Indiana University Press, 2001).

21 Frederick Bligh Bond, *The Gate of Remembrance: The Story of the Psychological Experiment which Resulted in the Discovery of the Edgar Chapel at Glastonbury* (Oxford: Oxford Blackwell, 1918).

22 Bowman, "Christianity, Plurality and Vernacular Religion."

23 See, for example, James P. Carley, *Glastonbury Abbey: The Holy House at the Head of the Moors Adventurous Glastonbury* (Glastonbury: Gothic Image Publications, 1996); Marion Bowman, "Drawn to Glastonbury," in *Pilgrimage in Popular Culture*, ed. Ian Reader and Tony Walter (Basingstoke and London: Macmillan, 1993); Marion Bowman and Ülo Valk (eds.), *Vernacular Religion in Everyday Life: Expressions of Belief* (Sheffield and Oakville, CT: Equinox, 2012); Katharine E. Maltwood, *A Guide to Glastonbury's Temple of the Stars: Their Giant Effigies Described from Air Views, Maps, and from "The High History of the Holy Grail."* (1929; reprinted, London: James Clarke, 1964); Patrick Benham, *The Avalonians* (Glastonbury: Gothic Image Press, 1993).

24 Dion Fortune, *Avalon of the Heart* (1934; reprinted London: Aquarian Press, 1971).

25 Geoffrey Ashe, *Avalonian Quest* (London: Methuen, 1982).

26 Marion Z. Bradley, *The Mists of Avalon* (London: Sphere Books, 1986).

27 Maltwood, *A Guide to Glastonbury's Temple of the Stars.*

28 Imbolc (February 1/2), Beltane (April 30/May 1), Lammas/ Lughnasa (August 1), and Samhain (October 31/November 1), Summer and Winter Solstice and Spring and Autumn Equinox.

29 John Michell, *The New View Over Atlantis* (London: Thames and Hudson, 1983).

30 Adrian J. Ivakhiv, "Power Trips: Making Sacred Space through New Age Pilgrimage," in *Handbook of New Age*, ed. Darren Kemp and James R. Lewis (Leiden: Brill, 2007), 283.

31 See Garrard, *Free State*.
32 Marion Bowman, "Ancient Avalon, New Jerusalem, Heart Chakra of Planet Earth: Localisation and Globalisation in Glastonbury," *Numen* 52, no. 2 (2005).
33 See, for example, Bowman, "Understanding Glastonbury as a Site of Consumption"; Bowman, "Valuing Spirituality."
34 Dawson, "Consuming the Self," 311.
35 Hopkinson-Ball, *Rediscovery of Glastonbury*.
36 Guy Redden, "The New Age: Towards a Market Model," *Journal of Contemporary Religion* 20, no. 2 (2005): 237.
37 Bowman, "Going with the Flow."
38 For example Lourdes, see, John Eade, "Order and Power at Lourdes: Lay Helpers and the Organization of a Pilgrimage Shrine," in *Contesting the Sacred: The Anthropology of Christian Pilgrimage*, ed. J. Eade and M. Sallnow (Urbana and Chicago: University of Illinois Press 2000), 51–76.
39 Garrard, *Free State*; Barry Taylor, *A Pilgrim in Glastonbury* (Glastonbury: Abbey Press, 2010).
40 Garrard, *Free State*; Taylor, *A Pilgrim in Glastonbury*.
41 "The Glastonbury Trust," accessed February 20, 2015, http://www.glastonburytrust.co.uk/.
42 The Chalice Well Trust exists to:1. Cherish, safeguard and beautify the holy place and living sanctuary called Chalice Well for the benefit of the people of Britain and the world.2. Encourage individual spiritual awareness and growth by offering this place to all people, of whatever religious persuasion or none, for pilgrimage, ceremony, quiet contemplation, and healing.3. Facilitate spiritual awareness and harmony in the local and wider community.
43 Gauthier, Woodhead, and Martikainen, "Introduction," 294.
44 "Glastonbury Online Ltd," *Glastonbury*, accessed February 22, 2015, http://www.glastonbury.co.uk/pages/site.php?pgid=420.
45 "The Glaston Group," accessed February 22, 2015, http://glastongroup.org/.
46 Ibid.
47 See Garrard, *Free State*.
48 *Glastonbury Reception Centre and Sanctuary*, accessed January 12, 2012, http://www.glastonbury-pilgrim.co.uk/#glastonbury-pilgrim-centre-about-us.php.
49 The range of technique's accessed through the online Glastonbury Therapists' Forum include: hypnotherapy; life coaching; NLP (Neuro Linguistic Programming); emotional freedom technique (EFT); drama, play, and integrative arts therapies; psychotherapy; rebirthing; dreamwork; aromatherapy; lymphatic drainage; reflexology; acupuncture; reiki: Chinese medicine; flower essences; herbal medicine; nutritional therapy; homeopathy; color healing/aura soma; crystal healing; shamanic healing; and space healing/geomancy.

50 "The Glastonbury Sanctuary," *Glastonbury Reception Centre and Sanctuary*, accessed October 29, 2014, http://www.unitythroughdiversity.org/the-sanctuary.html.
51 Ibid.
52 "The Glastonbury Unity Candle," *Glastonbury Reception Centre and Sanctuary*, accessed April 4, 2015, http://www.unitythroughdiversity.org/the-glastonbury-unity-candle.html.
53 *Glastonbury Reception Centre and Sanctuary* (blog), August 21, 2014, accessed February 4, 2015, http://www.unitythroughdiversity.org/blog—news.
54 See Marion Bowman, "Procession and Possession in Glastonbury: Continuity, Change and the Manipulation of Tradition," *Folklore* 115, no. 3 (2004): 1–13.
55 *Unity through Diversity*, accessed February 22, 2015, http://www.unitythroughdiversity.org/.
56 Henry Glassie, *Material Culture* (Indiana: Indiana University Press, 1999), 1.
57 Gauthier, Woodhead, and Martikainen, "Introduction," 11.
58 Ibid., 18.
59 Ibid.
60 Redden, "The New Age," 237.

Chapter 5

1 Information was collected at hoop workshops, online, and in-person interviews with hoopers. UCSB Office of Research/Human Subjects Approval granted July 21, 2010. Sub-ID 10–531, Pro. No: RELG-BU-RU-022–2N Participants in the online survey have remained anonymous.
2 Catherine L. Albanese, *A Republic of Mind and Spirit: A Cultural History of American Metaphysical Religion* (New Haven, CT: Yale University Press, 2007), 1.
3 Ibid., 4.
4 See Robert C. Fuller, *Spiritual, but Not Religious: Understanding Unchurched America* (Oxford : New York: Oxford University Press, 2001); Linda A. Mercadante, *Belief without Borders: Inside the Minds of the Spiritual but Not Religious* (New York: Oxford University Press, 2014).
5 Albanese, *Republic*, 13.
6 Ibid., 6, 13.
7 Ibid., 6.
8 Ibid.
9 Ibid., 14.
10 Ibid., 6.
11 Ibid., 14.

12 Ibid., 15.
13 Ibid., 15.
14 Ibid., 8.
15 Ibid.
16 Wade Clark Roof, *A Generation of Seekers: The Spiritual Journeys of the Baby Boom Generation*, 1st ed. (San Francisco: HarperSanFrancisco, 1993), 251.
17 Ibid., 256.
18 Robert Wuthnow, *After the Baby Boomers: How Twenty- and Thirty-Somethings Are Shaping the Future of American Religion* (Princeton, NJ: Princeton University Press, 2007), 14.
19 Flory and Miller's work on Post-Boomer Christian traditions has found similar tendencies in GenX religion. See Richard W. Flory and Donald E. Miller, *Finding Faith: The Spiritual Quest of the Post-Boomer Generation* (New Brunswick, NJ: Rutgers University Press, 2008).
20 Tom Beaudoin, *Virtual Faith: The Irreverent Spiritual Quest of Generation X*, 1st ed. (San Francisco: Jossey-Bass, 1998), 43.
21 Ibid., 122.
22 Jan M. Camp, *Hoopdance Revolution: Mindfulness in Motion* (Berkeley: Arc Light Books, 2013), 136–7.
23 Stewart M. Hoover, *Religion in the Media Age*, Religion, Media and Culture (London and New York: Routledge, 2006), 1–2 and 40–1.
24 Ibid., 1–2.
25 Ibid., 32–3.
26 Ibid., 23–6.
27 Ibid., 34–5.
28 Ibid., 35.
29 Ibid., 84.
30 Ibid., 21.
31 Ibid., 55–6.
32 Camp, *Hoopdance*, 119.
33 Ibid.
34 *Hoop Path: The First Steps*, DVD, 2008.
35 Ibid.
36 Hooping with blindfolds on, "swaying" in the hoop (dancing meditatively with or without the hoop on the body), utilizing first and second "hoop currents," and a variety of other HoopPath techniques all develop mental awareness and intuition. In HoopPath, the body of the hooper also becomes a part of the Maidan story through correspondence.
37 "Baxter's Credentials," HoopPath.com, accessed February 9, 2015, http://hooppath.com/about/baxters-credentials.html
38 Camp, *Hoopdance*, 119.

39 Jonathan Baxter (HoopPath founder) in discussion with Jenna Gray-Hildenbrand, August 2014.

40 Jonathan Baxter began teaching hooping workshops and began HoopPath, Inc. in 2005, but he began dedicating a significant portion of his time and energy into HoopPath in 2008, when he increased the number of his workshop tours and released a HoopPath DVD. In 2010 he joined Facebook, creating both a personal page (which currently has nearly 5,000 friends) and a business page for HoopPath (which currently has over 4,500 likes). In addition, Baxter has a Twitter account (@ HoopPather) established in 2010 and a HoopPath website (http://www.hooppath.com/). However, the oldest and most consistent means of communication between Baxter and his audience is YouTube (www.YouTube.com/user/jlbaxter), where he began posting videos in 2006. Since July 2006, Baxter has posted over forty videos. His YouTube channel has nearly 3,000 subscribers, with some videos viewed over 21,000 times.

Chapter 6

1 Gilles Deleuze, *Proust & Signs: The Complete Text*, trans. Richard Howard; Theory Out of Bounds, vol. 17 (Minneapolis: University of Minnesota Press, 2000. [Orig. pub. Presses Universitaires de France, 1964.]), 92.

2 Interviews as well as weekly transcription of gathering times material were collected using participant observation from August 2009 to August 2010. Participants were over the age of 21 and signed permissions. IRB protocol from the University of Denver is 2009–1124. All respondent names are changed.

3 Thomas R. Lindlof, "Media Audiences as Interpretive Communities," in *Communication Yearbook* 11, ed. J. A. Anderson, (1988): 81–107; Thomas R. Lindlof, "Interpretive Community: An Approach to Media and Religion," *Journal of Media and Religion* 1, no. 1 (2002): 61–74.

4 Lindlof, "Interpretive Community," 63.

5 Stolow's work, as defined below, blurs the lines between "religion" as connection (tied to the original Latin meaning of religio, "that which binds") and media as connection (i.e., an object or communicative activity that conveys meaning or affect). Another Way participants subconsciously identify both religion and media as connective, but also recognize their disjunctive or sedimentary properties.

6 Stanley Fish, *Is There a Text in This Class? The Authority of Interpretive Communities* (Cambridge, MA: Harvard University Press, 1980).

7 "If meaning develops, and if it develops in a dynamic relationship with the reader's expectations, projections, conclusions, judgments, and assumptions, these activities (the things the reader does) are not merely instrumental, or mechanical,

but essential, and the act of description must both begin and end with them. In practice, this resulted in the replacing of one question—what does this mean?—by another—what does this do? . . . The reader was now given joint responsibility for the production of a meaning that was itself redefined as an event rather than an entity . . . In this formulation, the reader's response is not to the meaning; it is the meaning." Fish, *Is There a Text*, 3.

8 "An interpreting entity, endowed with purposes and concerns, is, by virtue of its very operation, determining what counts as the facts to be observed. . . . linguistic and textual facts, rather than being the objects of interpretation, are its products." Fish, *Is There a Text*, 8.

9 Fish, *Is There a Text*, 14.

10 Ibid., 16.

11 Ibid., 171.

12 Jeremy Stolow, "Religion and/as Media," *Theory, Culture, & Society* 22, no. 4 (2005): 119–45.

13 Ibid., 122–3.

14 Ibid., 125.

15 Ibid., 127.

16 Lindlof, "Media Audiences," 81–2.

17 Ibid., 103.

18 Lindlof, "Interpretive Community," 63–5.

Chapter 7

* The broader research project from which this chapter was drawn used a combination of historical analysis, ethnographic work among performance-oriented subcultures, interviews with fans, as well as promoters, nonprofit organizations, and others who advertise or offer services at concerts and festivals, and a survey that asked respondents to report on environmental behaviors, religious practices, and convictions, and their relationship to musical and other artistic performance (WFU IRB: 00021450). I am grateful to the Wake Forest Center for Energy, Environment, and Sustainability (CEES) for their generous support of this project.

1 This recollection of a miracle story was supplied by an informant on February 9, 2015. When the subject reports that his friend was puddled with some good liquid, it means that his friend received a complimentary dose of liquid LSD from a "hippie" in a neighboring seat.

2 Many scholars have found it important to distinguish between religions and spiritualities for specific research aims, but such distinctions are not necessary to

any case I hope to make here. Thus, I use religion and spirituality interchangeably in what follows, though I ultimately imagine various practical spiritualities to be a subset of what I mean by "religion." Religions should not be imagined as related only to the categories of the so-called world religions, rather analyses ought to focus on the religious dimensions of human life wherever they are found, including among individuals who do not identify with specific institutionalized religions.

3 Colin Campbell, "The Cult, The Cultic Milieu and Secularization," in *A Sociological Yearbook of Religion in Britain* (London: SCM Books, 1972), 119–36.

4 See Bron Taylor, "Diggers, Wolves, Ents, Elves and Expanding Universes: Bricolage, Religion, and Violence from Earth First! and the Earth Liberation Front to the Antiglobalization Resistance," in *The Cultic Milieu: Oppositional Subcultures in an Age of Globalization,* ed. Jeffrey Kaplan and Helen Loow (Walnut Creek, CA: Alta Mira, 2002); Bron Raymond Taylor, *Dark Green Religion: Nature Spirituality and the Planetary Future* (Berkeley: University of California Press, 2010).

5 Lucas F. Johnston, *Religion and Sustainability: Social Movements and the Politics of the Environment* (Sheffield; Bristol, CT: Equinox, 2013).

6 See Mary Evelyn Tucker and Duncan Ryūken Williams, Buddhism and Ecology: The Interconnection of Dharma and Deeds (Cambridge, MA: Harvard University Center for the Study of World Religions : Distributed by Harvard University Press, 1997); Mary Evelyn Tucker and John H. Berthrong, Confucianism and Ecology: The Interrelation of Heaven, Earth, and Humans (Cambridge, MA: Distributed by Harvard University Press for the Harvard University Center for the Study of World Religions, 1998); Christopher Key Chapple, Hinduism and Ecology: The Intersection of Earth, Sky, and Water (Cambridge: Harvard University Press, 2000); Dieter T. Hessel and Rosemary Radford Ruether, Christianity and Ecology: Seeking the Well-Being of Earth and Humans (Cambridge, MA: Distributed by Harvard University Press for the Harvard University Center for the Study of World Religions, 2000); John Grim, Indigenous Traditions and Ecology: The Interbeing of Cosmology and Community (Cambridge, MA: Distributed by Harvard Press for the Center for the Study of World Religions, Harvard Divinity School, 2001); Christopher Key Chapple, Jainism and Ecology: Nonviolence in the Web of Life (Cambridge, MA: Harvard University Press, 2002); Tirosh-Samuelson 2002; Richard Foltz, Frederick Mathewson Denny, and Azizan Haji Baharuddin, Islam and Ecology: a Bestowed Trust (Cambridge, MA: Center for the Study of World Religions, Harvard Divinity School : Distributed by Harvard University Press, 2003); John Grim and Mary Evelyn Tucker, Ecology and Religion (Washington, DC: Island Press, 2014).

7 Important genealogical critiques of the category of "world religions" have illustrated that such categorizations are at best ethnocentric, and at worst perpetuate a colonialist imposition of Western categories on cultural, ethnic, and ethical "others" (see Tomoko Masuzawa, *The Invention of World Religions, or, How*

European Universalism Was Preserved in the Language of Pluralism [Chicago: University of Chicago Press, 2005]; Russell T. McCutcheon, *Studying Religion: An Introduction* [London; Oakville, CT: Equinox Pub, 1997]; Russell T. McCutcheon, *Critics Not Caretakers: Redescribing the Public Study of Religion* [Albany: State University of New York Press, 2001]; Dubuisson 2003; Talal Asad, *Genealogies of Religion: Discipline and Reasons of Power in Christianity and Islam* [Baltimore, MD: Johns Hopkins University Press, 1993]).

8 The number of such festivals seems to have increased over time. The website jambase.com listed 335 jam-oriented music festivals in the United States scheduled for 2015. *Jambase.com*, accessed February 9, 2015.

9 Kesey received positive critical attention for his novel *One Flew Over the Cuckoo's Nest* (1962). LSD is ultimately derived from a grain fungus, first synthesized in a laboratory in 1938 by Albert Hoffman, and the psychedelic properties of which were accidentally discovered by him in 1943. The term "entheogen" literally translates as "god generated within," a term that religious studies scholar Chas Clifton suggests "better describes the drugs' religious use than do such words as 'intoxicant' (literally, poisonous), 'hallucinogenic' (causing hallucinations) . . . or 'psychedelic' (soul-showing)." Chas Clifton, "Entheogens," in *Encyclopedia of Religion and Nature*, ed. Bron Taylor (London: Continuum, 2005), 596–7.

10 This was certainly true for many, but not all participants in this scene. No doubt there were people whose primary concerns were experimentation with psychotropic substances and a good party. But this spiritual motivation certainly seems to have been formative for many of the charismatic leaders of these movements. I am grateful to Todd LeVasseur for suggesting that I make this explicit.

11 Johnston, *Religion and Sustainability*, 52–3.

12 Charles Y. Glock, Robert N. Bellah, and Randy Alfred, *The New Religious Consciousness* (Berkeley: University of California Press, 1976).

13 Kevin Michael DeLuca, *Image Politics: The New Rhetoric of Environmental Activism* (New York: Guilford Press, 1999).

14 Robert Bellah, "The New Consciousness and the Berkeley New Left," in *The New Religious Consciousness*, ed. Charles Glock and Robert Bellah (Berkeley: University of California Press, 1976), 77–92.

15 Leary and Alpert were famous for encouraging students to experiment with LSD and to drop out of college. Their argument was essentially that there were higher forms of knowledge, accessible through psychedelic journeys, that ought to be pursued, and universities were some of the primary purveyors of the status quo.

16 Victor Turner, "Process, System, and Symbol: A New Anthropological Synthesis," in *Daedalus* 106 (1977): 71, quoted in Mihai Coman, "Liminality in Media Studies: From Everyday Life to Media Events," in *Victor Turner and Contemporary Cultural Performance* (New York: Berghahn Books, 2008), 94–108, esp. 95.

17 Victor Turner, *The Ritual Process: Structure and Anti-Structure* (New York: Aldine Publishers, 1969).

18 Douglas Martin, "Swami Satchidananda, Woodstock's Guru, Dies at 87," *The New York Times*, sec. World, August 21, 2002, http://www.nytimes.com/2002/08/21/world/swami-satchidananda-woodstock-s-guru-dies-at-87.html.

19 Michael Wadleigh, et al., *Woodstock 3 Days of Peace & Music* (Burbank, CA: Warner Bros. Pictures, Distributed by Warner Home Video, 2009).

20 This specific scene in the film is worthy of more precise dissection that cannot be performed here, but there is an irony to the teacher's note that he is imparting to the gathered group ancient techniques (at least 6,000 years old), which he learned in Los Angeles while experimenting with entheogenic substances.

21 DMT is short for the entheogenic compound N-dimethyltryptamine.

22 Wadleigh et al., *Woodstock*.

23 Ibid.

24 Will Keepin, "Breathwork," in *Encyclopedia of Religion and Nature*, ed. Bron Taylor (London: Continuum, 2005), 215.

25 Holotropic breathwork typically results in a "journey" in which "breathers become aware of deeper dimensions of their own consciousness, often evoking experiences of tremendous insight, healing, or psychological or spiritual significance." Keepin, "Breathwork," 215.

26 See Bron Taylor, "Diggers," and *Dark Green Religion*.

27 Graham Harvey, *Food, Sex, and Strangers: Understanding Religion as Everyday Life* (Durham, UK: Acumen, 2013).

28 See http://guides.library.ucsc.edu/c.php?g=119783&p=780833, accessed December 3, 2014.

29 See http://www.gdao.org/exhibits/show/posters/second-wave, accessed December 3, 2014.

30 See http://www.gdao.org/exhibits/show/posters/bob-fried, accessed November 11, 2014.

31 See http://www.gdao.org/exhibits/show/posters/end-of-fillmore, accessed November 13, 2014.

32 See Glock, Bellah, and Alfred, *New Religious Consciousness*.

33 Ibid., xi.

34 Jeff Wood' s website, accessed November 18, 2014, http://zendragongallery.com/collections/rock-posters/products/christmas-jam-2013-conscious-alliance. Conscious Alliance is a Boulder, Colorado-based organization that focuses on youth empowerment and feeding the hungry.

35 Bron Taylor, *Dark Green Religion*.

36 The term theriomorphic refers to a preternatural or supernatural being that takes animal form.

37 For examples, see https://www.etsy.com/search?q=Phish%20shirt (a search for any specific band will reveal a bevy of merchandise), or http://www.bravefriend.net/, accessed December 3, 2014. Figure 7.2 is a photo of such a shirt, produced by a vendor who identifies as "Doin' Good Things." The shirt depicts lyrics from a song titled "Plastic Jesus" and includes a small Jesus statuette on a car dashboard. The song was first performed by The Goldcoast Singers, three men who made up the group name and sang the song as a parody on a radio show in 1962. The song was made famous by an appearance in the film *Cool Hand Luke*. This shirt was marketed to Widespread Panic fans after the band covered the song during their 2014 fall tour. The lyrics are credited to Ed Cromarty and George Rush (the Goldcoast Singers), with more verses added over the years. The song illustrates the perception among many scene participants that traditional religious groups and beliefs are ambiguous.

38 *Backyardrevolution*, accessed December 3, 2014, http://backyardrevolution.com.

39 Thomas Wolfe, *The Electric Kool-Aid Acid Test* (New York: Farrar, Strauss, and Giroux, 1968).

40 "Grateful Dead Biography," *Rock and Roll Hall of Fame*, accessed July 2, 2014, http://rockhall.com/inductees/the-grateful-dead/bio/#sthash.DwTXcmtq.dpuf.

41 See Bron Taylor, *Dark Green Religion*.

42 I found these quotes in letters during a visit to the Grateful Dead archives at University of California, Santa Cruz, on August 1–2, 2014.

43 The term "headiness" to describe individual concert-goers is likely traceable to the term "deadhead," the term typically used to describe Grateful Dead fans. Today fans will self-identify as "Phishheads" (for the band Phish) or "Spreadheads" (for Widespread Panic). In addition, however, many of the drugs, paraphernalia, and other merchandise sold in the lots or within concert venues are described as "heady," which supposedly denotes their high quality. Both terms are possibly related to its application to individual concert-goers, also.

44 The so-called Gaia Hypothesis was proposed by James Lovelock and Lynn Margulis in 1972.

45 *Bonnaroo*, accessed December 3, 2014, http://www.bonnaroo.com/festival-info#the-code.

46 Fans of Widespread Panic often refer to them simply as "the boys," in some sense expressing the familial sensibility that obtains across the performance-oriented milieu.

47 Personal communication, October 16, 2014.

48 Author survey, August 12, 2014.

49 John Bell et al., "Reflections: Jerry Garcia's Life and Legacy," *Relix*, 2014, accessed December 8, 2015, https://web4.relix.com/articles/detail/reflections-jerry-garcia-s-life and legacy john bell del mccoury ethan mill.

50 The religion scholar Russell McCutcheon (2005) uses the phrase "domestication of dissent" in the title of a book that examines the boundaries and "authenticity" of public discourses related to Islam in the United States post-9/11.

Chapter 8

1 Garry Tregidga, "Stratton to St Keverne; Sites of Memory from the Early Modern Period," in *Memory, Place and Identity: The Cultural Landscapes of Cornwall*, ed. Garry Tregidga (London: Francis Boutle Publishers, 2012), 40–53; for an introduction to the territorial dimension to Cornish politics, see Bernard Deacon, Dick Cole, and Garry Tregidga, *Mebyon Kernow and Cornish Nationalism* (Cardiff: Welsh Academic Press, 2003).

2 Bernard Deacon, *Cornwall: A Concise History* (Cardiff: University of Wales Press, 2007), 2.

3 Amy Hale, "Genesis of the Celto-Cornish Revival? L.C. Duncombe Jewell and the Cowethas Kelto-Kernuak," in *Cornish Studies: Five*, ed. Philip Payton (Exeter: University of Exeter Press, 1997), 101.

4 Derek Williams (ed.), *Henry and Katharine Jenner: A Celebration of Cornwall's Culture, Language and Identity* (London: Francis Boutle Publications, 2004), 69.

5 Philip Payton, "Paralysis and Revival: The Reconstruction of Celtic-Catholic Cornwall 1890–1945," in *Cornwall: The Cultural Construction of Place*, ed. Ella Westland (Signal Mountain, TN: Patten Press, 1997), 28.

6 Sean Kay, *Celtic Revival? The Rise, Fall and Renewal of Global Ireland* (Lanham, MD: Rowman & Littlefield, 2011).

7 *Royal Cornwall Gazette*, January 4, 1878, 6.

8 Garry Tregidga, "Celtic Comparisons: Brittany and the Revivalist Movement in Cornwall," in *Brittany/Cornwall: What Relations?* ed. Anne Goarzin and Jean-Yves Le Disez (Centre de Recherche Bretonne et Celtuque, 2013), 63.

9 Ibid., 62–3.

10 Dudley Baines, *Migration in a Mature Economy and Internal Migration in England and Wales, 1861–1900* (Cambridge: Cambridge University Press, 1985), 159.

11 Sharron Schwartz, "Cornish Migration Studies: An Epistemological and Paradigmatic Critique," in *Cornish Studies: Ten*, ed. Phillip Payton (Exeter: University of Exeter Press, 2002), 142.

12 Phillip Payton, *The Cornish Overseas: The Epic Story of the Great Migration* (Fowey, UK: Cornwall Editions Limited, 1999), 398.

13 Parker, *Cornwall Marches On*.

14 *Royal Cornwall Gazette*, August 20, 1924.

15 Philip Payton, *The Making of Modern Cornwall: Historical Experience and the Persistence of Difference* (Trewirgie, UK: Dyllansow Truran, 1992), 132; Payton, *Cornwall*, 267.

16 *Cornish Guardian*, March 15, 1912.

17 Ibid., August 17, 1933.

18 *Cornish Culture online*, accessed January 8, 2015, http://www.cornishculture.co.uk/pagan.htm.

19 *Meyn Mamvro*, accessed January 8, 2015, http://www.meynmamvro.co.uk/.

20 *Gemma Gary*, accessed January 8, 2015, http://www.gemmagary.co.uk/about/.

21 "Calendar Customs: A Guide to British Calendar Customs and Local Traditions," accessed January 8, 2015, http://calendarcustoms.com/articles/montol-festival/.

22 Amy Hale, "'In the Eye of the Sun': The Relationship Between the Cornish Gorseth and Esoteric Druidry,'" in *Cornish Studies: Eight*, ed. Phillip Payton (Exeter: University of Exeter Press, 2000), 182–96; see also Chantal Laws and Susan Stuart, "Myth, Magic and the Marketplace: The Preservation and Interpretation of Cornwall's Heritage within a Spiritual Tourism Context," in *Proceedings of the Things That Move: The Material Worlds of Tourism and Travel Conference* (Leeds: Leeds Metropolitan University, 2007).

23 Monica Emerich, email message to author, March 5, 2014.

24 Monica Emerich, "A New American Dream: Taking the Celtic Cure in Mediated Landscapes," in *Memory, Place and Identity: The Cultural Landscapes of Cornwall*, ed. Garry Tregidga (London: Francis Boutle Publications, 2012), 86.

25 Fernand Braudel, *The Identity of France: History and Environment*, Vol. 1 (Waukegan, IL: Fontana Press, 1989).

26 Christopher Tilley, *A Phenomenology of Landscape* (London: Berg Publishers, 1994), 33.

27 Daniele Conversi, "Language or Race? The Choice of Core Values in the Development of Catalan and Basque Nationalisms," *Ethnic and Racial Studies* 13, no. 1 (1990): 212.

28 Bernard Deacon, "And Shall Trelawny Die? The Cornish Identity," in *Cornwall since the War: The Contemporary History of a European War*, ed. Phillip Patyon (Trewirgie: Dyllansow Truran, 1993), 212–4; see also Danile Conversi, "Language or Race? The Choice of Core Values in the Development of Catalan and Basque Nationalisms." *Ethnic and Racial Studies* 13, no. 1 (1990): 50–70.

29 Kayleigh Milden, "'Are you Church or Chapel?" Perceptions of Spatial and Spiritual Identity Within Cornish Methodism," in *Cornish Studies: Twelve*, ed. Philip Payton (Exeter: University of Exeter Press, 2004), 144–65.

30 L. E. Elliott-Binns, *Medieval Cornwall* (London: Methuen, 1955), 6.

31 Kenneth Pelmear, *Cornwall For Ever!* (Trewirgie, UK: Dyllansow Truran, 1985).

32 Garry Tregidga Facebook Page, Photos December 14 and 21, 2014, (modified January 9, 2015). www.facebook.com/photo.php?fbid=10152945913312806&set=a.10151200151217806.517011.632262805&type=1&theater.
33 Parker, *Cornwall Marches On*, 44–89.
34 Andrew Collins, "Pobol y Cwm at 40: Welsh-Language TV Has Never Been Stronger," *Guardian* (London), October 16, 2014. http://www.theguardian.com/tv-and-radio/tvandradioblog/2014/oct/16/pobol-y-cwm-40-welsh-language-tv-never-been-stronger; S4C website, accessed January 9, 2015, http://www.s4c.co.uk/en/; TG4 website, accessed January 9, 2015, http://www.tg4.ie/; Gov.UK website, accessed January 9, 2015, https://www.gov.uk/government/news/additional-1-million-for-mg-alba-announced-by-government.
35 Douglas Fraser, "Further Declines in Scottish Newspaper Sales," *BBC Scotland Business*, accessed January 9, 2015, http://www.bbc.co.uk/news/uk-scotland-scotland-business-26366464; "Concern over Newspapers' Decline in Wales," *BBC Wales*, accessed January 9, 2015, http://www.bbc.co.uk/news/uk-wales-11111396.
36 *BBC Spotlight*, accessed January 9, 2015, http://www.bbc.co.uk/programmes/b006pfr1.
37 Payton, "Territory and Identity," 225; Kenneth Mackinnon, "Cornish at Its Millennium: An Independent Study of the Language Undertaken in 2000," in *Cornish Studies: Ten*, ed. Phillip Payton (Exeter: University of Exeter Press, 2002), 274.
38 Garry Tregidga, "Competing Narratives of Religious and Cultural Identity in Cornwall," in *Media, Spiritualties and Social Change*, ed. Stewart M. Hoover and Monica Emerich (London: Continuum), 15–24.
39 Hale, "Genesis of the Celto-Catholic Revival?" 104.
40 *Royal Cornwall Gazette*, August 20 and 27, 1880.
41 Kenneth O. Morgan, *Wales in British Politics, 1868–1922* (Cardiff: University of Wales Press, 1970), 112–19.
42 Brian Elvins, "Cornwall's Newspaper War: The Political Rivalry between the *Royal Cornwall Gazette* and the *West Briton,* 1810–1831," in *Cornish Studies: Ten*, ed. Phillip Payton (Exeter: University of Exeter Press, 2002), 145–73.
43 *Cornish Guardian*, September 6, 1912, February 20, 1914, and February 16, 1923.
44 Callum Brown, *The Death of Christian Britain: Understanding Secularisation 1800–2000* (New York: Routledge, 2009).
45 *Cornish Guardian*, March 3, 1922.
46 *Royal Cornwall Gazette*, May 14, 1891 and July 14, 1892.
47 Ibid., January 30, 1890.
48 David Crowther and Chris Carter, "Community Identity and Cyberspace: A Study of the Cornish Community," in *Cornish Studies: Nine*, ed. Philip Payton (Exeter: University of Exeter Press, 2001), 241.

49 Ibid., 242.

50 Ibid., 243; See also Payton, *The Cornish Overseas*, 398.

51 California Cornish Cousins Facebook page, accessed January 10, 2015, https://www.facebook.com/pages/California-Cornish-Cousins/189038067798500; Cornish in New England Facebook page, accessed January 10, 2015, https://www.facebook.com/CORNISH.IN.NEW.ENGLAND; Cornish Downunder Facebook page, accessed January 10, 2015, https://www.facebook.com/groups/543390335722263/?fref=ts.

52 Mebyon Kernow—the Party for Cornwall Facebook page, accessed January 10, 2015, https://www.facebook.com/MebyonKernow?fref=ts; Cornwall Green Party Facebook page, accessed January 10, 2015, https://www.facebook.com/cornwallgreenparty?fref=ts; Cornwall Conservatives Facebook page, accessed January 10, 2015, https://www.facebook.com/CornwallConservatives?fref=ts.

53 Kernow King Facebook page, accessed January 10, 2015, https://www.facebook.com/kernowking?fref=ts.

54 Cornish Oafs Facebook page. accessed January 10, 2015, https://www.facebook.com/CornishOafs?fref=ts; RanG – www.anradyo.com Facebook page, accessed January 10, 2015, https://www.facebook.com/groups/440741969376913/.

55 Crowther and Carter, "Community Identity and Cyberspace," 228.

56 California Cornish Cousins, accessed January 9, 2015, https://www.facebook.com/pages/California-Cornish-Cousins/189038067798500.

57 Wbchris,(July 2, 2014). Nostalgic Cornwall Facebook page rockets to 6,000 members in just four months. West Briton. Retrieved from http://www.westbriton.co.uk/Nostalgic-Camborne-Facebook-page-rockets-6–000/story-21317402-detail/story.html.

58 Bella Dicks, *Culture on Display: The Production of Contemporary Visitability* (Milton Keynes: Open University Press, 2003), 119 and 191.

59 Ibid.

60 Say No to the Pasty Tax Facebook page, accessed January 10, 2015, https://www.facebook.com/groups/351201738255278/?fref=ts.

Chapter 9

1 The author wishes to thank Jenell Johnson, Robert Glenn Howard, Whitney Gent, and Emily Sauter for their invaluable feedback on this chapter.

2 All quotations from The Icarus Project come from: "The Icarus Project," The Icarus Project, accessed December 4, 2014, www.theicarusproject.net. All quotations retain their original spelling, grammar, and punctuation.

3 The Icarus Project uses terms such as "madness," "extreme states of consciousness," and "dangerous gifts" throughout their publications and in their discussion forums.

Although these terms may seem strange, pejorative, or outdated, I choose to use them throughout this chapter in order to respect Icarus's linguistic choices.

4 Jose Esteban Muñoz, *Disidentifications* (Minneapolis: University of Minnesota Press, 1999).

5 Ibid., 4.

6 Ibid.,11.

7 A name taken up by individual members.

8 As of December 8, 2014.

9 Ibid.

10 Ibid.

11 Megan E. Morrissey, "A DREAM Disrupted: Undocumented Migrant Youth Disidentifications with U.S. Citizenship," *Journal of International & Intercultural Communication* 6, no. 2 (2013): 145–62; Tim Stuettgen, "Disidentification in the Center of Power: The Porn Performer and Director Belladonna as a Contrasexual Culture Producer (A letter to Beatriz Preciado)," *Women's Studies Quarterly* 35, no. 1/2 (2007): 249–70.

12 Gust A. Yep, "The Violence of Heteronormativity in Communication Studies: Notes on Injury, Healing, and Queer World-Making," *Journal of Homosexuality* 45, no. 2 (2003): 46.

13 Donna Haraway, "Situated Knowledges: The Science Question in Feminism and the Privilege of Partial Perspective," *Feminist Studies* 14, no. 3 (1988): 575–99.

14 Robert Orsi, *The Madonna of 115th Street: Faith and Community in Italian Harlem, 1880–1950* (New Haven, CT: Yale University Press, 1985), lxi.

15 Don Yoder, "Toward a Definition of Folk Religion," *Western Folklore* 33, no. 1 (1974): 14.

16 Leonard N. Primiano, "Vernacular Religion and the Search for Method in Religious Folklife," *Western Folklore* 54, no. 1 (1995): 43.

17 Robert Glenn Howard, "Toward a Theory of the World Wide Web Vernacular: The Case for Pet Cloning," *Journal of Folklore Research* 42, no. 3 (2005): 323–60; Howard, "The Vernacular Web of Participatory Media," *Critical Studies in Media Communication* 25, no. 5 (2008): 490–513; Howard, "Electronic Hybridity: The Persistent Processes of the Vernacular Web," *Journal of American Folklore* 121, no. 480 (2008a): 192–218; Howard, "The Vernacular Mode: Locating the Non-Institutional in the Practice of Citizenship," in *Public Modalities: Rhetoric, Culture, Media, and the Shape of Public Life*, ed. Robert Asen and Daniel Brouwer (Tuscaloosa, AL: University of Alabama Press, 2010): 240–61.

18 Robert Glenn Howard, *Digital Jesus: The Making of a New Christian Fundamentalist Community on the Internet* (New York: New York University Press, 2011), 6.

19 Ibid., 21.

20 Gordon Graham, *The Re-Enchantment of the World* (New York: Oxford University Press, 2007), 21.

21 Ibid., 74.

22 Paul Heelas, *Spiritualities of Life: New Age Romanticism and Consumptive Capitalism* (Malden, MA: Blackwell, 2008), 5.

23 Ibid., 5.

24 Because posters are identified by screen name, and not gender, I use they/them/their as pronouns when referring to posters who have not explicitly stated their gender.

25 Muñoz, *Disidentifications*, 39.

26 Many Icaristas reside in the United States and are *not* members of indigenous communities; that is to say, in some ways, members of The Icarus Project appropriate shamanism (as well as Eastern and Native religions). One of the founders of The Icarus Project is aware of this potential risk. Below is an extended quotation from the most recent edition of *Navigating the Space Between Brilliance and Madness* that illustrates their productive discomfort about the use of shamanism as a discursive frame to understand madness: "Since the writing of this piece we have become familiar with the complexities of taking a word like shaman from one corner of the world and applying it universally to indigenous healers and guides from many traditions. We're also aware of the ways that westerners often harm other cultures by adopting their practices and profiting from them. In a context of cultural appropriation and neocolonialism, it's complicated for Westerners to call ourselves shamans. Nonetheless, we still find this language useful if understood as a shorthand for wounded healers with magical or spiritual inclinations, and so many readers of *Navigating the Space* have found these articles helpful that we have decided to include them in their original forms. We hope these essays can spark discussions that include an analysis of the power dynamics involved when Western peoples who have lost our own indigenous practices seek authentic spiritual connection in the practices of the peoples we have colonized" (The Icarus Project, *Navigating the Space Between Brilliance and Madness: A Reader and Roadmap of Bipolar Worlds.* [New York: The Icarus Project, 2013], 67).Cultural appropriation perhaps grows increasingly inevitable in a globalized, networked, transnational world; however, when it is done with care and self-reflexivity, it is not necessarily a negative thing. Although some scholars find appropriation of any sort an unforgivable sin, I am inclined to take The Icarus Project at their word, and look for the ways that shamanism is used ethically and productively by members of The Icarus Project. A well-intentioned appropriation of shamanism certainly does not undo all of the valuable work that The Icarus Project does, and we ought not write the group off simply because they unselfconsciously claimed or possibly misused a term.

27 Symbols often related to magic, demons, ritual.

28 Muñoz, *Disidentifications*, 200.

Chapter 10

1 Anthony Giddens, *Modernity and Self-Identity* (Cambridge: Polity Press, 1991).
2 Sherry Turkle, *Alone Together: Why We Expect More From Technology and Less from Each Other* (New York: Basic Books, 2011).
3 Manuel Castells, *The Rise of the Network Society (The Information Age: Economy, Society and Culture, Volume 1)* (Malden, MA: Blackwell Publishers, 1996).
4 Henry Jenkins, *Convergence Culture: Where Old and New Media Collide* (New York: New York University Press, 2006).
5 Clay Shirky, *Here Comes Everybody: The Power of Organizing without Organizations* (New York: The Penguin Press, 2008).
6 "What Is the Story Behind PostSecret?" PostSecret, accessed October 10, 2014, http://postsecretcommunity.com/news-faq/postsecret-story.
7 Alyce Gilligan, "Our Dirty Little (Post)Secret," *Relevant*, October 12, 2009, accessed October 10, 2014, http://www.relevantmagazine.com/life/whole-life/our-dirty-little-postsecret.
8 Frank Warren, *PostSecret: Confessions on Life, Death, and God* (New York: HarperCollins, 2009), 274.
9 Heidi Campbell (ed.), *Digital Religion: Understanding Religious Practice in New Media Worlds* (London: Routledge, 2013).
10 Mark Oppenheimer, "Examining the Growth of the 'Spiritual but Not Religious,'" *New York Times*, July 19, 2014, A14, http://nyti.ms/1nFHDZn.
11 Linda Mercadante, *Belief without Borders: Inside the Minds of the Spiritual But Not Religious* (New York: Oxford, 2013).
12 Oppenheimer, "Examining the Growth," A14.
13 Liberman and Hoover, "Identity, Confession, and Performance in PostSecret," White Paper, 2012, http://cmrc.colorado.edu/wp-content/uploads/2011/06/Third-Spaces.pdf#page=31.
14 Neha Prakash, "Deepak Chopra: Spirituality in the Age of Social Media," *Mashable*, September 17, 2012, accessed October 15, 2014, http://mashable.com/2012/09/17/deepak-chopra-spirituality-social-media/.
15 Gavin Richardson, "Without Pants," (blog), accessed October 14, 2014, http://www.lifewithoutpants.com/is-twitter-the-new-town-square-an-introduction-to-spirituality-and-social-media/).
16 Ibid.
17 Hannah Goodwyn, "Postcard Confessions: A Perspective on *Post Secret*," *CBN.com*, accessed October 14, 2014, http://www.cbn.com/spirituallife/biblestudyandtheology/perspectives/goodwyn-postsecret-card-confessions.aspx.
18 Ibid.
19 Ibid.

20 "Secrets of Spirituality," *PostSecret Chat*, http://www.postsecretcommunity.com/chat/viewtopic.php?t=237932).
21 Matt, comment on *PostSecret Chat.*
22 Sanctuarygonewrong, comment on *PostSecret Chat.*
23 Kradilicious, comment on *PostSecret Chat.*
24 Michel Foucault, *The History of Sexuality: An Introduction* (New York: Vintage Books,1990).
25 Raymond Williams, *Marxism & Literature* (Oxford: Oxford University Press, 1971).
26 "Soul Secret," http://www.patheos.com/ blogs/soulsecret/.
27 "Whisper," http://whisper.sh.
28 Stewart Hoover and Nabil Echchaibi, "The 'Third Spaces' of Digital Religion." *The Center for Media, Religion, and Culture* (2012). http://cmrc.colorado.edu/wpcontent/uploads/2012/06/Hoover-Echchaibi-paper.pdf
29 Mercadante, 2013.
30 Goodwyn, 2009.

Chapter 11

1 American Psychological Association, "How Does the APA Define," January 1, 2015, accessed February 7, 2015, http://www.apa.org.
2 Pamela Rutledge, "What Is Media Psychology? And Why You Should Care," *Media Psychology Research Center*, (blog), June 2010, http://www.apa.org/divisions/div46/Rutledge_What-is-Media-Psychology.pdf.
3 Hazel Rose Markus and Kitayama Shinobu, "Cultures and Selves: A Cycle of Mutual Constitution," *Perspectives on Psychological Science* 5, no. 4 (2010): 421.
4 Ibid.
5 Leerom Medovoi, "Age Trouble: A Timely Subject in American Literary and Cultural Studies," *American Literary History* 22, no. 3 (2010): 658, accessed January 24, 2015, http://muse.jhu.edu/.
6 Victor G. Cicirelli, "Fear of Death in Older Adults Predictions From Terror Management Theory," *The Journals of Gerontology Series B: Psychological Sciences and Social Sciences* 57, no. 4 (2002): 37.
7 Michael B. Salzman, "Globalization, Culture, and Anxiety: Perspectives and Predictions from Terror Management Theory," *Journal of Social Distress and the Homeless* 10, no. 4 (2001): 337–52.
8 J. L. Henderson, "The Cultural Unconscious," *Quadrant* 21, no. 2 (1988): 7–16.
9 Henry Abramovitch, "The Cultural Complex: Linking Psyche and Society," *Jung Journal* 1, no. 1 (2007): 50.
10 Samuel L. Kimbles, "Cultural Complexes and the Transmission of Group Traumas in Everyday Life," *Psychological Perspectives* 49, no. 1 (2006): 96–110.

11 Abramovitch, "Cultural Complex," 49.
12 Kimbles, "Cultural Complexes and the Transmission of Group," 2006.
13 Martin Gold and Elizabeth Ann Malcolm Douvan, "Culture," *A New Outline of Social Psychology*, ed. M. Gold and E. Douvan (Washington, DC: American Psychological Association), 120.
14 Thomas Singer, "The Cultural Complex and Archetypal Defenses of the Group Spirit: Baby Zeus, Elian Gonzales, Constantine's Sword, and Other Holy Wars," in *The Cultural Complex: Contemporary Jungian Perspectives on Psyche and Society*, ed. Thomas Singer and Samuel L. Kimbles (New York: Routledge, 2004), 22.
15 Ibid., 20.
16 Betty Meador, "Light the Seven Fires—Seize the Seven Desires," in *The Cultural Complex: Contemporary Jungian Perspectives on Psyche and Society*, ed. Thomas Singer and Samuel L. Kimbles (New York: Routledge, 2004), 171–84.
17 United States Census Bureau, *Population Estimates* [Datasets], 2009, May 13, available August 5, 2009, http:/www.census.gov/popest/national/.
18 William Strauss and Neil Howe, *Generations: The History of America's Future, 1584 to 2069* (New York: Morrow, 1991), 301.
19 Karl Mannheim, *Essays on the Sociology of Knowledge*, ed. Paul Kecskemeti (New York: Oxford University Press, 1952), 298, 304.
20 Ibid., 303.
21 Ibid., 309.
22 Ron Eyerman and Bryan S. Turner, "Outline of a Theory of Generations," *European Journal of Social Theory* 1, no. 1 (1998): 91–106.
23 C. Gilleard and Paul Higgs, *Theorising Cohort and Generation in Empirical Research*, presented at *Age, Cohort and Generation: Conceptual and Empirical Approaches* symposium, ISA Forum of Sociology (Barcelona, Spain, September 2008).
24 Steve Gillon, *Boomer Nation: The Largest and Richest Generation Ever, and How It Changed America* (New York: Free Press, 2004), 4.
25 Ibid., 5
26 Landon Jones, *Great Expectations: American and Baby Boom Generation* (New York: Coward, McCann & Geoghegan, 1980), 1.
27 Mike Brake, *Comparative Youth Culture: The Sociology of Youth Cultures and Youth Subcultures in America, Britain, and Canada* (London, GBR: Routledge, 1985).
28 Jacques Janssen, Mark Dechesne, and Ad Van Knippenberg, "The Psychological Importance of Youth Culture a Terror Management Approach," *Youth & Society* 31, no. 2 (1999): 153.
29 Ken Dychtwald, *Age Power: How the 21st century Will Be Ruled by the New Old* (New York: Jeremy P. Tarcher/Putnam, 1999).
30 James Harkin and Julia Huber, *Eternal Youths: How the Baby Boomers Are Having Their Time Again* (London, GBR: Demos, 2004).

31 Theodore Roszak, *The Making of an Elder Culture: Reflections on the Future of America's Most Audacious Generation* (Gabriola Island, BC, CAN: New Society Publishers, 2009), 5.

32 Ibid.

33 Gillon, *Boomer Nation*, 110.

34 Ibid.

35 Wade Clark Roof, *Spiritual Marketplace: Baby Boomers and the Remaking of American Religion* (Princeton, NJ: Princeton University Press, 2001).

36 Richard Cimino and Don Lattin, "Choosing my Religion," *American Demographics* 21, no. 4 (1999): 60, para. 10.

37 Roof, *Spiritual Marketplace*, 17.

38 Robert Jay Lifton, *The Broken Connection: On Death and the Continuity of Life* (New York: Simon & Schuster, 1979).

39 David Weiss and Frieder R. Lang, "Thinking about My Generation: Adaptive Effects of a Dual Age Identity in Later Adulthood." *Psychology and Aging* 24, no. 3 (2009): 729–34.

40 See Robert C. Atchley, "A Continuity Theory of Normal Aging," *The Gerontologist* 29, no. 2 (1989): 183–90; Roy F. Baumeister, and Mark R. Leary, "The Need to Belong: Desire for Interpersonal Attachments as a Fundamental Human Motivation," *Psychological Bulletin* 117, no. 3 (1995): 497–529; Mannheim, *Essays on the Sociology of Knowledge*, 1952; Weiss and Lang, "Thinking about My Generation," 2009.

41 For example, see Joshua Correll and Bernadette Park, "A Model of the Ingroup as a Social Resource," *Personality and Social Psychology Review* 9, no. 4 (2005): 341–59. doi: 10.1207/s15327957pspr0904_4; Michael A. Hogg and Kipling D. Williams, "From I to We: Social Identity and the Collective Self," *Group Dynamics: Theory, Research, and Practice* 4, no. 1 (2000): 81–97. doi:10. I037//1089-2699.4.1.81.

42 Weiss and Lang, "Thinking about My Generation."

43 Harkin and Huber, *Eternal Youths,* 13–14.

44 Gillon, *Boomer Nation*, 2004.

45 Ibid.

46 Jamie Arndt, Jamie L. Goldenberg, Jeff Greenberg, Tom Pyszczynski, and Sheldon Solomon, "Death Can Be Hazardous to Your Health: Adaptive and Ironic Consequences of Defenses against the Terror of Death," in *Psychodynamic Perspectives on Sickness and Health*, ed. P. R. Duberstein and J. M. Masling (Washington, DC: American Psychological Association, 2000), 206–7.

47 Anne Maija Huffman, "Eternal Youths: A Narrative Inquiry into the Buffering Effects of a Generational Cultural Complex against the Anxiety of Aging and Death in the American Baby Boom Generation," (doctoral dissertation, Institute of

Transpersonal Psychology, 2012). Interviews were conducted using Survey Monkey in 2011.

48 Virginia Braun and Victoria Clarke, "Using Thematic Analysis in Psychology," *Qualitative Research in Psychology* 3, no. 2 (2006): 77–101.

49 For more on this method, see Angela Cora Garcia, Alecea I. Standlee, Jennifer Bechkoff, and Yan Cui, "Ethnographic Approaches to the Internet and Computer-mediated Communication," *Journal of Contemporary Ethnography* 38, no. 1 (2009): 54.

50 Jones, *Great Expectations.*

51 Gillon, *Boomer Nation*, 8.

52 Catherine Kohler Riessman, *Narrative Methods for the Human Sciences* (Los Angeles, CA: Sage, 2008), 69.

53 Internet World Stats, "Internet Usage Statistics for the Americas," in *Internet World Stats: Usage and Population Statistics* (Internet Users and Population Stats for the Americas), June 2010, http:/www.internetworldstats.com/stats2.htm.

54 Lee Rainie, "Presentations: Baby Boomers and Technology," March 28, 2012, http://www.pewinternet.org/2012/03/28/baby-boomers-and-technology/.

55 Lee Rainie, "Baby Boomers in the Digital Age," (Pew Internet & American Life Project, 2010).

56 Rafael Capurro and Christoph Pingel, "Ethical Issues of Online Communication Research," *Ethics and Information Technology* 4, no. 3 (2002): 189.

57 Garcia et al., "Ethnographic Approaches to the Internet and Computer-mediated Communication," 2009.

58 William H. Frey, "Baby Boomers and the New Demographics of America's Seniors," *Generations* 34, no. 3 (2010): 28.

59 United States Census Bureau.

60 Paco Underhill, *What Women Want: The Global Market Turns Female Friendly* (New York: Simon and Schuster, 2010).

61 J. Wortham, "Baby Boomers, Luddites? Not So Fast," *New York Times,* February 20, 2009, para. 2, http:/bits.blogs.nytimes.com/2009/02/20/baby-boomers-luddites-not-so-fast.

62 Roof, *Spiritual Marketplace*, 145.

63 Gold and Douvan, 120.

64 J. Walker Smith and Ann Clurman, *Generation Ageless: How Baby Boomers are Changing the Way We Live Today—and They're Just Getting Started* (New York: HarperCollins, 2007), 86.

65 Richard M. Lee and Steven B. Robbins, "Measuring Belongingness: The Social Connectedness and the Social Assurance Scales," *Journal of Counseling Psychology* 42, no. 2 (1995): 232.

66 Heinz Kohut, *How Does Analysis Cure?*, ed. Arnold Goldberg, Vol. 52 (Chicago: University of Chicago Press, 1984), 200.

67 Ernesto Caravantes, *From Melting Pot to Witch's Cauldron: How Multiculturalism Failed America* (Lanham, MD: Hamilton Books, 2010), 6.

68 Singer, "Cultural Complex and Archetypal Defenses," 5.

69 Thomas T. Lawson, *Carl Jung, Darwin of the Mind* (London: Karnac Books, 2008).

70 Roof, *Spiritual Marketplace.*

71 Maja Becker, Vivian L. Vignoles, Ellinor Owe, Rupert Brown, Peter B. Smith, Matt Easterbrook, Ginette Herman et al., "Culture and the Distinctiveness Motive: Constructing Identity in Individualistic and Collectivistic Contexts," *Journal of Personality and Social Psychology* 102, no. 4 (2012): 833–55; Harry Charalambos Triandis, *Individualism & Collectivism* (Boulder, CO; Oxford: Westview Press, 1995).

72 Weiss and Lang, "Thinking about My Generation."

73 Ibid.

74 Gilleard and Higgs, *Theorising Cohort.*

75 Christopher Bollas, *Being a Character* (New York: Hill & Wang, 1992), 252.

76 Bill Gibron, "The 10 Best Films about Aging and the Elderly," *Pop Matters* (Blog), July 30, 2013, para. 2, http://www.popmatters.com/post/174004-the-10-best-films-about-agingthe-elderly-of-all-time/.

77 Lachman, Margie E. and Stefan Agrigoroaei, "Promoting Functional Health in Midlife and Old Age: Long-Term Protective Effects of Control Beliefs, Social Support, and Physical Exercise," *PloS one* 5, no. 10 (2010): e13297.

78 Gillon, *Boomer Nation*; Smith and Clurman, *Generation Ageless.*

79 Pete Townshend, "My Generation," on *My Generation* [CD], recorded by R. Daltrey, P. Townshend, J. Entwistle, and K. Moon (London, GBR: Brunswick Records, 1965), track 1.

80 Doug Owram, *Born at the Right Time: A History of the Baby Boom Generation* (Toronto: University of Toronto Press, 1997).

81 Gillon, *Boomer Nation.*

82 Smith and Clurman, *Generation Ageless.*

83 Rainie, "*The Internet and Religion.*"

84 Agnieszka Golec de Zavala, Aleksandra Cichocka, Roy Eidelson, and Nuwan Jayawickreme, "Collective Narcissism and its Social Consequences," *Journal of Personality and Social Psychology* 97, no. 6 (2009): 1074.

85 Christopher Lasch, *The Culture of Narcissism: American Life in an Age of Diminishing Expectations* (New York: W. W. Norton, 1991), xv.

86 Ibid.

87 Roof, *Spiritual Marketplace.*

88 Ibid., 7.

89 J. Zogby, "The Way We'll Be: The Baby Boomers' Legacy," *Forbes* (July 23, 2009), http:/www.forbes.com/2009/07/22/baby-boomer-legacy-change-consumer-opinions-columnists-john-zogby.html, para. 11.

90 M. Bywater, “Baby Boomers and the Illusion of Perpetual Youth,” *New Statesman* (October 30, 2006), http:/www.newstatesman.com/node/154659.

91 Gillon. *Boomer Nation.*

92 Smith and Clurman, *Generation Ageless.*

93 Cheryl Russell, *The Master Trend: How the Baby Boom Generation Is Remaking America* (New York, NY: Plenum US, 1993), 22.

Chapter 12

1 Graham Harvey, *Food, Sex and Strangers: Understanding Religion as Everyday Life* (New York: Routledge, 2013).

2 Lewis Carroll, *Alice's Adventures in Wonderland and Through the Looking Glass* (London: Puffin, 1962 [1872]), 274–5.

3 Leonard N. Primiano, “Vernacular Religion and the Search for Method in Religious Folklife,” *Western Folklore* 54, no. 1 (1995): 37–56; Leonard N. Primiano, “Manifestations of the Religious Vernacular: Ambiguity, Power, and Creativity,” in *Vernacular Religion in Everyday Life: Expressions of Belief*, ed. Ülo Valk and Marion Bowman (London, Equinox, 2012).

4 David D. Hall (ed.), *Lived Religion in America: Toward a History of Practice* (Princeton, NJ: Princeton University Press, 1997); Meredith B. McGuire, *Lived Religion: Faith and Practice in Everyday Life* (Oxford: Oxford University Press, 2008).

5 Manuel A. Vásquez, *More Than Belief: A Materialist Theory of Religion* (Oxford: Oxford University Press, 2011).

6 Samuli Schielke and Liza Debevec (eds.), *Ordinary Lives and Grand Schemes: An Anthropology of Everyday Religion* (New York: Berghahn Books, 2012); Michel de Certeau. *The Practice of Everyday Life* (Berkeley: University of California Press, 1984).

7 Malory Nye, *Religion: The Basics* (London: Routledge, 2004).

8 Harvey, *Food, Sex and Strangers*, 43.

9 Robert A. Orsi, “Everyday Miracles: The Study of Lived Religion,” in *Lived Religion in America: Toward a History of Practice*, ed. David D. Hall (Princeton, NJ: Princeton University Press, 1997): 3–21.

10 William T. Cavanaugh, “A Fire Strong Enough to Consume the House: ‘The Wars of Religion’ and the Rise of the State,” *Modern Theology* 11, no. 4 (1995); Richard King, “The Association of ‘Religion’ with Violence: Reflections on a Modern Trope,” in *Religion and Violence in South Asia: Theory and Practice*, ed. John R. Hinnells and Richard King (London: Routledge, 2007).

11 Malcolm Ruel, *Belief, Ritual and the Securing of Life: Reflexive Essays on a Bantu Religion* (Leiden: Brill, 1997).

12 John Bowker, *Licensed Insanities. Religions and Belief in God in the Contemporary World* (London: Darton, Longman and Todd, 1987).

13 Bruno Latour, *We Have Never Been Modern* (New York: Harvester Wheatsheaf, 1993).

14 Jane Goodall, "Primate Spirituality" in *Encyclopedia of Religion and Nature*, ed. Bron Taylor (New York: Continuum, 2005), 1304.

15 Steven Mithen, *The Singing Neanderthals: The Origins of Music, Language, Mind and Body* (London: Weidenfeld & Nicolson, 2005).

16 Sommer, Volker, e-mail message to author, August 25, 2014; Volker Sommer and Amy Parish, "Living differences: The Paradigm of Animal Cultures" in *Homo Novus—A Human Without Illusions*, ed. Ulrich Frey, Charlotte Störmer, and Kai Willführ (Heidelberg: Springer, 2010), 17–31; Mary Douglas, *Purity and Danger: An Analysis of Concepts of Pollution and Taboo* (London: Routledge, 1992).

17 James B. Harrod, "The Case for Chimpanzee Religion," *Journal for the Study of Religion, Nature and Culture* 8, no. 1 (2014): 9; James B. Harrod, "A Trans-species Definition of Religion," *Journal for the Study of Religion, Nature and Culture* 5, no. 3 (2011): 327–53.

18 Harrod, "The Case for Chimpanzee Religion," 9.

19 Nancy R. Howell, "Embodied Transcendence: Bonobos and Humans in Community," *Zygon* 44, no. 3 (2009): 602, 609.

20 Edward Tylor, *Primitive Culture,* 2 vols. (London: John Murray, 1871).

21 Nurit Bird-David, "' Animism' Revisited: Personhood, Environment, and Relational Epistemology," *Current Anthropology* 40 (1999); A. Irving Hallowell, "Ojibwa Ontology, Behavior, and World View," in *Culture in History: Essays in Honor of Paul Radin*, ed. Stanley Diamond (New York: Columbia University Press, 1960); Graham Harvey (ed.), *Handbook of Contemporary Animism* (London: Routledge, 2013).

22 Graham Harvey, *Animism: Respecting the Living World* (London: Hurst, 2005), xi.

23 Elias Lönnrot, *The Kalevala* (Oxford: OUP, 1989 [1835]).

24 Graham Harvey and Robert J. Wallis, *Historical Dictionary of Shamanism* (Lanham, MD: Scarecrow Press, 2006), 3.

25 Mircea Eliade, *Shamanism: Archaic Techniques of Ecstasy* (New York: Pantheon, 1964 [1951]).

26 Carlos Castaneda, *The Teaching of Don Juan* (Berkeley: University of California Press, 1968).

27 Michael Harner, *The Way of the Shaman* (San Francisco: Harper & Row, 1980).

28 Carlos Faust, "A Blend of Blood and Tobacco: Shamans and Jaguars among the Parakanã of Eastern Amazonia," in *In Darkness and Secrecy: The Anthropology of Assault Sorcery and Witchcraft in Amazonia*, ed. Neil L. Whitehead and Robin Wright (Durham, NC: Duke University Press, 2004), 157–8.

29 Michael Harner, *The Jivaro: People of the Sacred Waterfalls* (Berkeley: University of California Press, 1972).

30 Harner, *The Way of the Shaman*.

31 Graham Harvey and Charles Thompson (eds.), *Indigenous Diasporas and Dislocations* (Aldershot: Ashgate, 2005).

32 Christopher Hartney and Daniel J. Tower (eds.), *Constructing the Indigenous* (Leiden: E. J. Brill, 2015).

33 Graham Harvey, "Performing Indigeneity and Performing Guesthood," in *Constructing the Indigenous*, ed. Christopher Hartney and Daniel J. Tower (Leiden: E. J. Brill, forthcoming).

34 Pemina Yellow Bird and Kathryn Milun, "Interrupted Journeys: The Cultural Politics of Indian Reburial," in *Displacements: Cultural Identities in Question*, ed. Angelika Bammer (Durham, NC: Duke University Press, 1994), 10.

35 Lisa Aldred, "Plastic Shamans and Astroturf Sun Dances: New Age Commercialization of Native American Spirituality," *American Indian Quarterly* 24, no. 3 (2000): 334.

36 Christina Welch, "Complicating Spiritual Appropriation: North American Indian Agency in Western Alternative Spiritual Practice," *Journal of New Age and Alternative Spiritualities* 3 (2007): 97–117.

37 Daniel Quinn, *Ishmael* (New York: Bantam, 1992).

38 David D. Shorter, "Spirituality," in *The Oxford Handbook of American Indian History*, ed. Fredrick Hoxie (London: Oxford University Press forthcoming).

39 Shorter, "Spirituality"; Kenneth M. Morrison, "Animism and a Proposal for a Post- Cartesian Anthropology," in *The Handbook of Contemporary Animism*, ed. Graham Harvey (New York: Routledge, 2013): 38–52; Kenneth M. Morrison, "Beyond the Supernatural: Language and Religious Action," *Religion* 22 (1992): 201–5.

40 Craig Martin, *Capitalizing Religion: Ideology and the Opiate of the Bourgeoisie* (London: Bloomsbury, 2014), 6; Jonathan Rowson, *Spiritualise: Revitalising Spirituality to Address 21st Century Challenges* (London: Royal Society for the encouragement of Arts, Manufactures and Commerce, 2014), 31.

41 Robert A. Orsi, "Afterword: Everyday Religion and the Contemporary World," in *Ordinary Lives and Grand Schemes: An Anthropology of Everyday religion*, ed. Samuli Schielke and Liza Debevec (New York and Oxford: Berghahn Books, 2012), 157.

42 Martin, *Capitalizing Religion*.

43 Orsi, "Afterword," 146.

44 Te Pakaka Tawhai, "Maori Religion," in *The World's Religions: The Study of Religion, Traditional and New Religion*, ed. Stewart Sutherland and Peter Clarke (London: Routledge, 1988), 101.

Bibliography

Abramovitch, Henry. "The Cultural Complex: Linking Psyche and Society." *Jung Journal* 1, no. 1 (2007): 49–52.

Albanese, Catherine L. *A Republic of Mind and Spirit: A Cultural History of American Metaphysical Religion*. New Haven, CT: Yale University Press, 2007.

Aldred, Lisa. "Plastic Shamans and Astroturf Sun Dances: New Age Commercialization of Native American Spirituality." *American Indian Quarterly* 24, no. 3 (2000): 329–52.

Ambrose, Meg Leta, and Jef Ausloos. "The Right to Be Forgotten across the Pond." *Journal of Information Policy* 3 (2013): 1–23.

American Psychological Association. "How Does the APA Define." *American Psychological Association*. January 1, 2015. Accessed February 7, 2015. http://www.apa.org.

Ammerman, Nancy. *Everyday Religion: Observing Modern Religious Lives*. Oxford: Oxford University Press, 2007.

Anderson, Benedict. *Imagined Communities: Reflections on the Origin and Spread of Nationalism*. London: Verso, 2006.

Andrejevic, Mark. *Reality TV: The Work of Being Watched*. Lanham, MD: Rowman and Littlefield Publishers, 2004.

Apple, Rima. *Perfect Motherhood: Science and Childrearing in America*. New Brunswick, NJ: Rutgers University Press, 2006.

Arndt, Jamie, Jamie L. Goldenberg, Jeff Greenberg, Tom Pyszczynski, and Sheldon Solomon. "Death Can Be Hazardous to Your Health: Adaptive and Ironic Consequences of Defenses against the Terror of Death." In *Psychodynamic Perspectives on Sickness and Health*, edited by P. R. Duberstein and J. M. Masling, 201–57. Washington, DC: American Psychological Association, 2000.

Asad, Talal. *Genealogies of Religion: Discipline and Reasons of Power in Christianity and Islam*. Baltimore, MD: Johns Hopkins University Press, 1993.

Ashe, Geoffrey. *Avalonian Quest*. London: Methuen, 1982.

Atchley, Robert C. "A Continuity Theory of Normal Aging." *The Gerontologist* 29, no. 2 (1989): 183–90.

Aubert, Alexandra. Le Portage à travers le monde et les époques. *Swiss Association for Babywearing* (Association Suisse de Portage des Bébés). Accessed November 6, 2012. http://www.aspb.ch/association/ASPB%20-%20Le%20portage%20a%20travers%20le%20monde%20et%20les%20epoques.pdf.

Badinter, Elisabeth. *Le Conflit. La femme et la mère*. Paris: Flammarion, 2010.

Baines, Dudley. *Migration in a Mature Economy and Internal Migration in England and Wales, 1861–1900.* Cambridge: Cambridge University Press, 1985.

Barlow, David, Philip Mitchell, and Tom O'Malley. *The Media in Wales: Voices of a Small Nation.* Cardiff: University of Wales Press, 2005.

Bauman, Zygmunt. *Liquid love: On the Frailty of Human Bonds.* John Wiley & Sons, 2013.

Baumeister, Roy F., and Mark R. Leary. "The Need to Belong: Desire for Interpersonal Attachments as a Fundamental Human Motivation." *Psychological Bulletin* 117, no. 3 (1995): 497–529.

Baxter, Jonathan. Interview with Jenna Gray-Hildenbrand. August 10, 2014.

Beaudoin, Tom. *Virtual Faith: The Irreverent Spiritual Quest of Generation X.* 1st ed. San Francisco, CA: Jossey-Bass, 1998.

Becker, Maja, Vivian L. Vignoles, Ellinor Owe, Rupert Brown, Peter B. Smith, Matt Easterbrook, Ginette Herman et al. "Culture and the Distinctiveness Motive: Constructing Identity in Individualistic and Collectivistic Contexts." *Journal of Personality and Social Psychology* 102, no. 4 (2012): 833–55.

Behar, Howard. *It's Not about the Coffee: Leadership Principles from a Life at Starbucks.* New York: Penguin, 2007.

Bell, John, Del McCoury, Neal Casal, Ethan Miller et al. "Reflections: Jerry Garcia's Life and Legacy," *Relix*, 2014. Accessed December 8, 2015. https://web4.relix.com/articles/detail/reflections-jerry-garcia-s-life-and-legacy-john-bell-del-mccoury-ethan-mill.

Bellah, Robert. "The New Consciousness and the Berkeley New Left." In *The New Religious Consciousness*, edited by Charles Glock and Robert Bellah, 77–92. Berkeley: University of California Press, 1976.

Benham, Patrick. *The Avalonians.* Glastonbury: Gothic Image Publications, 1993.

The Big Chill. Film. Directed by Lawrence Kasdan. 1983. USA: Columbia Pictures.

The Big Lebowski. Film. Directed by Joel Coen. 1998. USA: Gramercy Pictures.

Bird, S. Elizabeth. *The Audience in Everyday Life: Living in a Media World.* New York: Routledge, 2003.

Bird-David, Nurit. "'Animism' Revisited: Personhood, Environment, and Relational Epistemology." *Current Anthropology* 40 (1999): S67–91.

Bjorn, Krista. "Colleen Barrett: On Leadership at Southwest Airlines." *Character First the Magazine*, November 29, 2011. Accessed December 22, 2014. http://cfthemagazine.com/2011-12/colleen-barrett-on-leadership-at-southwest-airlines/.

Black, Renata M. "Deepak Chopra On The Future of Business." *Huffington Post*, July 15, 2014. Accessed December 22, 2014. http://www.huffingtonpost.com/renata-m-black/deepak-chopra-on-the-futu_b_5588250.html.

Blain, Neil, and David Hutchison, eds. *The Media in Scotland.* Edinburgh: Edinburgh University Press, 2008.

Bobel, Chris. *The Paradox of Natural Mothering.* Philadelphia, PA: Temple University Press, 2002.

—. "Resisting, But Not Too Much: Interrogating the Paradox of Natural Mothering." In *Maternal Theory. Essential Readings*, 782–91. Toronto: Demeter Press, 2007.

Bollas, Christopher. *Being a Character: Psychoanalysis and Self Experience*. New York: Hill & Wang, 1992.

Bond, Frederick Bligh. *The Gate of Remembrance: The Story of the Psychological Experiment which Resulted in the Discovery of the Edgar Chapel at Glastonbury*. Oxford: 1918.

Bowker, John. *Licensed Insanities. Religions and Belief in God in the Contemporary World*. London: Darton, Longman, and Todd, 1987.

Bowman, Marion. "Ancient Avalon, New Jerusalem, Heart Chakra of Planet Earth: Localisation and Globalisation in Glastonbury." *Numen* 52, no. 2 (2005): 157–90.

—. "Christianity, Plurality and Vernacular Religion in Early Twentieth Century Glastonbury: A Sign of Things to Come." *Studies in Church History 51*. Woodbridge: Boydell, 2015.

—. "Drawn to Glastonbury." In *Pilgrimage in Popular Culture*, edited by Ian Reader and Tony Walter, 29–62. Basingstoke and London: Macmillan, 1993.

—. "Going with the Flow: Contemporary Pilgrimage in Glastonbury." In *Shrines and Pilgrimage in the Modern World: New Itineraries into the Sacred*, edited by Peter Jan Margy, 241–80. Amsterdam: Amsterdam University Press, 2008.

—. "Procession and Possession in Glastonbury: Continuity, Change and the Manipulation of Tradition." *Folklore* 115, no. 3 (2004): 1–13.

—. "Taking Stories Seriously: Vernacular Religion, Contemporary Spirituality and the Myth of Jesus in Glastonbury." *Temenos* 39–40, no. 1 (2003–4): 125–42.

—. "Understanding Glastonbury as a Site of Consumption." In *Religion, Media and Culture: A Reader*, edited by Gordon Lynch, Jolyon Mitchell, and Anna Strhan, 11–22. London: Routledge. 2011.

—. "Valuing Spirituality: Commodification, Consumption and Community in Glastonbury." In *Religion in Consumer Society: Brands, Consumers and Markets*, edited by Francois Gauthier and Tuomas Martikainen, 207–24. Farnham and Burlington, VA: Ashgate, 2013.

Bowman, Marion, and Ülo Valk, eds. *Vernacular Religion in Everyday Life: Expressions of Belief*. Sheffield, Oakville, CT: Equinox, 2012.

Brack, Jessica. "Maximizing Millenials in the Workplace." UNC Kenan-Flagler Business School, 2012. Accessed Februrary 16, 2015. http://www.kenan-flagler.unc.edu/executive-development/custom programs/~/media/DF1C11C056874DDA8097271A1ED48662.ashx.

Bradley, Marion Zimmer. *The Mists of Avalon*. London: Sphere Books, 1986.

Brake, M. *Comparative Youth Culture: The Sociology of Youth Cultures and Youth Subcultures in America, Britain, and Canada*. London, GBR: Routledge, 1985.

Braudel, Fernand. *The Identity of France: History and Environment*, Vol. 1. Waukegan, IL: Fontana Press, 1989.

Braun, Virginia, and Victoria Clarke. "Using Thematic Analysis in Psychology." *Qualitative Research in Psychology* 3, no. 2 (2006): 77–101.

Brown, Callum. *The Death of Christian Britain: Understanding Secularisation 1800–2000.* New York: Routledge, 2009.
The Bucket List. Film. Directed by Rob Reiner. 2007. USA: Warner Bros. Pictures.
Butler Bass, Diana. *Christianity after Religion.* New York: Harper One, 2013.
Bywater, M. "Baby Boomers and the Illusion of Perpetual Youth. *New Statesman.* October 30, 2006. http:/www.newstatesman.com/node/154659.
Calendar Customs: A Guide to British Calendar Customs and Local Traditions. Accessed January 8, 2015. http://calendarcustoms.com/articles/montol-festival/.
California Cornish Cousins. Accessed January 9, 2015. https://www.facebook.com/pages/California-Cornish-Cousins/189038067798500.
Campbell, Colin. "The Cult, The Cultic Milieu and Secularization." In *A Sociological Yearbook of Religion in Britain* 5, 119–36. London: SCM Books, 1972.
Campbell, Heidi A., ed. *Digital Religion: Understanding Religious Practice in New Media Worlds.* London: Routledge, 2013.
—. *Exploring Religious Community Online: We Are One in the Network.* Vol. 24. New York: Peter Lang, 2005.
—. "Understanding the Relationship between Religion Online and Offline in a Networked Society." *Journal of the American Academy of Religion* 80, no. 1 (2012): 64–93.
—. *When Religion Meets New Media.* New York: Routledge, 2010.
Camp, Jan. *Hoopdance Revolution: Mindfulness in Motion.* Berkeley, CA: Arc Light Books, 2013.
Capurro, Rafael, and Christoph Pingel. "Ethical Issues of Online Communication Research." *Ethics and Information Technology* 4, no. 3 (2002): 189–94.
Caravantes, Ernesto. *From Melting Pot to Witch's Cauldron: How Multiculturalism Failed America.* Lanham, MD: Hamilton Books, 2010.
Carey, William. *Communication as Culture: Essays on Media And Society.* New York: Routledge, 1992.
Carley, James P. *Glastonbury Abbey: The Holy House at the Head of the Moors Adventurous.* Glastonbury: Gothic Image Publications, 1996.
Carrette, Jeremy R., and Richard King. *Selling Spirituality: The Silent Takeover of Religion.* London: Routledge, 2005.
Carroll, Lewis. *Alice's Adventures in Wonderland and Through the Looking Glass.* London: Puffin, 1962 [1872].
Castaneda, Carlos. *The Teaching of Don Juan.* Berkeley. University of California Press, 1968.
Castells, Manuel. *The Rise of the Network Society (The Information Age: Economy, Society and Culture, Volume 1.* Malden, MA: Blackwell Publishers, 1996.
Cavanaugh, William T. "A Fire Strong Enough to Consume the House: "The Wars of Religion" and the Rise of the State." *Modern Theology* 11, no. 4 (1995): 397–420.
Centre for the Study of Media and Culture in Small Nations. Accessed January 9, 2015. http://culture.research.southwales.ac.uk/.

"Chalice Well." Accessed January 12, 2012. http://www.chalicewell.org.uk/index.cfm/glastonbury/Trust.Home.

Chapple, Christopher Key. *Hinduism and Ecology: The Intersection of Earth, Sky, and Water*. Cambridge, MA: Harvard University Press, 2000.

—. *Jainism and Ecology: Nonviolence in the Web of Life*. Cambridge, MA: Harvard University Press, 2002.

Chayko, Mary. *Portable Communities.* Albany: University of New York Press, 2008.

Chiam, Natasha. "Babywearing: Beyond the Cute Baby Carriers." *The Feminist Breeder*. Accessed January 30, 2015. http://resources.thefeministbreeder.com/babies-toddlers/babywearing/babywearing-beyond-the-cute-baby-carriers/.

Chidester, David. "'Classify and Conquer' Friedrich Max Muller, Indigenous Religious Traditions, and Imperial Comparative Religion." In *Beyond Primitivism: Indigenous Religious Traditions and Modernity*, edited by Jacob Olupona, 71–88. New York: Routledge, 2003.

Cicirelli, Victor G. "Fear of Death in Older Adults Predictions from Terror Management Theory." *The Journals of Gerontology Series B: Psychological Sciences and Social Sciences* 57, no. 4 (2002): P358–P366.

Cimino, Richard, and Don Lattin. "Choosing My Religion." *American Demographics* 21, no. 4 (1999): 60.

Clark, Lynn Schofield. *The Parent App: Understanding Families in the Digital Age.* Oxford: Oxford University Press, 2013.

—, ed. *Religion, Media and the Marketplace.* New Brunswick, NJ: Rutgers, 2007.

Clifton, Chas. "Entheogens." In *Encyclopedia of Religion and Nature*, edited by Bron Taylor, 596–97. London: Continuum, 2005.

Coats, Curtis D. *From Mediascape to Meaning and Back Again: An Interactionist Analysis of Spiritual Tourism in Sedona, Arizona*. Ann Arbor, MI: ProQuest, 2008.

Coleman, James William. *The New Buddhism: The Western Transformation of an Ancient Tradition*. New York: Oxford, 2001.

Collins, Andrew. "Pobol y Cwm at 40: Welsh-language TV Has Never Been Stronger." *Guardian*, London, October 16, 2014. Accessed January 9, 2015. http://www.theguardian.com/tv-and-radio/tvandradioblog/2014/oct/16/pobol-y-cwm-40-welsh-language-tv-never-been-stronger.

Coman, Mihai. "Liminality in Media Studies: From Everyday Life to Media Events." In *Victor Turner and Contemporary Cultural Performance*, edited by Graham St. John, 94–108. New York: Berghahn Books, 2008.

"Community." Tom's of Maine. Accessed December 22, 2014. http://www.tomsofmaine.com/goodness-report/community#Volunteer.

"Concern Over Newspapers' Decline in Wales." *BBC Wales*. Accessed January 9, 2015. http://www.bbc.co.uk/news/uk-wales-11111396.

Connors, Peter. *JAMerica: The History of the Jam Band and Festival Scene*. Boston: DaCapo, 2013.

Conversi, Daniele. "Language or Race? The Choice of Core Values in the Development of Catalan and Basque Nationalisms." *Ethnic and Racial Studies* 13, no. 1, (1990): 50–70.

Cornish Culture Online. Accessed January 8, 2015. http://www.cornishculture.co.uk/pagan.htm.

Cornish Downunder Facebook page. Accessed January 10, 2015. https://www.facebook.com/groups/543390335722263/?fref=ts.

Cornish Guardian. Newspaper collection, Cornwall Centre/Kresen Kernow. Redruth, United Kingdom.

Cornish in New England Facebook page. Accessed January 10, 2015. https://www.facebook.com/CORNISH.IN.NEW.ENGLAND.

Cornish Oafs Facebook page. Accessed January 10, 2015. https://www.facebook.com/CornishOafs?fref=ts.

Cornish Witchcraft/Pystry Kernewek. Accessed January 8, 2015. http://www.cornishwitchcraft.co.uk/.

Cornwall Conservatives Facebook page. Accessed January 10, 2015. https://www.facebook.com/CornwallConservatives?fref=ts.

Cornwall Green Party Facebook page. Accessed January 10, 2015. https://www.facebook.com/cornwallgreenparty?fref=ts.

Correll, Joshua, and Bernadette Park. "A Model of the Ingroup as a Social Resource." *Personality and Social Psychology Review* 9, no. 4 (2005): 341–59. doi: 10.1207/s15327957pspr0904_4.

Couldry, Nick. "Media Ethics: Towards a Framework for Media Producers and Media Consumers." In *Media Ethics Beyond Borders*, edited by Stephen J. A. Ward and Herman Wasserman, 59–73. New York: Routledge, 2010.

—. *Media, Society, World: Social Theory and Digital Media Practice*. Cambridge: Polity, 2012.

—. "Mediatization and the Future of Field Theory." *Communicative Figurations*, Working paper, no. 3 (2013).

—. "When Mediatization Hits the Ground." In *Mediatized Worlds. Culture and Society in a Media Age,* edited by F. Krotz and A. Hepp, 54–71. New York: Palgrave Macmillan, 2014.

Couvares, Francis G. "Hollywood, Main Street, and the Church: Trying to Censor the Movies Before the Production Code," *American Quarterly* 44, no. 4 (1992): 584–616.

"Credo." Q's for Good Leadership. Accessed November 24, 2014. http://danahzohar.com/www2/?page_id=612.

Crowther, David, and Chris Carter. "Community Identity and Cyberspace: A Study of the Cornish Community." In *Cornish Studies: Nine,* edited by Philip Payton, 227–46. Exeter: University of Exeter Press, 2001.

Cunliffe, Daniel. "'Young Bilinguals': Language Behaviour in Social Networking Sites: The Use of Welsh on Facebook." *Journal of Computer-Mediated Communication* 18, no. 3, (2013): 339–61.

Dawson, Andrew. "Consuming the Self: New Spirituality as 'Mystified Consumption.'" *Social Compass* 58, no. 3 (2011): 309–15.

Dawson, Lorne L., and Douglas E. Cowan, eds. *Religion Online: Finding Faith on the Internet.* New York: Routledge, 2013.

de Certeau, Michel. *The Practice of Everyday Life*. Berkeley: University of California Press, 1984.

de Zavala, Agnieszka Golec, Aleksandra Cichocka, Roy Eidelson, and Nuwan Jayawickreme. "Collective Narcissism and its Social Consequences." *Journal of Personality and Social Psychology* 97, no. 6 (2009): 1074.

Deacon, Bernard. *Cornwall: A Concise History.* Cardiff: University of Wales Press, 2007.

—. "The Electoral Impact of Cornish Nationalism." In *For a Celtic Future: A Tribute to Alan Heusaff,* edited by C. O'Luain, 243–52. Dublin: Celtic League, 1983.

Deacon, Bernard. "And Shall Trelawny Die? The Cornish Identity." In *Cornwall since the War: The Contemporary History of a European War,* edited by Philip Payton, 212–4. Trewirgie, UK: Dyllansow Truran, 1993.

Deacon, Bernard, Dick Cole, and Garry Tregidga. *Mebyon Kernow and Cornish Nationalism.* Cardiff: Welsh Academic Press, 2003.

Deleuze, Gilles. *The Fold: Leibniz and the Baroque.* Foreword and translation by Tom Conley. Minneapolis: University of Minnesota Press, 1993 [orig. *Le Pli: Leibniz et la baroque*, Paris: Editions de Minuit, 1988].

—. *Proust & Signs: The Complete Text.* Translated by Richard Howard. Theory Out of Bounds, Vol. 17. Minneapolis: University of Minnesota Press, 2000. [Orig. pub. Presses Universitaires de France, 1964.]

Deleuze, Gilles, and Felix Guattari. *Anti-Oedipus: Capitalism and Schizophrenia.* Translated by Robert Hurley et al. New York: Viking, 1972.

—. *Kafka: Toward a Minor Literature.* Translated by Dana Polan; foreword by Réda Bensmaïa. Theory and History of Literature series, Vol. 30. Minneapolis: University of Minnesota Press, 1986.

—. *A Thousand Plateaus: Capitalism and Schizophrenia.* Translated by Brian Massumi. Minneapolis: University of Minnesota Press, 1987.

DeLuca, Kevin Michael. *Image Politics: The New Rhetoric of Environmental Activism.* New York: Guilford Press, 1999.

Diamond, Irene and Lee Quinby, ds. *Feminism and Foucault: Reflections on Resistance.* Boston: Northeastern University Press, 1988.

Dicks, Bella. *Culture on Display: The Production of Contemporary Visitability.* Milton Keynes: Open University Press, 2003.

Didierjean-Jouveau, Claude-Suzanne. *Porter bébé. Avantages et bienfaits.* Genève-Bernex - Saint-Julien-en-Genevois: Jouvence, 2006.

Douglas, Mary. *Purity and Danger: An Analysis of Concepts of Pollution and Taboo.* London: Routledge, 1992.

Douglas, Mary, and Baron Isherwood. *The World of Goods.* London: Routledge, 1996.

Dubuisson, Daniel. *The Western Construction of Religion: Myths, Knowledge, and Ideology*. Baltimore, MD: Johns Hopkins University Press, 2003.

Dychtwald, Ken. *Age Power: How the 21st Century Will Be Ruled by the New Old*. New York: Jeremy P. Tarcher/Putnam, 1999.

Eade, John "Order and Power at Lourdes: Lay Helpers and the Organization of a Pilgrimage Shrine." In *Contesting the Sacred: The Anthropology of Christian Pilgrimage*, edited by John Eade and Michael J. Sallnow, 51–76. Urbana & Chicago: University of Illinois Press, 2000.

Einstein, Mara. *Brands of Faith*. New York: Routledge, 2008.

Ek, Richard. "Media Studies, Geographical Imaginations and Relational Space." In *Geographies of Communication: The Spatial Turn in Media Studies,* edited by Jesper Falkheimer and André Jansson, 45–66. Göteborg, Sweden: Nordicom, 2006.

Eliade, Mircea. *Shamanism: Archaic Techniques of Ecstasy*. New York: Pantheon, 1964 [1951].

Elliott, Anthony, and John Urry. *Mobile Lives*. New York: Routledge, 2010.

Elliott-Binns, Leonard Elliott. *Medieval Cornwall*. London: Methuen, 1955.

Elvins, Brian. "Cornwall's Newspaper War: The Political Rivalry Between the *Royal Cornwall Gazette* and the *West Briton*, 1810–1831." In *Cornish Studies: Ten*, edited by Phillip Payton, 145–73. Exeter: University of Exeter Press, 2002.

Emerich, Monica M. *The Gospel of Sustainability: Media, Market and LOHAS*. Urbana: University of Illinois Press, 2011.

Emerich, Monica M. "A New American Dream: Taking the Celtic Cure in Mediated Landscapes." In *Memory, Place and Identity: The Cultural Landscapes of Cornwall*, Garry Tregidga, 80–9. London: Francis Boutle Publications, 2012.

Engelke, Mathew. "Material Religion." In *The Cambridge Companion to Religious Studies*, edited by Robert A. Orsi, 209–29. Cambridge: Cambridge University Press, 2011.

Eyerman, Ron, and Bryan S. Turner. "Outline of a Theory of Generations." *European Journal of Social Theory* 1, no. 1 (1998): 91–106.

Fausto, Carlos. "A Blend of Blood and Tobacco: Shamans and Jaguars among the Parakanã of Eastern Amazonia." In *In Darkness and Secrecy: The Anthropology of Assault Sorcery and Witchcraft in Amazonia*, edited by Neil L. Whitehead and Robin Wright, 157–78. Durham, NC: Duke University Press, 2004.

Festinger, Leon. "A Theory of Social Comparison Processes." *Human Relations* 7, no. 2 (1954): 117–40.

Fish, Stanley E. *Is There a Text in This Class?:The Authority of Interpretive Communities*. Cambridge, MA: Harvard University Press, 1980.

Flory, Richard W., and Donald E. Miller. *Finding Faith: The Spiritual Quest of the Post-Boomer Generation*. New Brunswick, NJ: Rutgers University Press, 2008.

Foltz, Richard, Frederick Mathewson Denny, and Azizan Haji Baharuddin. *Islam and Ecology: A Bestowed Trust*. Cambridge, MA: Center for the Study of World Religions, Harvard Divinity School : Distributed by Harvard University Press, 2003.

Fortune, Dion. *Avalon of the Heart*. London: Aquarian Press, 1971 [1934].

Foucault, Michel. "After Word: The Subject and Power." In *Michel Foucault*, edited by H. Dreyfus and P. Rabinow, 206–26. Chicago: University of Chicago Press, 1982.

—. *Discipline and Punish: The Birth of the Prison*. New York: Pantheon Books, 1977.

—. *The History of Sexuality: An Introduction*. New York: Vintage Books, 1990.

Fraser, Douglas. "Further Declines in Scottish Newspaper Sales." *BBC Scotland Business*. Accessed January 9, 2015. http://www.bbc.co.uk/news/uk-scotland-scotland-business-26366464.

Freeman, GT. "Spirituality and Servant Leadership: A Conceptual Model and Research Proposal." *Emerging Leadership Journeys* 4, no. 1 (2011): 129.

Frey, William H. "Baby Boomers and the New Demographics of America's Seniors." *Generations* 34, no. 3 (2010): 28–37.

Friedman, M. *Mommyblogs and the Changing Face of Motherhood*. Toronto: University of Toronto Press, 2013.

Fry, Louis W. et al. "Spiritual Leadership as an Integrating Paradigm for Servant Leadership." In *Integrating Spirituality and Organizational Leadership*, edited by Sunita Singh-Sengupta and Dail Fields, 70–82. London: Macmillan, 2007.

Fuller, Robert C. *Spiritual, but Not Religious: Understanding Unchurched America*. New York: Oxford University Press, 2001.

Garcia, Angela Cora, Alecea I. Standlee, Jennifer Bechkoff, and Yan Cui. "Ethnographic Approaches to the Internet and Computer-Mediated Communication." *Journal of Contemporary Ethnography* 38, no. 1 (2009): 52–84.

Garrard, Bruce. *Free State: Glastonbury's Alternative Community, 1970 to 2000 and Beyond*. Glastonbury: Unique Publications, 2014.

Garry Tregidga Facebook page. Accessed January 9, 2015. www.facebook.com/photo.php?fbid=10152945913312806&set=a.10151200151217806.517011.632262805&type=1&theater.

Gauthier, Françoise, Linda Woodhead, and Tuomas Martikainen. "Introduction: Consumerism as the Ethos of Consumer Society." In *Religion in Consumer Society: Brands, Consumers and Markets*, edited by Françoise Gauthier and Tuomas Martikainen, 1–24. Farnham and Burlington, VT: Ashgate, 2013.

Gauthier, Françoise, Tuomas Martikainen, and Linda Woodhead. "Introduction: Religion et Société de Consommation/ Religion in Consumer Society." *Social Compass* 58, no. 3, (2011): 291–301.

Gemma Gary. Accessed January 8, 2015. http://www.gemmagary.co.uk/about.

Giacalone, Robert, and Carole L. Jurkiewicz. *Handbook of Workplace Spirituality and Organizational Performance*. New York: M. E. Sharpe, 2002.

Gibron, Bill. "The 10 Best Films About Aging and the Elderly." *Pop Matters* (Blog). July 30, 2013. http://www.popmatters.com/post/174004-the-10-best-films-about-agingthe-elderly-of-all-time/

Giddens, Anthony. *Modernity and Self-Identity: Self and Society in the Late-Modern Age.* Stanford: Stanford University Press, 1991.

Gilhus, Ingvild Saelid. "'All Over the Place': The Contribution of New Age to a Spatial Model of Religion." In *New Age Spirituality: Rethinking Religion*, edited by Steven J. Sutcliffe and Ingvild Saelid Gilhus, 35–50. Durham: Acumen, 2013.

Gilleard, C., and Paul Higgs. "Theorising Cohort And Generation in Empirical Research." Presentation at "Age, Cohort and Generation: Conceptual and Empirical Approaches" Symposium, ISA Forum of Sociology, Barcelona, Spain, September 2008.

Gillon, Steve. *Boomer Nation: The Largest and Richest Generation Ever, and How It Changed America.* New York: Free Press, 2004.

"Glastonbury Online Ltd." *Glastonbury.* Accessed February 22, 2015. http://www.glastonbury.co.uk/pages/site.php?pgid=420.

Glastonbury Reception Centre and Sanctuary. Accessed January 12, 2012. http://www.glastonbury-pilgrim.co.uk/#glastonbury-pilgrim-centre-about-us.php.

"The Glastonbury Sanctuary." *Glastonbury Reception Centre and Sanctuary.* Accessed October 29, 2014. http://www.unitythroughdiversity.org/the-sanctuary.html.

"The Glastonbury Trust." Accessed February 20, 2015. http://www.glastonburytrust.co.uk/.

"The Glastonbury Unity Candle." *Glastonbury Reception Centre and Sanctuary.* Accessed April 4, 2015. http://www.unitythroughdiversity.org/the-glastonbury-unity-candle.html. "The Glaston Group." Accessed February 22, 2015. http://glastongroup.org.

Glock, Charles Y., Robert N. Bellah, and Randy Alfred. *The New Religious Consciousness.* Berkeley: University of California Press, 1976.

Gold, Martin, and Elizabeth Ann Malcolm Douvan. "Culture." In *A New Outline of Social Psychology*, edited by M. Gold & E. Douvan, 117–139. Washington, DC: American Psychological Association. doi:10.1037/10225–006.

Goodall, Jane. "Primate Spirituality." In *Encyclopedia of Religion and Nature*, edited by Bron Taylor, 1303–6. New York: Continuum, 2005.

Goodwyn, Hannah. "Postcard Confessions: A Perspective on *Post Secret*." *CBN.com.* Accessed October 14, 2014. http://www.cbn.com/spirituallife/biblestudyandtheology/perspectives/goodwyn-postsecret-card-confessions.aspx.

Gov.UK. Accessed January 9, 2015. https://www.gov.uk/government/news/additional-1-million-for-mg-alba-announced-by-government.

The Graduate. Film. Directed by Mike Nichols. 1967. USA: United Artists.

Graham, Gordon. *The Re-Enchantment of the World.* New York: Oxford University Press, 2007.

Greenleaf, Robert. *The Servant as Leader.* Westfield, IN: Greenleaf Center for Servant Leadership, 2008.

Grim, John. *Indigenous Traditions and Ecology: The Interbeing of Cosmology and Community.* Cambridge, MA: Distributed by Harvard Press for the Center for the Study of World Religions, Harvard Divinity School, 2001.

Grim, John, and Mary Evelyn Tucker. *Ecology and Religion*. Washington, DC: Island Press, 2014.

Hale, Amy. "Genesis of the Celto-Cornish Revival? L. C. Duncombe Jewell and the Cowethas Kelto-Kernuak." In *Cornish Studies: Five*, edited by Phillip Payton, 100–111. Exeter: University of Exeter Press, 1997.

—. "'In the Eye of the Sun': The Relationship Between the Cornish Gorseth and Esoteric Druidry." In *Cornish Studies: Eight*, edited by Philip Payton, 182–96. Exeter: University of Exeter Press, 2000.

Hall, David D., ed. *Lived Religion in America: Toward a History of Practice*. Princeton, NJ: Princeton University Press, 1997.

Hallowell, A. Irving. "Ojibwa Ontology, Behavior, and World View." In *Culture in History: Essays in Honor of Paul Radin*, edited by Stanley Diamond, 19–52. New York: Columbia University Press, 1960.

Haraway, Donna. "Situated Knowledges: The Science Question in Feminism and the Privilege of Partial Perspective." *Feminist Studies* 14, no. 3 (1988): 575–99.

Harkin, James, and Julia Huber. *Eternal Youths: How the Baby Boomers Are Having Their Time Again*. London, GBR: Demos, 2004.

Harner, Michael. "The Case for Chimpanzee Religion." *Journal for the Study of Religion, Nature and Culture* 8, no. 1 (2014): 8–45.

—. *The Jivaro: People of the Sacred Waterfalls*. Berkeley: University of California Press, 1972.

—. *The Way of the Shaman*. San Francisco: Harper & Row, 1980.

Harrod, James B. "A Trans-Species Definition of Religion." *Journal for the Study of Religion, Nature and Culture* 5, no. 3 (2011): 327–53.

Hartney, Christopher, and Daniel J. Tower, eds. *Constructing the Indigenous*. Leiden: E. J. Brill, 2015.

Harvey, Graham. *Animism: Respecting the Living World*. London: Hurst, 2005.

—. *Food, Sex and Strangers: Understanding Religion as Everyday Life*. New York: Routledge, 2013a.

—, ed. *Handbook of Contemporary Animism*. London: Routledge, 2013b.

—. "Performing Indigeneity and Performing Guesthood." In *Constructing the Indigenous*, edited by Christopher Hartney and Daniel J. Tower. Leiden: E. J. Brill, 2015.

Harvey, Graham, and Charles Thompson, eds. *Indigenous Diasporas and Dislocations*. Aldershot: Ashgate, 2005.

Harvey, Graham, and Robert J. Wallis. *Historical Dictionary of Shamanism*. Lanham. MD: Scarecrow Press, 2006.

Hays, Sharon. *The Cultural Contradictions of Motherhood*. New Haven, CT: Yale University Press, 1996.

Heelas, Paul. *Spiritualities of Life: New Age Romanticism and Consumptive Capitalism*. Oxford: Blackwell, 2008.

Heelas, Paul, Linda Woodhead, Benjamin Seel, Karin Tusting, and Bronislaw Szerszynski, *The Spiritual Revolution: Why Religion Is Giving Way to Spirituality*. Oxford: Blackwell, 2005.

Henderson, J. L. "The Cultural Unconscious." *Quadrant*, 21, no. 2 (1988): 7–16.

Hessel, Dieter T., and Rosemary Radford Ruether. *Christianity and Ecology: Seeking the Well-Being of Earth and Humans*. Cambridge, MA: Distributed by Harvard University Press for the Harvard University Center for the Study of World Religions, 2000.

Hexham, Irving. "'The "Freaks' of Glastonbury: Conversion and Consolidation in an English Country Town." *Update* 7, no. 1 (1983): 3–12.

Hill, Peter C. et al., "Conceptualizing Religion and Spirituality: Points of Commonality, Points of Departure." *Journal of the Theory of Social Behavior* 30, no. 1 (2000): 51–77.

Hogg, Michael A., and Kipling D. Williams. "From I to We: Social Identity and the Collective Self." *Group Dynamics: Theory, Research, and Practice* 4, no. 1 (2000): 81–97. doi:10.I037//1089-2699.4.1.81.

HoopPath. Official Website. http://www.hooppath.com/.

Hoover, Stewart M. *Religion in the Media Age*.Media, Religion, and Culture. New York: Routledge, 2006.

Hoover, Stewart M., and Lynn Schofield Clark, eds. *Practicing Religion in the Age of the Media: Explorations in Media, Religion, and Culture*. New York: Columbia University Press, 2002.

Hoover, Stewart M., and Nabil Echchaibi. "The 'Third Spaces' of Digital Religion." *The Center for Media, Religion, and Culture* (2012). http://cmrc.colorado.edu/wp-content/uploads/2012/06/Hoover-Echchaibi-paper.pdf

Hopkinson-Ball, Tim. *The Rediscovery of Glastonbury: Frederick Bligh Bond, Architect of the New Age*. London: Sutton, 2007.

Horsfield, Peter. "Media." In *Key Words in Media, Religion and Culture*, edited by David Morgan, 111–22. New York: Routledge, 2008.

"How a Life Coach Can Help Your Employees." Zappos. Accessed December 22, 2014. http://www.zapposinsights.com/blog/item/how-a-life-coach-can-help-your-employees

Howard, Robert Glenn. *Digital Jesus: The Making of a New Christian Fundamentalist Community on the Internet*. New York: New York University Press, 2011.

—. "Electronic Hybridity: The Persistent Processes of the Vernacular Web." *Journal of American Folklore* 121, no. 480 (2008a): 192–218.

—. "Toward a Theory of the World Wide Web Vernacular: The Case for Pet Cloning." *Journal of Folklore Research* 42, no. 3 (2005): 323–60.

—. "The Vernacular Mode: Locating the Non-Institutional in the Practice of Citizenship." In *Public Modalities: Rhetoric, Culture, Media, and the Shape of Public Life*, edited by Robert Asen and Daniel Brouwer, 240–61. Tuscaloosa, AL: University of Alabama Press, 2010.

—. "The Vernacular Web of Participatory Media." *Critical Studies in Media Communication* 25, no. 5 (2008): 490–513.

Howell, Nancy R. "Embodied Transcendence: Bonobos and Humans in Community." *Zygon* 44, no. 3 (2009): 601–12.

Hsieh, Tony. *Delivering Happiness: A Path to Profits, Passion, and Purpose*. New York: Business Plus, 2010.

Huffman, Anne Maija. *Eternal Youths: A Narrative Inquiry into the Buffering Effects of a Generational Cultural Complex against the Anxiety of Aging and Death in the American Baby Boom Generation*. Doctoral dissertation, Institute of Transpersonal Psychology, 2012. UMI Number: 3541712.

The Icarus Project. *Navigating the Space Between Brilliance and Madness: A Reader and Roadmap of Bipolar Worlds*. New York: The Icarus Project, 2013.

"Impact." Clif Bar. Accessed December 22, 2014. http://www.clifbar.com/hubs/impact

Internet World Stats. "Internet Usage Statistics for the Americas." In *Internet World Stats: Usage and Population Statistics* (Internet Users and Population Stats for the Americas). Accessed June 2010. http:/www.internetworldstats.com/stats2.htm.

It's Our Cornwall Facebook page. Accessed January 10, 2015. https://www.facebook.com/pages/Its-Our-Cornwall/274653485930072?fref=ts

Ivakhiv, Adrian J. *Claiming Sacred Ground: Pilgrims and Politics at Glastonbury and Sedona*. Bloomington: Indiana University Press, 2001.

—. "Power Trips: Making Sacred Space through New Age Pilgrimage." In *Handbook of New Age*, edited by Darren Kemp and James R. Lewis. Leiden: Brill, 2007.

Janssen, Jacques, Mark Dechesne, and Ad Van Knippenberg. "The Psychological Importance of Youth Culture a Terror Management Approach." *Youth & Society* 31, no. 2 (1999): 152–67.

Jenkins, Henry. *Convergence Culture: Where Old and New Media Collide*. New York: New York University Press, 2006.

Johnston, Lucas F. *Religion and Sustainability: Social Movements and the Politics of the Environment*. Sheffield; Bristol, CT: Equinox, 2013.

Jones, L. Y. *Great Expectations: American and Baby Boom Generation*. New York: Coward, McCann and Geoghegan, 1980.

Jurkiewicz, Carole L. and Robert A. Giacalone. "A Values Framework for Measuring the Impact of Workplace Spirituality on Organizational Performance." *Journal of Business Ethics* 49 (2004): 129–42.

Kay, Sean. *Celtic Revival? The Rise, Fall and Renewal of Global Ireland*. Lanham, MD: Rowman & Littlefield, 2011.

Keepin, Will. "Breathwork." In *Encyclopedia of Religion and Nature*, edited by Bron Taylor, 214–17. London: Continuum, 2008.

Kernow King Facebook page. Accessed January 10, 2015. https://www.facebook.com/kernowking?fref=ts.

Kesey, Ken. *One Few Over the Cuckoo's Nest*. New York: Viking Press, 1962.

Kimbles, Samuel L. "The Cultural Complex and the Myth of Invisibility.'" In *The Vision Thing: Myth, Politics, and the Psyche in the World*, edited by T. Singer, 157–69. London, GBR: Routledge, 2000.

—. "Cultural Complexes and the Transmission of Group Traumas in Everyday Life." *Psychological Perspectives* 49, no. 1 (2006): 96–110.

King, Richard. "The Association of 'Religion' with Violence: Reflections on a Modern Trope." In *Religion and Violence in South Asia: Theory and Practice*, edited by John R. Hinnells and Richard King, 226–57. London: Routledge, 2007.

Klassen, Pamela. "Practice. " In *Key Words in Religion, Media and Culture*, edited by David Morgan, 136–47. London and New York: Routledge, 2008.

Kofman, Fred. *Conscious Business: How to Build Value Through Values*. Boulder, CO: Sounds True, 2006.

Kohut, Heinz. *How Does Analysis Cure?* Edited by Arnold Goldberg, Vol. 52. Chicago: University of Chicago Press, 1984.

Krisnakumar, Sukumarakurup, and Christopher P. Neck. "The 'What,' 'Why,' and 'How' of Spirituality in the Workplace." *Journal of Managerial Psychology* 17, no. 3 (2002): 153–64.

Krotz, Friedrich. "Media, Mediatization and Mediatized Worlds: A Discussion of the Basic Concepts. " In *Mediatized Worlds. Culture and Society in a Media* Age, edited by F. Krotz and A. Hepp, 72–87. New York: Palgrave Macmillan, 2014.

Lachman, Margie E., and Stefan Agrigoroaei. "Promoting Functional Health in Midlife and Old Age: Long-Term Protective Effects of Control Beliefs, Social Support, and Physical Exercise." *PloS one* 5, no. 10 (2010): e13297.

Lalanne, Michèle, and Nathalie Lapeyre. "L'engagement Écologique Au Quotidien A-t-il Un Genre ?" *Recherches Féministes* 22, no. 1 (2009): 47. doi:10.7202/037795ar.

Lasch, Christopher. *The Culture of Narcissism: American Life in an Age of Diminishing Expectations*. W. W. Norton, 1991.

Latour, Bruno. *We Have Never Been Modern*. New York: Harvester Wheatsheaf, 1993.

Laws, Chantal, and Susan Stuart. "Myth, Magic and the Marketplace: The Preservation and Interpretation of Cornwall's Heritage within a Spiritual Tourism Context." In *Proceedings of the Things That Move: The Material Worlds of Tourism and Travel Conference*. Leeds, UK: Leeds Metropolitan University, 2007.

Lawson, Thomas T. *Carl Jung, Darwin of the Mind*. London: Karnac Books, 2008.

Lee, Richard M., and Steven B. Robbins. "Measuring Belongingness: The Social Connectedness and the Social Assurance Scales." *Journal of Counseling Psychology* 42, no. 2 (1995): 232.

Leff, Leonard J. and Jerrold Simmons, *Dame in the Kimono: Hollywood, Censorship and the Production Code*. Lexington: The University of Kentucky, 2010.

Lewine, Edward. "Tony Hsieh's Office: Welcome to the Rain Forest." *The New York Times*, December 28, 2013. Accessed November 16, 2014. http://www.nytimes.com/2013/12/29/business/tony-hsiehs-office-welcome-to-the-rain-forest.html?_r=0.

Liberman and Hoover, "Identity, Confession, and Performance in PostSecret," White Paper, 2012. http://cmrc.colorado.edu/wp-content/uploads/2011/06/Third-Spaces.pdf#page=31.

Lifton, Robert Jay. *The Broken Connection: On Death and the Continuity of Life*. New York: Simon & Schuster, 1979.

Lindlof, Thomas R. "Media Audiences as Interpretive Communities." In *Communication Yearbook*, ed. J. A. Anderson11 (1988): 81–107.

—. "Interpretive Community: An Approach to Media and Religion," *Journal of Media and Religion* 1, no. 1 (2002): 61–74.

Lindvall, Terry. *Sanctuary Cinema: origins of the Christian film industry.* New York: New York University Press, 2007.

Lönnrot, Elias. *The Kalevala*. Oxford: Oxford University Press, 1989 (1835).

Mackey, John, and Raj Sisodia. *Conscious Capitalism: Liberating the Heroic Spirit of Business*. Boston: Harvard Business Review Press, 2014.

MacKian, Sara. *Everyday Spirituality*. New York: Palgrave MacMillan, 2012, http://www.palgraveconnect.com/pc/doifinder/10.1057/9780230365028.0001.E-book.

Mackinnon, Kenneth. "Cornish at Its Millennium: An Independent Study of the Language Undertaken in 2000." In *Cornish Studies: Ten*, edited by Phillip Payton, 266–82. Exeter: University of Exeter Press, 2002.

Mahan, Jeffrey H. *Media, Religion and Culture: An Introduction*. New York: Routledge, 2014.

Maltwood, Katharine E. *A Guide to Glastonbury's Temple of the Stars: Their Giant Effigies Described from Air Views, Maps, and from 'The High History of the Holy Grail.'"* 1929. Reprint, London: James Clarke, 1964.

Mannheim, K. *Essays on the Sociology of Knowledge*. Edited by Paul Kecskemeti. New York: Oxford University Press, 1952.

Markus, Hazel Rose, and Shinobu Kitayama. "Cultures and Selves: A Cycle of Mutual Constitution." *Perspectives on Psychological Science* 5, no. 4 (2010): 420–30.

Martin, Craig. *Capitalizing Religion: Ideology and the Opiate of the Bourgeoisie*. London: Bloomsbury, 2014.

Martin, Douglas. "Swami Satchidananda, Woodstock's Guru, Dies at 87." *The New York Times*, August 21, 2002. http://www.nytimes.com/2002/08/21/world/swami-satchidananda-woodstock-s-guru-dies-at-87.html.

Masuzawa, Tomoko. *The Invention of World Religions, or, How European Universalism Was Preserved in the Language of Pluralism*. Chicago: University of Chicago Press, 2005.

Mauss, Marcel. "Techniques of the Body." In *Incorporation. Zone 6*, edited by J. Crary and S. Kwinter, 455–77. New York: Zone, 1992; 1934 for the original edition in French.

McChesney, Robert W. Global Media, Neoliberalism, and Imperialism. *Monthly Review 52*, no. 10 (2001, March). http://monthlyreview.org/2001/03/01/global-media-neoliberalism-and-imperialism.

McCutcheon, Russell T. *Critics Not Caretakers: Redescribing the Public Study of Religion*. Albany: State University of New York Press, 2001.

—. *Studying Religion: An Introduction*. London; Oakville, CT: Equinox Pub, 1997.

McGuire, Meredith B. *Lived Religion: Faith and Practice in Everyday Life*. Oxford: Oxford University Press, 2008.

McNamara, Brendan, "The 'Celtic' Dimension of Pre-First World War Religious Discourse in Britain: Wellesley Tudor Pole and the Glastonbury Phenomenon." *Journal of the Irish Society for the Academic Study of Religions* 1, no.1 (2014): 90–104.

Meador, Betty. "Light the Seven Fires—Seize the Seven Desires." In *The Cultural Complex: Contemporary Jungian Perspectives on Psyche And Society*, edited by Thomas Singer and Samuel L. Kimbles, 171–84. New York: Routledge, 2004.

Mebyon Kernow—the Party for Cornwall Facebook page. Accessed January 10, 2015. https://www.facebook.com/MebyonKernow?fref=ts.

Medovoi, Leerom. "Age Trouble: A Timely Subject in American Literary and Cultural Studies." *American Literary History* 22, no. 3 (2010): 657–72. Accessed January 24, 2015. http://muse.jhu.edu/.

Melchar, David E., and Susan M. Bosco. "Achieving High Organization Performance through Servant Leadership." *Journal of Business Inquiry* 9, no. 1 (2010): 74–88.

Mercadante, Linda A. *Belief without Borders: Inside the Minds of the Spiritual but Not Religious*. New York: Oxford University Press, 2014.

Meyer, Birgit, ed. *Aesthetic Formations: Media, Religion, and the Senses*. New York: Palgrave Macmillan, 2009.

Meyn Mamvro. Accessed January 8, 2015. http://www.meynmamvro.co.uk/.

Michell, John. *The New View Over Atlantis*. London: Thames and Hudson, 1983.

Milden, Kayleigh. "'Are you Church or Chapel?' Perceptions of Spatial and Spiritual Identity within Cornish Methodism." In *Cornish Studies: Twelve*, edited by Phillip Payton, 144–65. Exeter: University of Exeter Press, 2004.

Mitchell, Jolyon. "Narrative." In *Key Words in Media, Religion and Culture*, edited by David Morgan, 123–35. New York: Routledge, 2008.

Mithen, Steven. *The Singing Neanderthals: The Origins of Music, Language, Mind and Body*. London: Weidenfeld & Nicolson, 2005.

Molz, Jennie Germann. *Travel Connections: Tourism, Technology and Togetherness in a Mobile World*. New York: Routledge, 2012.

Moore, Kelly. "Fear and Fun: Science and Gender, Emotion and Embodiment Under Neoliberalism." *S&F Online*. Accessed July 10, 2014. http://sfonline.barnard.edu/gender-justice-and-neoliberal-transformations/fear-and-fun-science-and-gender-emotion-and-embodiment-under-neoliberalism/.

Morgan, David. *The Embodied Eye*. Berkeley: University of California Press, 2012.

—. "The Materiality of Cultural Construction." *Material Religion* 4, no. 2 (2008): 228–9.

Morgan, Kenneth O. *Wales in British Politics, 1868–1922*. Cardiff: University of Wales Press, 1970.

Morrison, Kenneth M. "Animism and a Proposal for a Post-Cartesian Anthropology." In *The Handbook of Contemporary Animism*, edited by Graham Harvey, 38–52. New York: Routledge, 2013.

—. "Beyond the Supernatural: Language and Religious Action." *Religion* 22 (1992): 201–5.

Morrissey, Megan E. "A DREAM Disrupted: Undocumented Migrant Youth Disidentifications with U.S. Citizenship." *Journal of International & Intercultural Communication* 6, no. 2 (2013): 145–62.

Muñoz, Jose Esteban. *Disidentifications*. Minneapolis: University of Minnesota Press, 1999.

Myler, Larry. "Why Are 70% of Employees Disengaged, and What Can You Do About It?" *Forbes*, September 2, 2013. Accessed December 22, 2014. http://www.forbes.com/sites/larrymyler/2013/09/02/why-are-70-of-employees-disengaged-and-what-can-you-do-about-it/

Nostalgic Cornwall Facebook page. Accessed January 10, 2015, https://www.facebook.com/groups/604486726292230/?fref=ts.

Nye, Malory. *Religion: The Basics*. London: Routledge, 2004.

Oppenheimer, Mark. "Examining the Growth of the 'Spiritual but not Religious.'" *New York Times*. July 19, A14. http://nyti.ms/1nFHDZn.

Orsi, Robert A. "Afterword: Everyday Religion and the Contemporary World." In *Ordinary Liives and Grand Schemes: An Anthropology of Everyday Religion*, edited by Samuli Schielke and Liza Debevec, 146–61. New York and Oxford: Berghahn Books, 2012.

—. "Everyday Miracles: The Study of Lived Religion." In *Lived Religion in America: Toward a History of Practice*, edited by David D. Hall, 3–21. Princeton, NJ: Princeton University Press, 1997.

—. *The Madonna of 115th Street: Faith and Community in Italian Harlem, 1880–1950.* New Haven, CT: Yale University Press, 1985, lxi.

Owram, Doug. *Born at the Right Ttime: A History of the Baby Boom Generation.* Toronto: University of Toronto Press, 1997.

Parker, Simon. *Cornwall Marches On: Keskerdh Kernow 500.* Cornwall: Bosco Books, 1998.

Pasche Guignard, Florence. "The In/Visibility of Mothering Against the Norm in Francophone Contexts: Private and Public Discourses in the Mediation of 'Natural Parenting.'" *Canadian Journal of Communication* 40, no. 1 (2015): 105–24.

Payton, Phillip. *The Cornish Overseas.* Fowey, UK: Alexander Associates, 1999.

—. *Cornwall.* Fowey, UK: Alexander Associates, 1996.

—. *The Making of Modern Cornwall: Historical Experience and the Persistence of Difference.* Trewirgie, UK: Dyllansow Truran, 1992.

—. "Paralysis and Revival: The Reconstruction of Celtic-Catholic Cornwall 1890–1945." In *Cornwall: The Cultural Construction of Place*, edited by Ella Westland, 25–39. Signal Mountain, TN: Patten Press, 1997.

—. "Territory and Identity." In *Cornwall Since the War: The Contemporary History of a European War*, edited by Philip Payton, 224–52. Trewirgie, UK: Dyllansow Truran, 1993.

Pelmear, Kenneth. *Cornwall For Ever!* Trewirgie, UK: Dyllansow Truran, 1985.

Petchsawang, Pawinee, and Dennis Duchon. "Workplace Spirituality, Meditation, and Work Performance." *Journal of Management, Spirituality and Religion* 9, no. 2 (2012): 189–208.

Pike, Sarah M. *New Age and Neopagan Religions in America.* New York: Columbia University Press, 2004.

Plate, S. Brent. *A History of Religion in 5½ Objects: Bringing the Spiritual to Its Senses.* Boston: Beacon Press, 2014.

Primiano, Leonard N. "Afterword. Manifestations of the Religious Vernacular: Ambiguity, Power and Creativity." In *Vernacular Religion in Everyday Life: Expressions of Belief*, edited by Marion Bowman and Ülo Valk, 382–94. Sheffield and Bristol, CT: Equinox, 2012.

—. "Manifestations of the Religious Vernacular: Ambiguity, Power, and Creativity." In *Vernacular Religion in Everyday Life: Expressions of Belief*, edited by Ülo Valk and Marion Bowman, 382–94. London: Equinox, 2012.

—. "Vernacular Religion and the Search for Method in Religious Folklife." *Western Folklore* 54, no. 1 (1995): 37–56, and 43.

Prince, Ruth, and David Riches. *The New Age in Glastonbury: The Construction of Religious Movements.* New York and Oxford: Berghahn Books, 2000.

Quinn, Daniel. *Ishmael.* New York: Bantam, 1992.

Rainie, Lee. "Baby Boomers and Technology." *Pew Research Center: Internet, Science and Tech.* March 28, 2012. http://www.pewinternet.org/2012/03/28/baby-boomers-and-technology/.

—. "Baby Boomers in the Digital Age." *Pew Internet & American Life Project*, 2010.

—. "The Internet and Religion: The Great Disruption" (PowerPoint presentation). *Pew Internet Research Center.* February 24, 2014. http://www.pewinternet.org/2014/02/24/the-internet-and-religion-the-great-disruption/.

RanG Facebook page. Accessed January 10, 2015. https://www.facebook.com/groups/440741969376913/.

Ransom, Diana. "Finding Success by Putting Company Culture First." *Entrepreneur*, April 19, 2011. Accessed November 1, 2014. www.entrepreneur.com/article/219509.

Ray, Paul H., and Sherry Ruth Anderson. *The Cultural Creatives: How 50 Million People Are Changing the World.* New York: Three Rivers Press, 2000.

Redden, Guy. "The New Age: Towards a Market Model," *Journal of Contemporary Religion*, 20, no. 2 (2005): 231–46.

Richardson, Gavin. "Without Pants" (blog). Accessed October 14, 2014. http://www.lifewithoutpants.com/is-twitter-the-new-town-square-an-introduction-to-spirituality-and-social-media/.

Riessman, Catherine Kohler. *Narrative Methods for the Human Sciences.* Los Angeles, CA: Sage, 2008.

Ritter, RuthAnn. "Buddhism in the Western Workplace: Implications for a Spiritual Employee and Organization." Master's thesis, Iliff School of Theology, 2014.

Roof, Wade Clark. *A Generation of Seekers: The Spiritual Journeys of the Baby Boom Generation.* 1st ed. San Francisco: HarperSanFrancisco, 1993.

Roof, Wade Clark. *Spiritual Marketplace: Baby Boomers and the Remaking of American Religion.* Princeton, NJ: Princeton University Press, 1999.

Roof, Wade Clark, Anne E. Patrick, Ronald L. Grimes, and Bill J. Leonard. "Forum: American Spirituality." *Religion and American Culture—A Journal of Interpretation* 9, no. 2 (1999): 131–57.

Rosenthal, Michele, Rivka Ribak, Rachael Liberman, Nabil Echchaibi, and Laura Portwood-Stacer. "Navigating Media Ambivalence: Strategies of Resistance, Avoidance, and Engagement with Media Technology in Everyday Life." *Selected Papers of Internet Research* 3 (2013). Accessed February 20, 2015. http://spir.aoir.org/index.php/spir/article/viewFile/898/pdf.

Roszak, Theodore. *The Making of An Elder Culture: Reflections on The Future of America's Most Audacious Generation.* Gabriola Island, BC, CAN: New Society Publishers, 2009.

Rowson, Jonathan. *Spiritualise: Revitalising Spirituality to Address 21st Century Challenges.* London: Royal Society for the encouragement of Arts, Manufactures and Commerce, 2014.

Royal Cornwall Gazette. Newspaper collection, Cornwall Centre/Kresen Kernow. Redruth, United Kingdom.

Ruel, Malcolm. *Belief, Ritual and the Securing of Life: Reflexive Essays on a Bantu Religion.* Leiden: Brill, 1997.

Russell, Cheryl. *The Master Trend: How the Baby Boom Generation Is Remaking America.* Boston: Da Capo Press, 1993.

Rutledge, Pamela. "What Is Media Psychology? And Why You Should Care." *Media Psychology Research Center.* June 2010. http://www.apa.org/divisions/div46/Rutledge_What-is-Media-Psychology.pdf.

S4C website. Accessed January 9, 2015. http://www.s4c.co.uk/en/.

Salzman, Michael B. "Globalization, Culture, and Anxiety: Perspectives and Predictions from Terror Management Theory." *Journal of Social Distress and the Homeless* 10, no. 4 (2001): 337–52.

Say No to the Pasty Tax Facebook page. Accessed January 10, 2015. https://www.facebook.com/groups/351201738255278/?fref=ts.

Schielke, Samuli, and Liza Debevec, eds. *Ordinary Lives and Grand Schemes: An Anthropology of Everyday Religion.* New York: Berghahn Books, 2012.

Schwartz, Sharron. "Cornish Migration Studies: An Epistemological and Paradigmatic Critique." In *Cornish Studies: Ten*, edited by Philip Payton, 136–65. Exeter: University of Exeter Press, 2002.

Searle, Travis P. and John E. Barbuto Jr. "Servant Leadership, Hope, and Organizational Virtuousness: A Framework for Exploring Positive Micro and Macro Behaviors and Performance Impact." *Journal of Leadership & Organizational Studies* 18 (2011): 107–17.

Sendjaya, Sen and James C. Sarros. "Servant Leadership: Its Origin, Development, and Application in Organizations." *Journal of Leadership & Organizational Studies* 9, no. 2 (2002): 57–64.

Shirky, Clay. *Here Comes Everybody: The Power of Organizing Without Organizations.* New York: The Penguin Press, 2008.

Shorter, David D. "Spirituality." In *The Oxford Handbook of American Indian History*, edited by Fredrick Hoxie. London: Oxford University Press, 2015.

Singer, T. "The Cultural Complex and Archetypal Defenses of the Group Spirit: Baby Zeus, Elian Gonzales, Constantine's Sword, and Other Holy Wars." In *The Cultural Complex: Contemporary Jungian Perspectives on Psyche and Society*, edited by T. Singer and S. L. Kimbles, 13–34. New York: Routledge, 2014.

Singer, T. (with C. Kaplinsky). "Cultural Complexes in Analysis." In *Jungian Psychoanalysis: Working in the Spirit of C. G. Jung*, edited by M. Stein, 22–37. Chicago, IL: Open Court, 2010.

Smith, J. Walker, and Ann Clurman. *Generation Ageless: How Baby Boomers Are Changing the Way We Live Today—and They're Just Getting Started.* New York: HarperCollins, 2007.

Smythe, Dallas W. "On the Audience Commodity and Its Work." *Media and Cultural Studies: Keyworks* (1981): 230–56.

Snodgrass, Judith. *Presenting Japanese Buddhism to the West.* Chapel Hill: University of North Carolina Press, 2003.

Sommer, Volker, and Amy Parish. "Living differences: The Paradigm of Animal Cultures." In *Homo Novus—A Human Without Illusions*, edited by Ulrich Frey, Charlotte Störmer, and Kai Willführ, 17–31. Heidelberg: Springer, 2010.

Stadtman Tucker, Judith. "Mothering in the Digital Age: Navigating the Personal and Political in the Virtual Sphere." In *Mothering in the Third Wave*, edited by A. Kinser, 199–212. Toronto: Demeter Press, 2008.

Stanczak, Gregory, and Donald Miller. *Engaged Spirituality: Spirituality and Social Transformation in Mainstream American Religious Traditions: Report Supplement.* Los Angeles: The University of Southern California Center for Religion and Civic Culture, 2002.

Sterne, Jonathan. "Bourdieu, Technique and Technology." *Cultural Studies* 17, no. 3–4 (2003): 367–89.

Steven Sutcliffe, *Children of the New Age: A History of Spiritual Practices.* London: Routledge, 2003.

Stolow, Jeremy. "Religion and/as Media." *Theory, Culture, & Society* 22, no. 4 (2005): 119–145.

Strauss, William, and Neil Howe. *Generations: The History of America's Future, 1584 to 2069.* New York: Morrow, 1991.

Stuettgen, Tim. "Disidentification in the Center of Power: The Porn Performer and Director Belladonna as a Contrasexual Culture Producer (A letter to Beatriz Preciado)." *Women's Studies Quarterly* 35, no. 1/2 (2007): 249–70.

Sutcliffe, Steven J., and Ingvild Saelid Gilhus. *New Age Spirituality: Rethinking Religion.* Durham & Bristol: Acumen, 2013.

Takeshita, Chikako. "Eco-Diapers. The American Discourse of Sustainable Motherhood." In *Mothering in the Age of Neoliberalism*, edited by M. Vandenbeld Giles, 117–31. Bradford: Demeter Press, 2014.

Tawhai, Te Pakaka. "Maori Religion." In *The World's Religions: The Study of Religion, Traditional and New Religion*, edited by Stewart Sutherland and Peter Clarke, 96–105. London: Routledge, 1988.

Taylor, Bron Raymond. "Diggers, Solves, Ents, Elves and Expanding Universes: Bricolage, Religion, and Violence from Earth First! and the Earth Liberation Front to the Antiglobalization Resistance." In *The Cultic Milieu: Oppositional Subcultures in an Age of Globalization*, edited by Jeffrey Kaplan and Helen Loow, 26–74. Walnut Creek, CA: Alta Mira, 2002.

—. *Dark Green Religion: Nature Spirituality and the Planetary Future.* Berkeley: University of California Press, 2010.

Taylor, Janelle S., Linda L. Layne, and Danielle F. Wozniak, eds. *Consuming Motherhood.* New Brunswick, NJ: Rutgers University Press, 2004.

Taylor, Timothy. *The Artificial Ape. How Technology Changed the Course of Human Evolution.* New York: Palgrave Macmillan, 2010.

Teusner, Paul. "Imaging Religious Identity: Intertextual Play Among Postmodern Christian Bloggers." *Online-Heidelberg Journal of Religions on the Internet* 4, no. 1 (2010).

TG4. Accessed January 9, 2015. http://www.tg4.ie/.

Tilley, Christopher. *A Phenomenology of Landscape.* London: Berg, 1994

Tirosh-Samuelson, Hava, ed. *Judaism and Ecology: Created World and Revealed Word.* Cambridge, MA: Harvard University Press, 2002.

Toalston, Art. "Truett Cathy, Faith Rooted Business Entrepreneur Dies." *Baptist Press*, September 8, 2014. Accessed December 22, 2014. http://www.bpnews.net/43315/truett-cathy-faithrooted—business-entrepreneur-dies.

Tokyo Story. Film. Directed by Yasujirō Ozu. 1953. Japan: Shochiku.

Townshend, Pete. "My Generation." On *My Generation* [CD]. Recorded by R. Daltrey, P. Townshend, J. Entwistle, and K. Moon. London: Brunswick Records, 1965.

Tregidga, Garry. "Celtic Comparisons: Brittany and the Revivalist Movement in Cornwall." In *Brittany/Cornwall: What Relations*, edited by Anne Goarzin and Jean-Yves Le Disez, 51–66. CRBC (Centre de Recherche Bretonne et Celtuque), 2013.

—. "Competing Narratives of Religious and Cultural Identity in Cornwall." In *Media, Spiritualties and Social Change*, edited by Stewart M. Hoover and Monica Emerich, 15–24. London: Continuum, 2011.

—. "Representing the Duchy: Francis Acland and Cornish Politics, 1910–1922." In *Cornish Studies: Fifteen*, edited by Phillip Payton, 164–83. Exeter: University of Exeter Press, 2007.

—. "Stratton to St Keverne; Sites of Memory from the Early Modern Period." In *Memory, Place and Identity: The Cultural Landscapes of Cornwall*, edited by Garry Tregidga, 40–53. London: Francis Boutle Publishers, 2012.

Triandis, Harry Charalambos. *Individualism & Collectivism*. Boulder, CO; Oxford: Westview Press, 1995.

Tucker, Mary Evelyn, and Duncan Ryūken Williams. *Buddhism and Ecology: The Interconnection of Dharma and Deeds*. Cambridge, MA: Harvard University Center for the Study of World Religions : Distributed by Harvard University Press, 1997.

Tucker, Mary Evelyn, and John H. Berthrong. *Confucianism and Ecology: The Interrelation of Heaven, Earth, and Humans*. Cambridge, MA: Distributed by Harvard University Press for the Harvard University Center for the Study of World Religions, 1998.

Turkle, Sherry. *Alone Together: Why We Expect More From Technology and Less from Each Other*. New York: Basic Books, 2011.

Turner, Victor. "Process, System and Symbol." *Daedalus* 106, no. 1 (1977): 61–80.

—. *The Ritual Process: Structure and Anti-Structure*. New York: Aldine Publishers, 1969.

Tylor, Edward. *Primitive Culture*. 2 vols. London: John Murray, 1871.

Underhill, Paco. *What Women Want: The Global Market Turns Female Friendly*. New York: Simon and Schuste, 2010.

United States Census Bureau. "Population Estimates." *U.S. Census Bureau*. August 5, 2009. http:/www.census.gov/popest/national/.

van Hout, Itie C. ed. *Beloved Burden. Baby-Wearing around the World*. Amsterdam: Royal Tropical Institute, 2011.

Vásquez, Manuel A. *More than Belief: A Materialist Theory of Religion*. Oxford: Oxford University Press, 2011.

Veblen, Thorstein. *The Theory of the Leisure Class*. New York: Cosimo, 1899, 2007.

Wadleigh, Michael, Bob Maurice, Richie Havens, Joan Baez, Joe Cocker, Joe McDonald, Arlo Guthrie et al. *Woodstock 3 days of Peace & Music*. Burbank, CA: Warner Bros. Pictures : Distributed by Warner Home Video 2009.

Wagner, Rachel. *Godwired: Religion, Ritual and Virtual Reality*. New York: Routledge, 2012.

Warren, Frank. Comments on PS archives. Accessed November 2, 2014. http://www.postsecretcommunity.com/lifedeathgod/secrets.php.

—. *PostSecret: Confessions on Life, Death, and God*. New York: HarperCollins, 2009.

Wbchris. "Nostalgic Cornwall Facebook Page Rockets To 6,000 Members in just four months." *West Briton* (Turo, UK), July 2, 2014. http://www.westbriton.co.uk/Nostalgic-Camborne-Facebook-page-rockets-6–000/story-21317402-detail/story.html.

Weiss, David, and Frieder R. Lang. "Thinking about My Generation: Adaptive Effects of a Dual Age Identity in Later Adulthood." *Psychology and Aging* 24, no. 3 (2009): 729–34. doi:10.1037/a0016339

—. "The Two Faces of Age Identity." *GeroPsych: The Journal of Gerontopsychology and Geriatric Psychiatry* 25, no. 1 (2012): 5–14. doi: 10.1024/1662–9647/a000050.

Welch, Christina. "Complicating Spiritual Appropriation: North American Indian Agency in Western Alternative Spiritual Practice." *Journal of New Age and Alternative Spiritualities* 3 (2007): 97–117.

Williams, Derek, ed. *Henry and Katharine Jenner: A Celebration of Cornwall's Culture, Language and Identity*. London: Francis Boutle Publications, 2004.

Williams, Raymond. "Culture Is Ordinary." In *Resources of Hope: Culture, Democracy, Socialism*, edited by Raymond Williams and Robin Gables, 3–18. London: Verso, 1989.

—. *Marxism & Literature*. Oxford: Oxford University Press, 1971.

Wolfe, Thomas. 1968. *The Electric Kool-Aid Acid Test*. New York: Farrar, Strauss, and Giroux.

Wortham, J. "Baby Boomers, Luddites? Not So Fast." *New York Times*. February 20, 2009, http:/bits.blogs.nytimes.com/2009/02/20/baby-boomers-luddites-not-so-fast.

Wuthnow, Robert. *After the Baby Boomers: How Twenty- and Thirty-Somethings Are Shaping the Future of American Religion*. Princeton, NJ: Princeton University Press, 2007.

Yellow Bird, Pemina, and Kathryn Milun. "Interrupted Journeys: The Cultural Politics of Indian Reburial." In *Displacements: Cultural Identities in Question*, edited by Angelika Bammer, 3–24. Durham, NC: Duke University Press, 1994.

Yep, Gust A. "The Violence of Heteronormativity in Communication Studies: Notes on Injury, Healing, and Queer World-Making." *Journal of Homosexuality* 45, no. 2 (2003): 46.

Yoder, Don. "Toward a Definition of Folk Religion." *Western Folklore* 33, no. 1 (1974): 14.

Yoder, John Howard. *Body Politics: Five Practices of Christian Community before the Watching World*. Scottdale, PA: Herald Press, 1992.

—. *Discipleship as Political Responsibility*. Scottdale, PA: Herald Press, 2003.

—. *The Original Revolution: Essays on Christian pacifism*. Scottdale, PA: Herald Press, 1971.

—. *The Politics of Jesus*. 2nd ed. Grand Rapids, MI: Eerdmans, 1994.

—. *The Priestly Kingdom: Social Ethics as Gospel*. Notre Dame, IN: Univ. of Notre Dame Press, 1984.

Zogby, J. "The Way We'll Be: The Baby Boomers' Legacy." *Forbes*. July 23, 2009. http:/www.forbes.com/2009/07/22/baby-boomer-legacy-change-consumer-opinions-columnists-john-zogby.html.

Zohar, Danah, and Ian Marshall. *Spiritual Capital: Wealth We Can Live By*. San Francisco, CA: Berrett-Koehler Publishers, 2004.

Index

www.ingramcontent.com/pod-product-compliance
Ingram Content Group UK Ltd.
Pitfield, Milton Keynes, MK11 3LW, UK
UKHW020135290926
15471UKWH00003B/511

9 781474 223157